POLITICAL INFLUENCE

Political Influence

Influence

BY EDWARD C. BANFIELD

THE FREE PRESS OF GLENCOE

Preface

THIS study was financed by the Governmental Affairs Foundation with funds from the Edgar B. Stern Family Fund. The sponsors gave the author the utmost freedom in the formulation of the problem and in the design and execution of the research. Their only requirement was that it delineate political realities — "influence" was the key category — which should be taken into account by anyone seeking to bring about an improvement in the structure of government in the metropolitan area of Chicago. With a very few exceptions, proposals for metropolitan reorganization have failed to win acceptance in the United States. A better understanding of the workings of influence in the metropolitan areas, the sponsors reasoned, might lead to sounder and more feasible proposals for reform. It was not a part of the author's task to propose any reforms, however, or even to suggest the tactics that reformers should follow in Chicago. While the author sincerely hopes that the sponsors' purposes are served by the study, these were not the only ones he had in mind in making the study.

Peter B. Clark is the principal author of Chapter 5, "The Fort Dearborn Project." Interviews collected by him have been used in other chapters as well, and a general debt is owed him for advice and criticism.

Dr. Luther Gulick, president of the Public Administration Institute, and Professor Norton E. Long, now of Northwestern University, initiated the study and have encouraged and stimulated it in many ways. Warm thanks are due them both.

v

Acknowledgement and appreciation are also due two students, Miss Mary Cahn and Robert F. Stout, who assisted in the interviewing, and several friends and colleagues who read part or all of the manuscript. Professors Gilbert Y. Steiner, of the University of Illinois, and Grant McConnell, Herbert J. Storing, and James Q. Wilson, of the University of Chicago, made many valuable suggestions. Professors Richard Meier, of the University of Michigan, and Walter Isard, of the University of Pennsylvania, commented helpfully on Chapter 11, as did Professors Jerome Rothenberg, of the University of Chicago, and Charles E. Lindblom, of Yale University, on the first draft of Chapter 12. My old friend and collaborator, Martin Meyerson, who got me interested in urban affairs in the first place, was a lively and provocative critic, and the Joint Center for Urban Studies of the Massachusetts Institute of Technology and Harvard University, of which he is Director, made its facilities available generously in the final stages of the work.

E. C. B.

Contents

Contents

POLITICAL INFLUENCE

I

Introduction

THIS is a study of the way influence works in a large American city. Its purpose is twofold: to describe and analyze an urban political system in one of its aspects and to contribute to the theoretical understanding of influence in political settings of all kinds.

By "influence" is meant ability to get others to act, think, or feel as one intends.[1] A mayor who persuades voters to approve a bond issue exercises influence. A businessman whose promises of support induce a mayor to take action exercises influence. A precinct captain who controls votes by doing favors exercises influence. A department head who improves the morale of his subordinates exercises influence.

To concert activity for any purpose — to arrange a picnic, build a building, or pass an ordinance, for example — a more or less elaborate system of influence must be created: the appropriate people must be persuaded, deceived, coerced, inveigled, or otherwise induced to do what is required of them. Any co-operative activity — and so any organization, formal or informal, ephemeral or lasting — may be viewed as a system of influence.[2] This is as true of the co-operative activity called government as of any other.

Government, from this standpoint, consists of acts of influence, acts which proceed from many quarters (e.g., the businessman as well as the mayor) and which produce their effect in many ways

3

(e.g., by reasonable discussion as well as the authority of office). To study the patterns of influence by which action is concerted in public matters is to study government.

Any empirical study must reflect the criteria, implicit or explicit, by which it is decided what data are relevant and what are not. The criteria of relevance employed here — the conceptual scheme, in other words — may conveniently be summarized under four leading questions:

1. *Who has influence and who is subject to it?* A person does not, of course, have the same influence (as he has the same muscular strength) in every encounter. To ask which of several persons has the most influence is meaningless unless it is specified, influence with whom? With the mayor? The city-planning commission? The press? Similarly, the range of matters to which influence extends must be specified. A department head has great influence with regard to the affairs of his own department, but he may have little or none with regard to that of other departments. Thus the relevant questions are: Who has influence with whom and with regard to what? And (the mirror image, so to speak, of the first question): who can be influenced by whom with regard to what?

2. *How does influence "work"?* What is wanted is a description of the means the influencer employs (or could employ) to affect the behavior of the influencee and of how these means act upon the motivations and expectations of the influencee. From this standpoint, the following distinctions are almost inescapable: (*a*) influence which rests upon a sense of obligation ("authority," "respect"); (*b*) influence which depends upon the wish of the influencee to gratify the influencer ("friendship," "benevolence"); (*c*) influence which works by improving the logic or the information of the influencee ("rational persuasion"); (*d*) influence which works by changing the influencee's perception of the behavior alternatives open to him or his evaluation of them, and which does so otherwise than by rational persuasion (e.g., "selling," "suggestion," "fraud," "deception"), and (*e*) influence which works by changing the behavior alternatives objectively open to the influencee, thus either absolutely precluding him from adopting an alternative unacceptable to the influencer ("coercion") or inducing him to select as his preferred (or least objectionable)

alternative the one chosen for him by the influencer ("positive or negative inducement"). These are analytical distinctions, of course, and a concrete act of influence is almost always a mixture of these elements. (A mayor, for example, is likely to employ in a single act of influence the authority of his office, the respect he commands as a man, rational persuasion, "selling," and perhaps both rewards and punishments as well.) The mixtures into which these analytical elements are characteristically combined are therefore particularly relevant to a description of influence.

3. *What are the terms upon which influence is expended?* When one speaks of the influence of a person, the reference is usually not to what he is doing or has done but rather to what he could do if he tried. A governor, for example, is not without influence merely because he does not choose to exercise any. The pertinent question, usually, is not how the governor *does* change the situation but how he *could* change it. It is seldom enough, however, to know that a person could (or could not) achieve a certain result by exerting all of his influence. Usually there are circumstances that prevent him from exercising more than a part of it. A man with a very modest property may, strictly speaking, have the ability to take a luxury cruise around the world, but he is not likely to take one because he has a family to feed, clothe, and shelter. Similarly, a governor may have ample influence to secure the passage of a certain bill but may fail to exercise it because he must save his influence for other uses.

Thus there are really two separate questions: What is A's ability to achieve the intended result? And, what is his ability to achieve it without incurring disadvantages ("costs") which he regards as equal to or greater than the advantage of the result?

Ideally, one would like to have a complete schedule of the amounts of influence the actor could exercise under all possible "cost" conditions. How much of his legislative program could the governor get approved by the legislature if he were willing to accept any sacrifice whatever (e.g. even impeachment for bribing legislators)? How much could he get accepted if he were willing to make a somewhat smaller sacrifice (e.g., loss of the chance of re-election)? How much if he were to sacrifice still less (e.g., hard work, day and night, persuading legislators)? How much if he were willing to make no sacrifice at all?

4. *How is action concerted by influence?* A political stiuation may often be viewed as one in which a proposal is to be adopted or not adopted. From this standpoint, it is relevant to inquire what acts are necessary for the adoption of the proposal, on what terms the actors who have it within their ability to give or withhold these acts can be influenced to give (or withhold) them, and through what mechanisms these terms can all be arranged (or not arranged) so that the proposal will be adopted (or not adopted).

In the following chapters this conceptual scheme is employed successively at three levels of generality. At the first and lowest level are six case studies of political influence in Chicago (Chapters 2 through 7). These tell in considerable detail how influence was used in certain recent civic controversies. Each case study is intended to answer all of the leading questions listed above.

At the second level of generality are three chapters (Chapters 8 through 10) which interpret the case studies, drawing from them a set of "low level" empirical generalizations. These generalizations also answer, although less comprehensively, the leading questions listed above.

The picture that emerges from these chapters should not be taken as typical of all metropolitan political systems. New York is very different politically from Chicago, and Los Angeles is still more different; the political system of every major metropolitan area, in fact, has some striking peculiarities. Until social scientists have made more progress in the comparative study of political systems, the observations that can be made about the similarities and differences of these cities will be too impressionistic to be of much value.[3] One of the purposes of the present study is to help prepare the way for systematic comparative analysis.

At the third and highest level of generality are two chapters (Chapters 11 and 12) in which an effort is made to explore the logical structure of certain aspects of influence. These chapters generalize further some of the material of the earlier chapters and they restate certain empirical generalizations as analytical ones. Both of these chapters go beyond the empirical material and present theories which apply generally to situations involving political influence.

The advantage of studying government as patterns of influence is that attention is directed beyond the legal-formal arrangements by which things are "supposed" to be done to the much more complicated ones by which they are "really" done. It may be that the mayor and the other officials are mere puppets who dance on strings pulled by private persons from behind the scenes. If this is the case, a study which limits itself to an account of the legal-formal relations of the mayor and the officials is so incomplete as to be downright untruthful.

As this suggests, the appropriateness of the category "influence" for the study of government depends in part upon how wide the discrepancy is between the way the city is "supposed" to be run and the way it "really" is run. If, indeed, nothing were ever done except upon the basis of a purely official exercise of authority, i.e., if no unofficial influence were ever brought to bear, the use of "influence" as a guiding concept would be awkward and perverse. "Official authority" would be enough. In fact, of course, some "outside" influence almost always exists; no matter how conscientious (or how jealous of his authority!) an official may be, he is not — and in a democracy nobody thinks he should be — an "unmoved mover." Yet some governments are influenced from the "outside" relatively little and then only in ways that are easy to see; "influence" is probably not a reasonable way to approach the study of governments such as these.

The current popularity in the United States of the influence approach to the study of the community is to be accounted for in part by the importance of "outside" influence in official decisions. Just how important these influences are is a matter of opinion. Some writers, impressed with inequalities of wealth and status and inferring from these corresponding inequalities of influence, have concluded that what we have been taught to call democracy is mostly sham. The formal machinery of government, they say, is really of little importance. The big decisions are made elsewhere. They are made by private persons, especially the very rich, who meet in homes and clubhouses to "set the line on policy" and who use their corporate positions (most of them are heads of big corporations) to enforce the decisions they have secretly made. Other persons lower down on the scale of wealth and status take orders from these higher ones, and nothing is done which has not first been approved by the "top power leaders." Anyone who resists the decisions of the "power elite" is ignored or crushed, if necessary by force.

Whether the situation in any American city corresponds to this account may be doubted. Certainly the extreme version of it wildly caricatures the way things are normally done in most of our large cities. Yet the account is plausible enough to justify careful inquiry.

Most recent studies of influence are essentially opinion polls: a more or less carefully selected sample of informants is asked to rank the prominent people of a community, or of some larger public, according to relative "power" or "leadership position" (such terms are used interchangeably in the literature), and the hierarchy that results is called a "power structure." Several very serious objections may be made to this procedure. Informants are seldom clear about what is meant by such terms as "power," "leadership," and "influence." Even if they are clear about the terms, they may not know the facts: the workings of influence are hard to see and easy to imagine. Often the questions asked are so hypothetical ("Who can make others do what he wants?") as to be meaningless; "answers" are then necessarily mere rearrangements of the verbalisms in the "questions." That the informants tend to agree in the attributions they make does not prove the attributions "correct"; agreement may mean only that the informants share a common mythology. Or it may mean that the answers have been structured along the same lines by the form of the question. When an interviewer asks, "Who are the top power leaders in this community?" he suggests by his question that there *are* top power leaders. Probably few respondents are thoughtful enough, or cantankerous enough, to challenge the hidden premises of such questions.

The method employed in this study seeks to avoid these difficulties. The data here consist mainly of case studies of the actual workings of influence. The events recounted in the cases were all unfolding while the research was under way, and it was possible therefore to ask questions — not hypothetical ones, but concretely pointed ones — of most of the leading actors. The answers obtained could be checked against and supplemented by documents and other "objective" evidence, including that of subsequent behavior. In the main, therefore, the reliance here is not upon "opinion" but upon ascertainable fact. That the trustees of the Michael Reese Hospital failed to get their way in the Branch Hospital Dispute and that the Sponsors of the Fort Dearborn Project failed to carry that undertaking to realization are statements of fact that cannot be questioned in the way that general attributions of influence, even when made by well-informed people, can be questioned.

Given the conceptual framework summarized above, it is necessary to observe influence "at work" rather than "in repose." Controversy seems to provide the best setting for such observation, for in controversy the contending actors not only exercise influence but do so more or less competitively. The selection of the particular controversies to be studied did not pose a problem. The six described here are virtually a 100 per cent sample of those which were of city-wide or more than city-wide importance in the two years (1957-58) field work was under way. These studies, therefore, are not simply cases in the sense of unrelated instances or examples. Read together — and, especially, in conjunction with similar material that has been published elsewhere[4]— they constitute a fairly complete account of recent civic controversy in Chicago.

It must hastily be acknowledged, however, that the method employed here has its own peculiar limitations. For one thing, attention to controversy diverts attention from what is not controversial and even from what is not *actively* controversial (e.g., what is not in the headlines). That the Chicago Title and Trust Company levies a toll on every real estate transaction, that organized barbers charge the outrageous price of $2.00 for a haircut, that newspaper delivery trucks travel 70 miles an hour on streets closed to commercial traffic — these are all evidences of influence at work. But in these matters the influence relationship, having been established some time ago and not having been called into question recently, lies outside the ken of the researcher who

associates influence with controversy. In such "steady state" situations nothing "happens," and therefore case studies cannot be
written.

Some matters of importance — for example, the influence of
organized labor and of gangsters — are not discussed in the
present study because the six cases studied did not happen to
bring them to attention. In the analytical chapters some material
is introduced to supplement the case studies. This, however, does
not go beyond what was essential to the interpretation of the cases.
That it is possible to describe in detail the workings of influence
in the recent civic controversies of Chicago without mention of
organized labor or gangsters (and with mention of Negroes in
only one case) suggests something about the place of these in the
influence structure. Nevertheless, these are omissions, and it must
be emphasized that this book is far from being a complete or
systematic account of political influence in Chicago.

Such omissions would be more serious if other researchers were
not supplying some of them.[5]

It must be acknowledged, too, that the case-study method does
not entirely eliminate opinion and conjecture from the data. That
someone tries to influence a politician and that the politician
responds as if he were influenced (perhaps even saying in so
many words that he has been influenced) does not prove that he
was influenced: he may have intended all along to act as the
would-be influencer wanted him to act (perhaps for reasons very
different from those of the would-be influencer), and he may have
found it convenient to claim that he was influenced. The only way
to find out about such things is to get a perfectly honest and
straightforward account of his motives from the actor who presumably was influenced. This, of course, is very seldom possible.
Although, with two important exceptions (Governor Stratton, who
agreed to be interviewed but never found time for it, and Wayne
Johnston, the president of the Illinois Central Railroad, who lost
his temper when he was shown a first draft of "The Chicago
Campus"), the actors in the cases co-operated surprisingly well
with the researchers' efforts to get the inside story, it would be
naive to suppose that any of them told the whole truth about
what "really" moved him. The chances are that most of them did

not know themselves the precise mixture of their motives. It is disappointing, certainly, to see how impressionistic and conjectural the case studies are at most crucial points. (In the Branch Hospital case, did Ryan merely respond to pressures or did he cleverly stage-manage the whole affair? In the Chicago Transit Authority case, did the Governor really try to get his legislative leaders to accept the subsidy proposal? And, for that matter, did the Mayor try as hard as he might to influence the Governor?)

But having acknowledged these limitations, it seems appropriate to say again that the merit of the case-study approach is that it keeps close to reality, especially to the objective facts of behavior that is not merely verbal.

Social science differs from most journalism and from most history in (among other things) concerning itself with what is typical rather than with what is unique. Accordingly, both the case studies and the analytical chapters, but especially the latter, focus upon what appear to be regularities in the "normal" situation and ignore, or pay little attention to, what appear to be "accidental," "peculiar," or "exceptional" circumstances. The interest here is not in individuals (e.g., Mayor Daley or Governor Stratton) but rather in roles (e.g., mayor of Chicago or governor of Illinois), and especially in what is most characteristic of roles.[6] Accordingly, both in the case studies and in the analysis an effort is made to describe the ends which pertain to roles and the constraints which the situation places upon roles (an especially important class of constraint is, of course, behavior shaped by other, antagonistic or competitive, roles) and to show what, given these ends and these constraints, must logically be the strategy of a skillful role-player. In reality, of course, a player may be very unskillful, and even if he is skillful he may make a mistake. For purposes of analysis, however, it is useful to assume that roles will be skillfully played. The justification for this assumption is that it leads to a more fruitful analysis. But the assumption is not generally as unrealistic as may at first be thought. People are ordinarily selected for roles according to their ability to play them skillfully, and those who cannot play them skillfully ordinarily lose them. (It is safe to say that any man who remains very long

as boss of the Chicago Democratic machine is a skillful politician!)
But apart from this, the role itself, if it is a well-established one,
is likely to have a good deal of skill built into it: ways of doing
things that have proved functional will have been institutionalized
in the role so that even an inept incumbent — one who could not
himself devise a rational strategy — may act "intelligently" merely
by doing what he is "supposed" to do.

This interest in describing the strategy that would be followed by
skillful role-players and, more generally, in describing what is
normal and typical, necessarily entails a sacrifice of realism. Some
readers will feel that the analytical chapters oversimplify the cases.
These readers may also find that some of the case material does
not altogether tally with the generalizations that are made, and
they will probably wonder why no effort is made to explain and
account for exceptions to the general rules.

The justification for this lack of realism is that it is the aim
of science to simplify, and that what is from one standpoint simplification is necessarily *over*simplification from another standpoint.
For example, the generalization is made (in Chapter 9) that civic
controversies in Chicago arise out of the maintenance and enhancement needs of large formal organizations. To one who wants
to predict behavior, this may be "a useful simplification" because
it economizes effort by directing attention to one variable instead
of many. But to one who wants to "understand the situation in
its complexity," the statement is a "gross oversimplification" because it leaves out of account much that common sense suggests
ought to be taken into account.

PART I

2

The Branch Hospital

Wɪᴛʜ 3,400 beds, the Cook County Hospital was said to be the biggest in the world. Big as it was, it was overcrowded In some wards beds were only a foot apart, and in others they overflowed into the corridors. The obstetrical ward, designed for 6,000 babies a year, actually had 16,000, which meant that, normally, a mother could spend only two days in the hospital.

This was the situation late in 1954 when Daniel Ryan, president of the Cook County Board, announced that the voters would soon be asked to approve a bond issue to finance an 800-bed addition to the hospital and other improvements.

Everyone agreed that the county hospital should be enlarged and improved. In the dispute that quickly arose, the issue was *where* the new facilities should be located. Ryan proposed adding to the existing hospital, which was centrally located on the West Side. This would increase the number of patients there very little, but by spreading them over a greater space it would relieve overcrowding. He recognized that the West Side hospital was not convenient to the fast-growing South Side, some parts of which were as much as two hours away. To mitigate this, he proposed building on the South Side an emergency hospital of not more than 100 beds and an outpatient clinic. Southsiders who needed something more would have to travel to the improved West Side hospital. Those who opposed this plan felt that the West Side hospital

15

was already too large and that all additional facilities should be built on the South Side.

From a formal standpoint, the issue was to be settled by a majority vote of the County Board. Actually it would be settled by Ryan, for Ryan controlled the Board.

Ryan, who was 62 in 1957, had been a member of the Cook County Board almost continuously for 31 years, and his acquaintance with its affairs went back even beyond that. His father, a contractor who came to this country in 1890, had been president of the Board, and it was because he had the same name as his father that he was asked to run when his father died. Since then he had had opportunities to run for Congress and for other offices, but he had never been tempted. "I like it here," he told an interviewer. "I know my way around and it suits me."

Unlike most local politicians, he did not have a business or professional practice on the side. Early in his career a money-making friend had put him onto some very good investments. For many years he had not depended upon his salary. Some said he was a very rich man, but this he denied.

He kept his friend's picture over his desk in his inner office as much, perhaps, from admiration as from gratitude. He admired a man who, starting from nothing, had made himself a multi-millionaire. This was probably the kind of success he would have preferred for himself.

Like all members of the County Board, Ryan held office because the slatemakers of his party put him on the ticket. (Ten commissioners were elected at large from Chicago; any Democrat who was nominated was certain to be one of these. Five commissioners were elected at large from the so-called country towns — that part of the county which lay outside of Chicago; any Republican who was nominated was certain to be one of these.) It did not follow from this that he was under the party leaders' control. On the contrary, once elected he was a power in his own right, for the law gave the president of the Board the right to appoint some 11,000 employees. If the party leaders had been foolish enough to challenge him, he could have thrown them into dismay by replacing 11,000 loyal Democrats with 11,000 others.

"Nobody makes my policy except me," Ryan responded sharply when an interviewer asked him if the County Committee of the Democratic Party had offered advice with regard to the hospital issue.

So much patronage was the source of great power. This power, wisely invested, could be made to yield more power. The additional power, wisely invested, could be made to yield still more. To take a hypothetical example: by giving some of his patronage to a ward committeeman, Ryan might increase his influence among the slatemakers. By using this influence with the slatemakers he might help a would-be candidate who, when elected, would do him favors in return. Having these favors ready to command, he might use them to earn still other favors from other people. Like the fabulous trader who started with a piece of string and ended with a kingdom, the machine politician who is single-minded and astute may build an empire by trading favors.

Ryan had made himself one of the key figures of the Democratic Party in the county. As such it was simple for him to control the Democrats on the Board. Most of them were heavily indebted to him for patronage. "If you don't go along with me," he could say, "four hundred of your friends will be walking the street tomorrow morning." Even without this direct hold over them, he could influence his fellow Democrats, for any one of them who crossed him might find himself left off the ticket at the next election.

There was one Democrat on the Board who could stand up to Ryan. This was John J. Duffy. Duffy's power arose from two circumstances. He was boss of the 19th ward. He was also an extremely able, experienced, and hard-working man — the only Democrat on the Board who had the capacity to share Ryan's responsibility for running the affairs of the county. Although Ryan did not let the reins pass out of his hands, he relied heavily upon Duffy.

The Republican minority of the Board met frequently in caucus and generally agreed to act in concert. The Democrats never found a caucus necessary. When Ryan and Duffy made a decision, the rest followed along.

There was no informal consultation between Ryan and Duffy on the one side and the Republicans on the other. They talked business only in Board meetings, all of which were open to the public. So firm was Ryan's control of the Democratic majority that he had no need to negotiate with the Republican minority.

To influence the Board, then, one would first have to influence Ryan. This would not be easy. He was rich, powerful, and unambitious enough to be independent. The hospital matter — or at any rate *inaction* on the hospital matter — was not likely to be an issue upon which an election would turn.

"If you want to understand Dan Ryan," a Board member said, "you must remember these things. He is getting old. He is not in good health. He is very rich. He likes people."

This meant that Ryan would be accommodating, especially to those who were not bad fellows. It meant also that he would not take as much trouble as a young man might to get to the bottom of an issue. He would hear all who wanted to be heard, and he would even make some effort to find the terms on which a satisfactory compromise might be reached. But he would not stay up all night fighting for a principle or trying to cajole unreasonable people to act as if they were reasonable. Instead, he would look for the course of action that promised to make the least trouble.

Civic leaders — even those who were very critical of machine politicians — believed Ryan was honest, fair, and well intentioned. "Dan is a fine fellow," a Republican of an old Chicago family told an interviewer during the hospital dispute. "He wants to do the right thing. I hate to oppose him."

The leaders of the Welfare Council of Metropolitan Chicago had long believed that the overcrowding of the West Side hospital should be relieved by building a large general hospital on the South Side. They had made their views clear to Ryan. In proposing his plan, he was in effect rejecting theirs.

The Council was an organization of organizations. It had been formed during the First World War to co-ordinate the activities of private and public welfare agencies. By 1954 it consisted of 253 such bodies — especially public health and family welfare agencies, homes for the aged, and medical, nursing, and other professional associations. The Council co-ordinated health and welfare services, planned for unmet needs, and rendered services — particu-

larly informational ones — to its constituent agencies. When the
hospital dispute arose, its budget was $533,000. Three-fifths of
this came from the Community Fund, an organization which was
housed in the same building and which appointed two of the
Council's 44 directors.

The directors were drawn largely from among the lay and professional leaders of the agencies constituting the Council. Administering welfare agencies had long been too technical a business for
amateurs — so, at least, a good many professionals thought —
but the boards of welfare agencies were nevertheless dominated
by lay people, even though the money to support the agencies came
mostly from public appropriations and from popular subscription.
The professionals had found that they could not operate successfully without the backing of lay leaders. The Council was one of
the vehicles through which co-optation of lay leaders by professionals took place. Accordingly, while almost a third of the
Council's directors were professionals, the president and three
vice-presidents were always lay.

It was highly desirable, of course, that the president of the
Council be one who presented the kind of image that would
attract support from its public. "The Council is interested in everyone's opinion," one of its officials told an interviewer. "It is
nothing without acceptance by the citizens. But naturally the support of the citizens who have a particular interest in welfare
matters is the most vital to us — the kind of people who make up
the boards of the agencies which belong to the Council and the
many others who are the civic leadership of the community."

By general consent and without the need for any formal discussion, this was taken to imply that its president (and hence the
three vice-presidents also, since they were being groomed as
possible successors to the president) should normally be: male
(the secretary was sometimes a woman, but no woman had ever
been president); if not rich, at least prosperous (most recent
presidents had been millionaires); neither radical nor reactionary
nor political in a partisan way (the social work movement had not
been dominated by crusaders for many years, but it was still no
place for the extremely tax-minded); not overly identified with
any sectarian or minority group (a clergyman could not have

been president, and only once had a Jew been president); able and willing to speak vigorously in behalf of the public interest (he had to be a person of "civic stature," a Council official said); willing to give the time necessary to the organization, whatever it might be (in the language of the organization, willing to "assume responsibility"); and, finally, able to work harmoniously with the heads of the Community Fund and others important to the Council, including, of course, its professional staff.

There was, doubtless, some tension between these requirements and the qualities which would make for success in dealing with politicians and even with civic leaders of another sort. A man who became president of the Council was not likely to be "self-made" in the way that the politician and the people especially admired by the politician were self-made; he was likely to be confident of his social status and of the moral and other correctness of his position — too confident, perhaps, to make him attractive to the politician; he was not likely to have had much experience in the ways of politicians or much knowledge of the realities with which they dealt, and he was certain to have been indoctrinated in the professional creed of the social worker to such an extent as to be almost one of them. Not the least important effect of this indoctrination would be to give him a high regard for the facts and figures — "research" — and for the views of the staff men — "experts" — who assembled data and interpreted them.

When the branch hospital dispute arose, the president of the Council was Frank H. Woods, a coal merchant of great inherited wealth. At the height of the dispute his term expired, and he left the Council to become head of the Community Fund. Thomas I. Underwood, a wealthy corporation lawyer, succeeded him. Neither Woods nor Underwood had much skill in political give-and-take. Underwood, however, (one of his principal opponents in the hospital dispute said after his death) was a "wonderful man who understood Chicago's needs and could see all sides of a question."

The Council had a staff of 90 persons, 34 of them professionals. The staff was organized in a number of departments and divisions; each division was under the direction of an executive committee elected by those constituent organizations concerned with its activities. Under the general direction of the whole board and of an executive director, the divisions were responsible for their own programs.

It was the Health Division which had responsibility in the county hospital matter. The executive secretary of this division was Alexander Ropchan. He had a Master's degree in economics and had done postgraduate work in social service administration. Twenty-five years as head of the Health Division had made him intimately familiar with health affairs in Cook County. His special knowledge put him in a position to influence the views of his executive committee. Some said he "brainwashed" it; others said this was a ridiculous calumny. Whether his influence was great or small, undue or not, depended upon how one looked at it. There was no doubt that in a matter upon which the executive committee had come to a conclusion Ropchan could not have followed a contrary course, nor would he have tried. On the other hand, being in possession of the facts gave him a great advantage; by showing grounds for preferring one course of action to another, he could help the lay leaders to make up their minds. There was nothing wrong in that, of course. It was, after all, one of the things he had been hired to do. Just how far one in his position should go in helping a lay board to make up its mind was the real question, and to it there could be no precise or generally acceptable answer.

Over the years, a number of studies by public agencies had recommended establishment of a South Side hospital. Ropchan was familiar with these, and he had no doubt that their conclusions were correct. In 1955 he and his staff, with the assistance of the Chicago Plan Commission, made a special study of the subject. In this connection, the chairman of the Health Division created a committee consisting of the presidents of three hospitals, two hospital administrators, five physicians, several businessmen, a social worker, a hospital architect, and others. After more than twenty meetings, the committee concluded that, while the West Side hospital should be repaired, the overcrowding should be relieved by building a 700-bed hospital and clinic on the South Side. It recommended also that the county consider purchasing care for its patients from voluntary hospitals.

The committee made three arguments against further building

on the West Side: (1) hospital and outpatient facilities were already too concentrated there; (2) the West Side hospital was already too big to be effectively administered; and (3) there was already congestion of traffic and parking facilities around the hospital.

On the positive side, it made these arguments for a South Side Branch:

Proximity to the population to be served is essential in meeting human needs. Outpatient departments, particularly, must be easily accessible to serve patients effectively. The values of hospital units for long-term patients are enhanced, if they are accessible to relatives and friends whose visits are important to the well-being of patients in hospitals for long periods of time.

For effective medical care, hospital bed units for long-term patients and outpatient departments must be integrated physically and functionally with general hospitals for acutely ill patients. This integration is essential in order that patients may have continuity of care from the same physicians and in order that wasteful duplication of specialized services such as x-ray and laboratory may be avoided. It is particularly not sound to establish an outpatient department in any outlying location without an adequate general hospital to which the department would be attached.

Outlying units of Cook County Hospital to serve the medically indigent would attract new groups of physicians. This would spread the burden of medical care for the medically indigent over more physicians. Furthermore, outlying units would help raise the level of medical practice in outlying communities by the increased opportunities for hospital affiliation afforded physicians in the community.

The report contained few facts to back up these assertions. It presented no evidence of diseconomies of scale at the West Side hospital, nor did it discuss what would be the optimum scale for such an institution.

It was doubtful if the Council's "research" had much more than a ceremonial function. In the branch hospital matter, at any rate, the data were very sketchy. It was doubtful, too, whether rigorous and extensive research could have helped greatly in the making of the decision. The optimum scale of the county hospital, for example, could not have been established without an extremely elaborate calculation of the costs and benefits of various alternatives — a calculation which, to be reasonably complete, would somehow have to weight a great many factors (e.g., morale of medical and nursing staffs) which could not be given a money value or be measured in any very meaningful way. And even if the optimum scale were established, it would still be necessary to calculate whether the saving in money, time, or other values from building on the West Side might not offset the economies to be had from building at the optimum.

Most of the crucial questions on which the branch hospital dispute was to turn were, like this one, not susceptible to being answered precisely on a purely technical basis. Even those which were entirely factual — e.g., would there be enough nurses to staff a South Side branch? — would turn out, on close examination, to be questions about which prudent men in possession of the same facts might honestly disagree.

The Welfare Council's conclusions were based not upon scientific knowledge but upon the common-sense judgment or "feel" of the specialist who had long been in intimate touch with these matters. Their "informed" common sense, Ropchan and his associates felt, was obviously better than "ordinary" common sense. Of course, others might not think so. It might be argued that social workers and hospital administrators, like other specialists, have a "trained incapacity" — that they are prone to certain errors because they have biases that come with specialization. It might be argued, too, that the common sense of businessmen is more to be trusted than that of the specialist — that there is in business a process of natural selection at work which brings to the fore those who have uncommon talent for making prudent judgments. But even if it were granted that the common sense of the expert is more to be trusted than the common sense of the unusually able amateur, the question would remain: *how much more* is it to be trusted? If, for example, specialists say (on the basis of judgment, not clearly demonstrable fact) that the health of patients will be adversely affected by the inaccessibility of a West Side hospital to families and friends, should contrary lay opinion be altogether disregarded? And even if lay opinion on this question is disregarded, does it follow that the issue is settled? For even if it were absolutely certain that building on the West Side would discourage visits and thus affect the health of patients so as to prolong the average stay in the hospital by, say three per cent, might not the net advantage, whether measured in dollars and cents or in other terms, conceivably lie, nevertheless, with the West Side?

As a practical matter, of course, specialists often disagree. ("Visitors just disturb patients," the medical head of the County Hospital told an interviewer. "We try to limit their visits to two a week; that causes enough trouble.") And so, in the end, "ordinary" common sense must be relied upon to choose between the conflicting opinions of the experts.

Between the Welfare Council, on the one side, and its opponents on the other side, there seemed to be a fundamental difference of opinion on these questions. The Council placed great weight on the opinions of experts who were in close practical touch with the problems under discussion. The politicians and businessmen who opposed the Council assumed that their judgment was as good as the experts' or maybe even better. Although they made no use of the rituals of research themselves, they nevertheless professed great respect for the Council's fact-gathering. This was science and scholarship, and they respected it. ("Those Welfare Council people are very well educated; they know what they're talking about," a businessman civic leader who opposed a South Side branch told an interviewer earnestly.) But despite their regard for research and facts, the politicians and businessmen could see clearly enough that the crucial questions were matters of judgment. Their judgment, they thought, was as good as — indeed, perhaps better than — that of the Welfare Council.

In some ways the Council's habit of "research" was a handicap. It prevented the Council leaders from communicating successfully with men who were accustomed to work by talking rather than by reading and writing. Ryan, for example, would not think of taking home Ropchan's lengthy memoranda for study. He did not even own a brief case. He never put anything in writing when he could avoid it. He did his business by talking, and he talked as little as possible. Very often his conversation consisted of a grunt, an expressive stare, and a wave of the hand.

When the Council leaders talked, they were ineffective. Often they read prepared statements. When they departed from these, they floundered. One reason for this was that the man who read the statement was not the one who had written it. (It was taken for granted that politicians, press, and public attached more weight to statements read by "big name" civic leaders than by the staff men who had written them and who knew much more about the subject.) But, in part, the trouble was that the Council leaders were not persuasive in the give-and-take of informal discussion. They were writers rather than talkers.

In part, also, the trouble was that they seemed to think the issue would be settled on its merits. In public hearings it was indispensable to preserve the fiction that the public interest was all that would enter into the decision. But the Council might have recognized, explicitly in private discussion and implicitly in its public statements, that it would be persuasive only if it showed that certain private interests would be served, or at least not harmed, by a South Side branch. Had it, for example, shown Ryan that a South Side branch would be an asset rather than a liability in his next campaign, it might have had more success with him. Perhaps it was impossible to show him this; but this was the direction effective arguments would have had to take. The Council, however, because it believed in facts and figures and expert opinion and because it assumed that decisions which *ought* to be made on public grounds *would* be made on them, did no research on the political realities of the situation.

As Ropchan later saw it, the Council failed to persuade because it was dealing with a man who had already made up his mind. There are times when persuasion is impossible. This, he concluded later, was one of them.

The proposal which Ryan put forward had been framed by the two career civil servants who ran the county hospital. These were Fred A. Hertwig, an engineer who had been warden of the hospital for ten years, and Dr. Karl A. Meyer, medical superintendent of Cook County institutions. Although the two men were active partners in developing and supporting the plan, Meyer was the dominant figure.

He had placed first in a competitive examination for his post in 1914 and had run the hospital with a firm hand ever since. A man of enormous vitality, he had at the same time carried on a large private surgical practice and been a professor of surgery at North-western University, a successful businessman and farmer, a member of the Board of Trustees of the University of Illinois, an elective office, for eighteen years, and president of the board for six.

More than forty years of such activity had made Meyer wealthy and had given him an extraordinarily wide circle of acquaintances. His private practice included many politicians and newspapermen. (Duffy, a leader of the County Board, was his patient.) In the eyes of those who favored a South Side branch, he was a master of intrigue and wire-pulling. "He is a very able surgeon," one of them remarked, "but he is a damn sight better politician."

Meyer had twice been offered the Democratic nomination for governor. Obviously, he had a good deal of political weight.

His management of the hospital had never been political in a party sense, however. He had run the hospital in his own fashion under both Democratic and Republican county administrations without interference. The county hospital, he told an interviewer, was freer of politics than any private one.

While it was true that the professional services of the hospital were free of party politics, Meyer had built up what professional politicians like Ryan called an "organization." This was a complex system of influence which helped maintain the great institution to which he had devoted most of his life and which helped also, of course, to maintain his own personal position. It was said by his critics that he was widely feared within the medical profession. This may have been a considerable exaggeration. But there was no doubt that he was a good man to know.

Meyer and Hertwig took the position that, if there was to be an expansion, the West Side plant should be enlarged because the presence there of core facilities — a central heating plant, elaborate new X-ray equipment, living quarters for doctors and nurses, and so on — and a well-functioning medical and adminis-trative staff made possible quicker and cheaper expansion. The hospital was in possession of land on which buildings could be erected. By building there, Meyer and Hertwig argued, the county could have the new facilities fully in operation within a year or two.

On the other hand, if a general hospital was to be built on the

South Side, it would first be necessary to secure a site. This would almost certainly involve a bitter and protracted struggle with any neighborhood chosen for the purpose. Experience had show that bringing people into a neighborhood, especially bringing Negroes and low-income people into one, was unpopular and politically difficult. At best, Meyer and Hertwig said, it would take five or six years to acquire land and build the hospital. Then the greatest difficulties would begin to appear. Unless the county was willing to pay a salaried medical staff (which Meyer assumed was out of the question), it would have to depend largely upon the services of "residents," i.e., young doctors serving at nominal pay in order to get training, and of those experienced physicians in private practice who were willing to contribute time for charity. To secure residents, the branch hospital would have to be accredited as a training hospital. That meant, among other things, that the most important medical specialties — internal medicine, surgery, pediatrics and obstetrics, and gynecology — would have to be practiced there. Unless the physicians who contributed their services as trainers were specialists, the training opportunities would not attract residents.

In Meyer's view, to build and operate a general hospital of good enough quality to attract an able medical staff would cost far more than it would cost to provide equivalent service at the West Side hospital. There a fine staff was already at work in association with the University of Illinois Medical School, the campus of which adjoined the hospital grounds, as well as Northwestern University, the Chicago Medical School, and the Stritch School of Medicine of Loyola University. At the West Side hospital all that was needed was to give the patients more space. Elsewhere it would be necessary to build and staff a new hospital. Even if money were no object, Meyer believed, the fact that the West Side plant could be expanded at once made that possibility obviously preferable.

To say that he wished to expand the West Side hospital was, Meyer said, a damnable lie. His proposal would merely relieve overcrowding. It would not add to the number of patients. Indeed, the number would even decrease a little, for reorganization of some wards would make it possible to move certain patients to other institutions.

Meyer agreed that a South Side hospital should be built. (It should have 1,500 beds, he said, not 700, as the Welfare Council proposed.) However, it should be in addition to, not in substitution for, expansion of the West Side plant. Moreover, since the need was urgent and action there would produce returns more quickly, the West Side plant should be expanded first.

Ropchan and others of the Welfare Council consulted Meyer and Hertwig several times in the course of their study of the hospital question. These contacts, however, did not result in a meeting of minds. Under the best of circumstances, Meyer was not an easy man to reason with. He was abrupt and testy, as if he were brimming over with indignation. When he listened to others, he did so impatiently, as if they were student nurses. That he had a vigorous mind could not be doubted. It was not, however, the kind of a mind which could enter into reasonable discussion.

In his dealings with the Welfare Council, Meyer was even more impatient than usual. Seeing that discussion could lead to nothing, the Council gave it up.

For his part, Meyer had nothing but contempt for many so-called experts on hospital planning and administration. "They were just a bunch of ribbon salesmen until they took a course somewhere," he told a visitor. If the people who were so anxious to tell him how to run the county hospital had the responsibility of running it themselves, they would, he thought, sing a very different tune. It was easy to make proposals when you did not have to carry them out. In his eyes, the Welfare Council was an organization of busybodies.

Meyer's views had great weight with Ryan, who had known him for more than thirty years, and with Erickson, the Republican who had preceded Ryan as president of the County Board and who was now a member of it. Over the years these men had come to rely on Meyer in much the same way that the Welfare Council relied on Ropchan. That finding an acceptable site on the South Side and getting money from the legislature to operate another hospital would both be painful processes Ryan took for granted. Meyer's assurance that health needs could best be met by expanding the West Side plant was sufficient for him, since it enabled him to do what was least troublesome.

There was no doubt that, had he wished to do so, Meyer could have persuaded Ryan to build on the South rather than on the West Side. In a sense, then, the decision rested with Meyer, since he could influence Ryan, and Ryan could control the Board.

In the spring of 1955, representatives of the Welfare Council called on Ryan to give him a pre-publication copy of the report of their study. He gave them what they thought was a receptive hearing and said that he planned to appoint a citizens' advisory committee to go into the whole matter. He would want advice from the Council in selecting the committee.

A year and a half later, when Ryan finally prepared to appoint the committee, the Council handed him a list of fifteen first choices and a number of alternates. "These were not stooges or people sold on our views," Ropchan said later. "They were top civic people — people like Laird Bell." (Bell, a partner in a leading law firm, was a former chairman of the board of trustees of the University of Chicago and former president of the Harvard Alumni Association.)

Ryan handed the list to his assistant, a career civil servant of long experience. "Ask them to serve on a committee," he said.

"Do you understand that these are all Welfare Council people?" the assistant asked, not realizing that the Council had deliberately listed people who were not its spokesmen.

"Then balance them off with others from our lists," Ryan told him.

The assistant sent out invitations to 49 persons, including nineteen who had been recommended by the Council. Some who were invited declined to serve, and others who accepted never actually met with the committee. (Virtually all of those who declined were from the Welfare Council's list. The reason was, perhaps, that "top" people were busier than others; at any rate, Bell and most of those nominated by the Council did not serve.)

As it turned out, more or less by accident, the "Committee of 49" (it was so called although only 29 persons actually participated), far from representing the Welfare Council, as Ryan supposed, was in fact weighted against it. Only one of the Council's officers or directors was a member, and only three of the civic leaders on the committee had close ties with the Council. On the other hand, the committee included Meyer, Hertwig, and two or three others from the staff of the hospital as well as others who were connected with it indirectly.

The Committee of 49 met on February 20, 1957, in the offices of the County Board. Ryan asked James A. Cunningham, a partner in a big firm of investment brokers, to be chairman. As far as Cunningham knew, this was a spur-of-the-moment choice. "Dan just dropped the handkerchief in my lap," he said later.

Cunningham was a logical choice. The committee's task was to make recommendations with regard to a bond proposal. Cunningham was a businessman whose views in such a matter would have weight with the voters who would be asked to authorize the bonds and with the financial community which would be asked to underwrite them. He was also a civic leader of prominence and long experience. As president of the Civic Federation, a taxpayers' group, he had, some years earlier, been a vigorous and effective chairman of a mayor's committee to study the revenue problems of Chicago. He was a Republican, and this was an advantage for Ryan's purposes: if Cunningham had anything to do with it, no one could claim that the hospital matter was a partisan Democratic maneuver.

There were some who said that Ryan made Cunningham chairman because Cunningham could be depended upon to bring in the recommendations that Ryan wanted. Cunningham's investment brokerage house, a politician said privately, did a big business in the county's bonds. "A partner in that firm isn't giving Dan a kick in the teeth," he remarked. "Why should he? Jim doesn't give a damn whether the hospital is on the South Side, the West Side, or any other side."

This was unfair. County bonds were always advertised and sold at competitive bidding. Cunningham's firm had only once, several years earlier, been a successful bidder. "Frankly," Cunningham wrote when the politician's comment was brought to his attention, "I am not beholden to any public official; I do not even live in

Cook County, and I do not give a damn whether my actions please or displease any individual in public office."

It was far-fetched, too, to suppose that Ryan, even if he could, would punish Cunningham for bringing in an inconvenient recommendation. The fact was that Ryan admired Cunningham ("Cunningham came up from nothing," he told an interviewer — "there's a man with brains . . . a real smart man") and believed that the county was fortunate to have his services. If Cunningham had concluded in favor of a South Side branch, Ryan might have been surprised, but it is hardly likely that he would have thought any worse of him. More likely, he would have reconsidered his own position. That Cunningham may more or less consciously have wished to please his friend Dan is possible. Like almost everybody, Cunningham probably enjoyed being well regarded by people in power. But it could not be assumed from this that his decision was a foregone conclusion.

When Cunningham took the chair and looked to the Welfare Council for testimony, he found that it had no representative present. Not having been invited to serve on the Committee of 49 and not having been informed of the meeting, the Council leaders had not come.

There must have been a misunderstanding, someone said.

"I think they seem to want to be misunderstood," Ryan replied.

The Chicago Hospital Council, an organization which was acting in close association with the Welfare Council, was represented, however. The chairman of its board of directors, Stanley Farwell, was himself a member of the Committee of 49. Farwell was the semi-retired head of a firm of business management consultants. He was a member of an old Chicago family and had for many years been a trustee of the Negro hospital, Provident. In his testimony he called attention to a set of recommendations drawn up by a committee of five hospital administrators. These were very similar to those made by the Welfare Council.

After brief statements by Ryan, Erickson, and others (including Dr. Lowell T. Coggeshall, dean of the Division of Biological Sciences at the University of Chicago, who observed that the number of people having adequate health insurance seemed likely to increase and that, therefore, more information on the future load on hospitals for the medically indigent was needed), Dr. Morris Fishbein, a former editor of the *Journal of the American Medical Association,* suggested that a small subcommittee be appointed to assemble what information was available on the questions involved and to present it in digested form to the full committee.

This suggestion was quickly accepted, and when the committee met again a week later, Cunningham announced the appointment of the following subcommittee:

Chester R. Davis, senior vice-president of the Chicago Title and Trust Company. Davis had recently returned from Washington where he had served for two years as Assistant Secretary of the Army, a post in which he developed a plan for medical and hospital care of all members of the armed forces. As a member of the board of trustees of the University of Illinois, he had been closely associated with Meyer. In 1952, he had served on another committee to consider the affairs of the county hospital. Those who knew Davis said that he was a man of independent mind; his association with Meyer did not mean that he was Meyer's man. He was a Republican.

Fishbein, a close friend of Meyer.

Col. Theophilus M. Mann, a Negro attorney. Mann was a commissioner of the Chicago Housing Authority and a Democrat.

William McFettridge, president of the Building Service Employees International Union (AFL). McFettridge, a Republican, was said never to refuse appointment to a committee of this kind and never to attend a meeting of one. He did not attend any of the subcommittee meetings.

Charles Murphy, an architect and former member of the Chicago Plan Commission.

Gilbert H. Scribner, Jr., a realtor and president of the Civic Federation.

Reuben Thorson, an investment banker and president of the board of directors of the Cook County School of Nursing, a public institution.

Cunningham was chairman of the subcommittee.

No representative of the Welfare Council was on the subcommittee. Colonel Mann's name was on the list given Ryan by the Council, but the Council leaders had no idea what position he might take. They recommended him simply because he was known to be a man of outstanding character and ability. Mrs. Bernice Van der Vries, a director of the Council, was invited to serve on the subcommittee, but declined on the grounds that she was too busy with other affairs.

When its composition was made known, the proponents of the South Side branch felt that the subcommittee had been selected to support and justify the West Side hospital.

"I was surprised at Jim Cunningham," said a civic leader who favored a South Side branch and who probably expected appointment to the subcommittee.

Cunningham, however, as he later explained to an interviewer, had a particular reason for each of his selections. There should be a Negro on the subcommittee; that accounted for Mann. Labor should be represented; that accounted for McFettridge (although Cunningham well knew that McFettridge never attended work sessions). There should be a woman; that accounted for the invitation to Mrs. Van der Vries. The supply of nurses would enter into the question in a crucial way; therefore Thorson was needed. Murphy's firm could give technical advice on building-cost estimates. Scribner was needed because it would be helpful to have the staff of the Civic Federation investigate some of the financial aspects of the problem. Davis and Fishbein would be valuable because of their general knowledge and experience.

At the second meeting of the Committee of 49, the Welfare Council was represented by its president, Underwood, by Dr. Kenneth B. Babcock, a member of its special committee, and others. Their assurances that doctors and nurses would be available to staff a South Side hospital were sharply questioned by Meyer and his associates. In the interchanges on this and other points, it appeared that the Council's case rested largely upon matters of judgment.

DR. BABCOCK: I am sure in that area there are graduate nurses that are not working, and if you put a hospital up close to them they would work. There is a universal shortage. There is no question of that.

DR. HOFFMAN: I don't know much about nursing. Maybe you have a special way of getting them. I should like to ask you about internes. We can't fill our complement at the County Hospital, and I know that a fine hospital like Evanston can't get the quota. What is your special formula?

DR. BABCOCK: You are going to be a teaching hospital, and if its excellence is good enough ——

FROM THE FLOOR: Where are you going to get your teaching hospital? Only one university and that is the University of Chicago.

DR. BABCOCK: When we say "teaching hospital" we don't necessarily mean a university hospital. There are thousands of good teaching hospitals in the United States that are not anywhere near a medical school. They are teaching hospitals; teach internes in residence.

FROM THE FLOOR: I want to say as hospital administrator that unless you have men connected with medical schools . . . you are going to have a second rate hospital. You are not going to draw internes and residents and nurses. They all go in line with hospital growth in reputation [and] with medical affiliation.

DR. BABCOCK: Well, I don't think [this is] a place to argue. I think the hospitals of the United States would disagree [with] classifying them as second-degree hospitals because they didn't have a university affiliation. You put up your hospital and you will attract them. There is no question about it.

Fishbein proposed circularizing South Side doctors to discover how many of them would contribute service to a branch hospital. (This was later done by the Welfare Council. Six hundred and eighty-nine, including at least 194 specialists, said they would serve. But the question was still unsettled. The replies, Meyer argued, indicated the doctors' good intentions. But how many of them would really find time to give regular service if called upon?)

The Welfare Council leaders left the meeting feeling that it had been called to embarrass them. "We were boxed in," one of them said later. "There was no interest in exploring the problem. Only in discrediting us. Their only interest was in getting people on their feet so that they could snipe at them."

In the following month the subcommittee met eight or nine times in Cunningham's office and elsewhere. Meyer and his associates submitted detailed estimates, and the subcommittee went over them line by line, cutting wherever it saw an opportunity. According to Meyer, it would cost $30 million to build a South Side hospital. This was twice what the Welfare Council (relying on the advice of a leading firm of hospital architects who contributed their services at the request of one of the Council's lay leaders) estimated to be adequate. Murphy, the architect member of the subcommittee, had the figures reviewed in his office and reported that Meyer's estimate was much too high and the Council's much too low.

When Cunningham asked the Council to send a representative to meet with the subcommittee, it replied that it would like to send seven or eight people to testify at a public hearing of which a stenographic record would be made. "It was obvious that Cunningham's strategy was, 'Let's be nice and make a deal — a compromise,'" a Council official said later. By asking for a public hearing, the Council meant to make it difficult for the subcommittee to disregard its recommendations.

Cunningham said that one or two representatives of the Council would be sufficient, and he flatly refused to open the sessions to the public or to make a formal record. The subcommittee wanted to discuss the problem, he said, not listen to speeches.

Finally, five representatives of the Council appeared at a closed session. Ropchan read a prepared statement, and there was discussion. The Council representatives felt that the mood of the subcommittee was antagonistic. Davis, for example, asked why the Council insisted that a general hospital, rather than an emergency hospital and clinic, was needed on the South Side. He lived in Wayne, forty miles west of Chicago, he said. If one of his family became ill, they consulted a local physician. If special treatment or hospitalization was needed, the local doctor sent them, with all the relevant records, to the Presbyterian Hospital in the center of Chicago, where they were taken care of by an appropriate specialist. This arrangement seemed all right for him, Davis said. Why shouldn't it be all right for the poor as well? Why was it essential that there be a general hospital within a few miles of everyone? After one of the Council's representatives (he was a physician and hospital administrator and a past president of the Chicago Hospital Council) had replied, Davis said: "Now I know your opinion. But I still don't think a clinic has to be a part of a hospital." This was recalled later by one of the Council leaders as an instance of the subcommittee's lack of regard for expert testimony. Here was Davis, a banker who had no technical knowledge of hospital administration, saying that he would ignore any opinion which did not coincide with his. Davis, no doubt, saw the matter in a very different light. He probably felt that since the Council's view was based *merely* on opinion — albeit "expert" opinion — and not, as it seemed to think, on technical information — there was no reason to regard its preferences or judgment as superior to his own.

Cunningham said little during the discussion. At the end of it, he asked what areas of agreement there were. No one replied. Then Woods, president of the Council, asked permission to read a formal statement. In it he served notice that the Council would campaign actively against any bond proposal for building on the West Side. The Council, he added, was very much dissatisfied with the procedure that had been adopted. The question was too important and too complex to have been left to a committee appointed at the last minute.

"This was a bombshell," one of the Council leaders said later. "They accused us of threatening. 'A very unwise statement,' one of them said."

The Council's strategy had been a poor one. If the Council had been able to force the subcommittee to hold public hearings, it might have gained some advantage by doing so. But it could not force it, and in trying to do so it only antagonized it, thus making friendly negotiation later impossible. "If the Welfare Council hadn't antagonized so many people they would have done better," a member of the subcommittee told an interviewer. "They built up an amazing degree of resistance. They did it by saying, 'This is it or else.' They took a meat-axe approach, trying to politic it."

This handicap might possibly have been overcome by persuasive arguments. But the Council's spokesmen were not effective in argument. Either they did not have what Davis and the others thought were convincing answers to the crucial questions or (as they themselves believed) Davis and the others had no intention of allowing themselves to be influenced by anything that might be said.

In part the trouble was that, with one or two exceptions, the Council leaders and the subcommittee members were different kinds of people, kinds that responded to each other with active hostility. Self-made men were inclined to be contemptuous of rich men who were not self-made. "They come from old families," one of the subcommittee members observed, speaking of the civic leaders active in welfare matters. "They won't sit down with politicians and talk with them, with their feet on the desk, as you or I would. It is a question of semantics. They don't understand each other. A ――――― is an example. He has an old family name. He opens the door, and then the bright, well-educated staff guys carry the ball. I set policy in *my* work. The staff is for research. I got out of the Community Fund."

The self-made man did not want to deal with staff men as if they and he were equals. They might be well educated, but he was rich and powerful. A member of the subcommittee, speaking of another member's attitude toward the Council, said:

They rubbed him the wrong way. He regards himself as a stout character. He said, "These goddam staff people are parasites living off our donations and they kick us around." He had no respect for the civic leaders who are the heads of the Council either. He said they are the captives of their staffs.

While the subcommittee considered, two prominent Negroes announced their opposition to a South Side branch. Dr. Nathaniel O. Calloway, president of the South Side branch of the Chicago Medical Society and president of the Chicago Urban League, and Edwin C. Berry, executive director of the League, told a press conference that the big problem was to get private hospitals to admit those Negroes who were able to pay. The county hospital, they said, was in the habit of taking Negroes who — but for racial discrimination — could go to private hospitals. If this practice were stopped, the county would gain about 1,500 beds for the care of those who were really indigent. (This estimate was wildly exaggerated, hospital authorities said.) The identification of "Negro" with "indigent" was both a calumny against the Negro and an imposition upon the taxpayer.

Moreover, Calloway and Berry said, if a branch hospital were built on the South Side, it would in effect be segregated because whites would not use it. The private hospitals of the South Side, they implied, wanted county facilities expanded in order to relieve themselves of the necessity of admitting Negroes on a non-discriminatory basis.

The newspapers assumed that Calloway and Berry were speaking for the Urban League. Actually, it had not taken a position. Calloway had merely used its office as a convenient place in which to hold a personal press conference, and Berry, who happened to be in the office at the time, had joined as an observer and had expressed his own personal views when he felt called upon to do so. That the League would support Calloway's and Berry's position was not at all certain. A few days before, the research director of the League had circulated a preliminary report which said that expansion on the South Side should await the end of discrimination in private hospitals. This opinion, which the research director had arrived at independently, drew angry protests from some of the League's white backers. One of these called a board member who, in turn, called Berry. Berry explained that a preliminary report did not necessarily reflect the policy of the organization. Later, after his press conference with Calloway, he had to explain matters to the board again. After a good deal of persuasion, a majority voted to take a position which was substantially the one he and Calloway recommended.

It was true, as Calloway and Berry said, that the Chicago Hospital Council was playing a leading part in the fight for a South Side branch. Hospitals, too, had been represented on the advisory committee which had helped formulate the Welfare Council's position.

It was true, too, that discrimination against Negroes was widespread. Some South Side hospitals admitted none. Others admitted a few and kept them segregated in private rooms or special wards. Others limited Negroes to 15-20 per cent of all patients and did not segregate them. Few hospitals had Negro physicians on their staffs.

The one hospital which had gone far toward treating the Negro fairly was Michael Reese, a Jewish-run hospital of 908 beds on the edge of the Negro slum. There, Negroes comprised 15-25 per cent of all patients, and a number of colored physicians were staff members. Because of its relative fairness, Michael Reese was in danger of being submerged. It was treating about one hundred patients a day in its accident room. Twenty-five per cent of its beds were for ward patients, most of whom could not, or did not, pay their bills in full. The cost of these charities amounted to more than a million dollars a year. If the hospital took many more low-income Negroes, it might lose the support of whites altogether and go bankrupt or, at least, fail to attract large donations and therefore cease to be progressive.

The South Side population was increasing rapidly, but the amount of hospital space there was actually declining. St. Lukes was closing its doors, and Mercy talked of moving away. The time was coming when Michael Reese, despite good intentions, would have to turn patients away. Outsiders might think of this as primarily a public relations problem: if someone turned away were to die on the street, there would be a nasty story in the papers and perhaps a lawsuit. But to the trustees and administrators of the hospital the problem was much more serious. "This is not a matter of diplomacy or public relations," one of them wrote, "but a true crisis in medical care." It was a crisis, they felt, not only for Michael Reese but for the whole of the South Side.

Michael Reese, accordingly, was a prime mover in the struggle for a South Side branch. Its administrator, Dr. Morris H. Kreeger, a man who curiously resembled Meyer in single mindedness and intensity of manner, devoted much of his time to stimulating and directing efforts to secure a South Side branch. In this he had the help of the hospital's full-time public relations man and of a special committee of its board of directors. The president of the hospital, Grant J. Pick, a philanthropist who devoted most of his time to the hospital's affairs, was chairman of this special committee, the members of which included some of the most influential Jews in the city.

Calloway and Berry were sympathetic to Michael Reese, but they felt that it was approaching its problem in the wrong way. "Instead of priming the pump of segregation," Berry said, "they should direct themselves toward getting the other hospitals to open their doors to Negroes as they have done. If all the hospitals took Negroes on a non-discriminatory basis, Michael Reese would have nothing to worry about."

Those who wanted to see justice done to the Negro, Calloway and Berry thought, should oppose expansion of the county hospital on either the South Side or the West Side. This, in their opinion, would force private hospitals to accept those Negroes who were able to pay. If the Negroes with money were not admitted to the county hospital, they would have to be admitted to private ones. As Berry explained:

> People who want to discriminate want to do it quietly. Discrimination is illegal as well as immoral, so people don't want to get caught doing it. Hospitals are operated mainly by religious bodies. They are very vulnerable when anybody calls attention to their discrimination. If they think they may be accused of murder for excluding someone because he is colored, they will take a very close look at their policy.
>
> If you follow the history of discrimination, you will find that many people will discriminate a lot when doing so is free, but they will discriminate less as the cost of doing it increases.

As president of the South Side branch of the medical society, Calloway was particularly concerned for the welfare of Negro doctors. The doctors, however, did not all have the same interest in the county hospital matter. A few had staff appointments in white hospitals, and many had them in Provident, the Negro hospital. Whether they liked it or not, these few profited by the exclusion of the others. Some of these others were satisfied not to have a hospital connection; they treated their patients in their offices, sending the ones who were very sick to the county hospital (but not to Provident, where the patient might form an attachment to another Negro doctor) with instructions to return for a "check-up" afer their release. Other Negro doctors, however, either because they wanted to use and improve their professional skill or because they resented the injustice of discrimination, desired hospital connections. These doctors could see that if Calloway succeeded in breaking down discrimination against Negro doctors, they would be worse off than before, since their patients would probably go to white doctors. Many, however, were glad to take the risk, perhaps because they were confident that if Negro patients entered the hospitals, Negro doctors would soon follow.

Calloway and Berry did not try to exert as much influence as they might have. Berry, for example, did not talk to the editors of the *Chicago Defender,* a paper with a wide circulation among Negroes. The *Defender* featured a series of articles by Calloway in which he attacked the branch hospital proposal. Later, however, the newspaper editorially supported it. Had Calloway and Berry gone into the issue fully with the editors, they might perhaps have brought them around.

Neither Calloway nor Berry approached Congressman William L. Dawson, the powerful Democratic boss of the Negro wards. (Dawson, Ryan said later, did not interest himself in the dispute.) Probably, even if they had been asked to, most of the Negro politicians would not have fought the county hospital merely to vindicate the principle of non-discrimination. Like all politicians, they had to consider their political futures. Only one or two were "race men." The others had accommodated themselves to a situation in which whites held the upper hand.

However, the main reason why Calloway and Berry did not do more with the *Defender,* the politicians, and others was lack of time. Calloway was a physician with a crowded waiting room. Berry had only recently joined the Urban League. It had virtually ceased functioning the year before his coming, and, accordingly, his first task was to assemble a staff and formulate a program. It was because the former staff had not worked closely with the board of directors that reorganization had been necessary, and Berry was determined not to repeat the others' error. Collaboration with the Board took a great deal of his time. Therefore, he had not been able to do everything he wanted.

Berry did mention the hospital matter to Ernest R. Rather, the public relations consultant of an automobile club which had offices in the same building as the Urban League. Some years earlier, Rather and other young business and professional men had organized "The Chicago Committee of One Hundred" to promote racial understanding. At the time of the branch hospital dispute, the committee was a letterhead organization which Rather operated from a drawer in his desk. Now and then he sent letters of congratulations in its name to the mayor or to the publisher of a newspaper. He preserved the replies under cellophane in a big scrapbook. When he learned about the branch hospital dispute from Berry over a mid-morning coffee, Rather found that he — and therefore the committee — disagreed entirely with the League. "We reject the thinking of some observers who cloud the picture by injecting the poisonous serum of segregation into issues merely for the sake of winning some irrelevant point," he wrote the newspapers, two of which published his letter.

Rather found time for a discussion of the issue with the editors of the *Defender,* for which he had once worked. When he and County Commissioner Sneed met in a barbershop, he told Sneed that he favored a South Side branch hospital. Sneed replied that a branch would surely be segregated.

Despite Rather's support, the Welfare Council's position had been weakened by the opposition of Calloway and Berry. People who would otherwise have taken the correctness of its position for granted began to wonder when they found it bitterly challenged by the Urban League.

The leaders of the Council were well acquainted with Calloway, and, the year before, some of them had attended a meeting sponsored by the Urban League at which he had made his views known. The Council and the League had not been in close communication on the branch hospital question, however. In part, this was because the leading figures in both organizations were very busy. In part, it was because some of the Council thought Calloway was difficult to work with. But it was also in part because the Council was not particularly sensitive to Negro opinion. "When we started to work on the branch hospital problem," Ropchan said, "we blithely thought in terms of poor people, not in terms of Negroes and whites. But once we got into it, we quickly realized that the new location would have to be such as would not lead to a segregated hospital. It would have to be accessible to both races. We had not thought much about the argument that some Negroes are now advancing — that any new public hospital will delay integration in private ones."

Insofar as it had taken account of Negro opinion in the hospital matter, the Council had relied mainly for advice upon a businessman who, although a member of the Urban League's Board, was not in a position to speak for it. Finding Negro lay leaders who could and would participate effectively in its affairs had always been difficult for the Council. There were few Negroes who could be regarded as spokesmen for the interests of Negroes as a whole, although there were some who could speak authoritatively on particular matters. Of the recognized Negro leaders, some, like Calloway, would take part in the Council only if they could use it as a vehicle for the radical reform of race relations. Those few who were "reasonable" the Council had to use over and over again, first in one capacity and then in another.

According to Berry, however, the Council's problem was less a shortage of Negro leaders than a lack of regard for Negro opinion. As he explained later:

The Welfare Council made a bad goof. There was no mutuality with the Negro community. It was like Uncle Charley on the plantation. We have great confidence in them and they have given us great help. (We think we have helped them at times too!) But in this day, no group can dictate in matters of this kind. No group can say, "We have decided what is good for you and here it is."

Whether Calloway and Berry themselves knew what was good for the Negro was, of course, open to question. There were some who thought that they were so preoccupied with discrimination that they failed to give due importance to the non-ideological or practical side of things. Observing that the county hospital question had aroused interest only because the issue of discrimination was involved, a columnist for the *Defender* wrote that there was need for an organization which would not over emphasize the importance of discrimination.

We seemed to have reached a point in history where the children of these alert ancestors have waged an increasingly successful fight against prejudice, but they are now handicapped by the fact that they must carry on their shoulders people who only want to use the cry of discrimination as an excuse for not working.

Basically, this phenomenon is exploited by nationalist leaders and rabble rousers around the world, who know they can achieve prominence not by developing constructive solutions to complex problems but merely by "blaming" all problems on the other side.

Some whites were sure that the colored man-on-the-street was more interested in hospital facilities and less interested in discrimination than Calloway and Berry seemed to think. When a "race man" told one of the county commissioners that Negro patients would gladly crawl on their hands and knees to the West Side if that would help end discrimination, the Commissioner snorted. "Nonsense", he said. "The ordinary Negro doesn't give a damn for your principles."

Colonel Theophilus Mann, the Negro on the subcommittee, was thoroughly familiar with the differences of opinion within the Negro community. As a trustee of Provident Hospital, he had, besides, an intimate knowledge of the ways of hospitals and doctors.

In his opinion, the crucial features of the branch hospital issue were not racial at all. The issue appeared to him very much as it did to Cunningham, Davis, Scribner, and the other civic leaders. Was it more economical to expand on the West Side or to build a branch? Since the tax rate could not be raised without action of the legislature, would it be possible to support another hospital? To him, these were the key questions.

Mann resisted the temptation to see discrimination everywhere. "Sometimes," he said, "I think that much of this holler about discrimination is an excuse — something to complain about. I remember when I was a student at the University of Illinois I used to hear other Negro students say, 'That professor doesn't like colored people; he never gives a colored person better than a C.' I knew different."

During the war, he came to the conclusion that there was no longer a "race" problem in the United States:

> During the war I spent two years in Europe. In England, France, and Belgium it dawned on me that we don't have a race problem in this country — we have a class problem. The Negro was brought here to be a peasant. At first he was a distinct race. He had his distinct language, his distinct tribal customs, his religion, and he was definitely distinguishable in his physical characteristics. After he had been here a while, he took up one religion or another — mostly Methodist or Baptist because those were the common religions of the South. Gradually he ceased to be a different race. What we have now is largely a class problem, not a race problem.

Mann was, of course, perfectly well aware that most hospitals excluded Negroes or placed quotas on their admission. To him this did not necessarily mean that the people who ran them were prejudiced. It was obvious that most Negroes were in the low-income group. In America, low-income people are usually excluded from "nice" places because it is bad for business to serve them. Hospitals, however, are in a special situation; they cannot admit a patient on their own responsibility: the patient must be brought to the hospital by a doctor who will be responsible for him. There are few colored doctors on the staffs of the hospitals; for this reason — not simply because of discrimination — few Negro patients are admitted.

That there were few Negro doctors on the staffs of the hospitals was not, in Mann's view, altogether due to discrimination either. Some of the doctors cannot meet the high requirements. This, he felt, is not the hospital's fault any more than it is the Negro's; it is the result of two centuries of history. It is a shame that the Negro doctor does not generally have a better medical education, but it is a fact that cannot be ignored by the hospitals.

Many Negroes are not graduates of Grade A schools. That is through no fault of the Negro. But it is not necessarily evidence of discrimination by the medical schools either. As you know, education has been segregated in the South from the first grade. Many Negroes do not get enough elementary school education to qualify them for entrance into good medical schools. It's not their fault, but it's a fact. You can't say, "Well, it was unfair that you didn't get a better education so we'll let you practice in our hospital anyway." You can't play with people's lives. The hospital has some responsibility to keep out men who are not qualified, whatever the reason for their lack of qualification.

Although he did not share, in the least, their view that curtailing public hospital facilities would — and should — force private institutions to take all Negroes who applied, Mann nevertheless agreed with Calloway and Berry that those who could afford to pay for care should not be admitted to the county hospital. Obviously, if they were refused admission to private hospitals because they did not have accredited doctors, and to public ones because they could afford to pay, some would have nowhere at all to go. But Mann thought this might not be as bad as it was sometimes made to sound. "I think maybe in medical practice we've gone overboard for the idea of putting everybody in the hospital," he told an interviewer. "I was born in my parents' home. I can understand the tendency of doctors to put the patient in the hospital. It takes the worry off the doctor and makes it easy for him to see a dozen or so patients all at the same time. But I don't know that it is really essential for the welfare of the patient."

During most of the subcommittee's discussions, Mann did not

allude to the racial aspects of the issue. In one of its final meetings, however, he remarked that the more enlightened and financially responsible Negroes favored private rather than public hospital facilities. By this time, the subcommittee had reached its conclusions on other grounds.

While the subcommittee deliberated, various interested parties were trying to influence the County Board and especially its president, Ryan.

The Welfare Council was one of the most active of these. In 1955 it had retained a public relations service. The public relations professionals now advised on strategy: they outlined the political situation as they saw it and told Ropchan how strong a stand he should take. In addition, they prepared public statements and promotional materials. On their advice the Council published a newsletter, *Panorama,* which distributed to the several thousand lay civic leaders who were members of the boards of directors of its constituent organizations. This large but select group, the Council leaders decided, was to be prepared to take political action when the time for it came. Whenever possible, Council representatives were to speak before the constituent organizations to prepare them, and especially their leaders, for the action to come.

The Council's own board of directors was "briefed." Some of the board members had served on the special hospital committee and were therefore well informed. But others knew little of the issue. Two or three were even dubious of the need for a South Side branch. Accordingly, from the beginning of the year on, the staff brought the issue before the Board at many of its monthly meetings and now and then circulated copies of favorable newspaper editorials. Gradually, the board members became committed to the position of the staff and the advisory committee.

Negotiating with Ryan, when the time for that came, would have to be done by the principal lay officers of the Council. Accordingly, they received special indoctrination from the staff. Two or three meetings of the executive committee were devoted exclusivly to discussion of policy to be followed.

The Council had long been regarded by the newspapers as a

source of reliable information on health and welfare matters. When it distributed "data sheets" on the branch hospital matter, they were well received. Editorial writers for the *Daily News, Tribune,* and *Sun-Times* called Ropchan occasionally to ask the views of the Council on this or that development. All of the papers supported the South Side branch.

On one occasion the *Sun-Times* invited Ropchan and others of the Council to discuss the issue with Meyer and Hertwig at an editorial conference. Three editorial writers sat at the ends of a long table with the opposing sides facing each other between. "We'd like to hear you argue it out," one of them said. Before long, however, the editorial writers themselves got into the argument on the side of the Council.

"What plans do you have for expansion on the South Side?" one of them asked Meyer.

Meyer admitted that there was need for a South Side branch. But it would take $45 million to rehabilitate the existing hospital *and* build a branch. First things should come first, he said.

"Why not ask for the $45 million to do the whole job," one of the editorial writers inquired.

"Would the newspapers support us?" Meyer countered.

"You might ask us," the editorial writer replied.

When Ropchan asked a question of him, Meyer snapped, "I won't answer that. We've given you too much information already."

"Isn't this public information we're talking about?" one of the newspapermen asked.

"If you'll permit me to say so," another said to Meyer, "your public relations are terrible and you should do something about it."

Meanwhile, the Welfare Council was seeing to it that Ryan and Cunningham got letters favoring a South Side branch from the heads of welfare agencies.

Ryan was irked by these letters. He believed that the writers of them did not understand what was involved and that they would not have written if they had not been stirred up to do so by Ropchan. It exasperated him to find that the CIO, for example, would write a strong letter on the basis of nothing more (as he thought) than the Welfare Council's advice and prompting. It was unfair, he felt, that the writers should criticize him merely on the basis of Ropchan's say-so and without having investigated the matter for themselves. At least two or three of the lay civic leaders who put their names to letters were surprised to get telephone calls from him the next morning. He wanted to convince them that they had been taken in by the Council.

With the same object in mind, he paid a call on two editors of the *Daily News*. They talked for two hours, but the paper's position remained unchanged.

Like Ryan, Cunningham believed that the letters he was receiving were inspired by the Council and were therefore of little or no significance. One letter was from General Robert Wood, chairman of the board of the Sears-Roebuck Company, who wrote as a patron of the Chicago Boys Club, one of the Council's constituent organizations. One day Cunningham happened to meet Wood at lunch.

"Bob," he said, "do you know both sides of this hospital story?"

"No," Wood replied. "I know nothing about it. They asked me to sign the letter and I did."

"Well," Cunningham said, "If you had X dollars to spend and if the question were building on the South Side or rehabilitating the West Side facility which we already have and which is in dreadful shape, which you do?"

"Why," said Wood, "of course I'd clean up what we already have."

The Council encountered resistance from a few of its member organizations. The head of one complained to Cunningham that a representative of the Council had threatened to have her organization, a maternity hospital, cut out of the Community Fund if she did not write a letter supporting a South Side branch. When the *Daily News* called Underwood, the president of the Council, to ask about reports that it was forcing its constituent organizations to back its position, he denied the report. Naturally, he said, they were trying to get the support of their members. But there was no coercion involved. How could there be? The Council had no way of coercing anybody.

The fact was that Frank Woods, the recently retired president of the Council who was about to become head of the Community Fund, had personally urged the leaders of some welfare agencies to put pressure on the County Board. In at least one of these conversations he had given the impression — perhaps unintentionally — that an agency which did not support the Council's position would fare ill at the hands of the Community Fund.

Ropchan and two assistants also sought to stir the constituent agencies into activity. According to his later account, they made about thirty telephone calls one day to the heads of welfare agencies, asking them to go to their boards of directors for resolutions to be sent to the County Board. In these calls no threats were made; they were simply appeals for co-operation.

The Council was not the only source of pressure, however. Farwell, the head of the hospital council, arranged a private meeting with Ryan and Meyer. There had been reason to expect that Farwell, who had been on good terms with Ryan for many years and who had long been a leader in hospital affairs, would be made chairman of the Committee of 49. Cunningham had been named instead, and Farwell had not even been included on the subcommittee. (He was left off it because someone thought he might be after a contract for his management firm, which once before had studied the hospital problem for the county. This suspicion, his friends said, was grossly unjust; he had sometimes given the services of his firm in worthwhile causes.) Despite these indications that his views were not favored, Farwell was confident that he could persuade Ryan to accept a compromise. His plan called for rehabilitation of the West Side hospital but no expansion there, getting authority from the legislature to pay private hospitals in full for care of indigent patients "farmed out" to them by the county, buying or renting for temporary use one of the South Side hospitals which were moving away, and acquiring land immediately for construction of a branch on the far South Side to be built in stages over the next decade or two to a capacity of 1,500 beds. The segregation issue was "phony," he told Ryan. A South Side hospital might have 80 per cent Negroes, but that would make it no more "segregated" than a bus which carried 80 per cent Negroes when it passed through a Negro area.

Unless some compromise could be agreed upon, Farwell said, there would surely be opposition to the proposed bond issue.

To Meyer the compromise was wholly unacceptable. As long as

it was possible to build upon the staff and facilities which already existed on the West Side, it was nonsense, he said, to talk of starting from scratch on the South Side. Ryan, too, showed no interest in the compromise. Getting authority from the legislature to pay private hospitals for service to county patients would not be easy. Nor would it be easy to get the tax rate increased to support a second hospital. In any case, the plants which could be bought or rented for temporary use were not well located. A South Side hospital should be much farther south.

Meanwhile, the directors of the Michael Reese hospital exerted themselves to find a satisfactory solution to the problem.

Lester Crown went to Jacob Arvey, an old friend and associate who was a Democratic national committeeman and who had long been a power in the Cook County machine. Arvey's identification with the Jewish community was strong, but he did not see fit to intervene. Crown had better talk to Ryan, he said. It was up to Ryan. Crown knew Ryan very well (as a youth, Ryan had been employed by Crown's father), but he could not get him to promise a South Side branch.

Ferd Kramer, another member of the Michael Reese board, asked Mayor Daley to help. Kramer was a partner in a big real estate and property management firm and had, for many years, played a leading part in civic affairs relating to housing and slum clearance. Daley, in addition to being mayor, was chairman of the county Democratic committee. The two men had high regard for each other. But when Kramer asked him to intercede with Ryan in favor of a South Side hospital, Daley declined.

Crown, Kramer, and others, having no success with Arvey and Daley, went to Ryan. They found him sympathetic, but unwilling to come out in favor of decentralizing Cook County Hospital.

The reason Ryan was so impervious to influence, some surmised, was that the Catholic church had got to him first. Mercy Hospital, a Catholic institution on the South Side, was to move and be re-established with a medical school named in honor of Cardinal Stritch. At first the plan was to locate the new Catholic medical center in Skokie, a North Side suburb. But Skokie was becoming largely Jewish, and it was found that hospital facilities there were adequate. Since the medical center was to be moved, there was much to be said for locating it in the Cal-Sag area on the extreme South Side; this was a district which was growing at a fantastic rate because of the St. Lawrence Seaway and related port-development projects. And if it were to be in the Cal-Sag area, there was much to be said for having a branch of the county hospital alongside of it. A county hospital would be a priceless resource to the Stritch medical school and, of course, it would have the added advantage of relieving Mercy Hospital from the necessity of taking an undue number of charity cases. The politicians, some people thought, would "stall" until the Church acted; but once the Cardinal had made up his mind, something would be done.

The theory was plausible, but wrong. Ryan had not been asked by the Church to delay the building of the hospital. ("The Chancellery did not get to me on this," he said later. "I wouldn't have paid any attention if they had. I have been asked by them to do things and I have refused when I thought I should. You don't get elected that way, by serving any one special group.") At the beginning of the dispute the director of Catholic hospitals had favored a South Side branch. Later, in the course of the dispute, he became convinced that in view of financial limitations it would be best to expand on the West Side at once and to build on the South Side as soon as possible afterward. This he had told Ryan in informal conversation. Nor was there any truth in the story that Mercy Hospital was to be moved to the South Side; when the hospital dispute ended, the plan was still to locate it in Skokie.

There had been organized, meanwhile, an Emergency Committee for Cook County Medical Care which proposed to raise several thousand dollars to secure the defeat of an unsatisfactory bond proposal. The Emergency Committee came into being in the following way:

At a dinner party, Kreeger, the administrator of Michael Reese, had spoken with great feeling of the South Side's plight and the politician's callousness. One of the guests was Arnold H. Maremont. Maremont was a very rich man — he was the guiding light in four corporations with assets of $35 million and a partner in a million-acre ranch — who had recently come to have a decided taste for civic service. He was an active Democrat.

As Kreeger explained it, the branch hospital issue was drawn between callous politicians on the one hand and the forces of democracy on the other.

"Do you mean to say," Maremont asked him, "that there is no way of making one's voice heard in this matter? You people are naive. You don't know how to organize. You flounder. No wonder they call you do-gooders."

Kreeger should call Commissioner Chaplin, Maremont said. (Chaplin was a Republican county commissioner and the president of a large corporation. Maremont, it developed, was the owner of this corporation and chairman of its board of directors. The two men had offices in the same building.)

Chaplin at once took a very active interest in the hospital dispute. On two or three occasions he went to Michael Reese and stood watching the accident cases being brought in by police ambulances and taxicabs. This gave him a vivid sense of Michael Reese's problem. There was little he could do to help, however, for the Republican minority on the board was not a factor with which Ryan had to reckon.

Maremont soon called a meeting in his office to announce that he was indignant and wanted to do something. If others felt as he did, he would join in financing an effort to create a favorable climate of opinion. He would have his personal public relations man do what he could to help along these lines.

The Welfare Council and Michael Reese Hospital had been thinking for some time of organizing a "citizen's committee." A committee, acting for all of the proponents of a South Side branch, could hire a publicity man who would give the issue his full attention. By this device, too, the sponsoring organizations could stay out of the limelight when it was to their advantage to do so. In this joint effort, Michael Reese, the Welfare Council, and the Hospital Council hoped to secure the participation of the University of Chicago (the University clinics were under much the same pressure as was Michael Reese), the Catholic hospitals, and a prominent Negro.

In this they did not succeed. The University acknowledged that a South Side branch was needed, but it said there was no real possibility of getting one, since neither the Negroes nor any neighborhood in which a branch might be located would tolerate one. The archdiocesan director of Catholic hospitals believed he could do the cause more good by not joining the committee. The Negro who was invited to join never replied definitely to the invitation despite repeated inquiries.

These arrangements were being attempted at the time Maremont offered to sponsor a citizens' committee. When Ryan promised to appoint an advisory committee, the arrangements were called off temporarily and Maremont was told that action then would be premature. Later, when the proponents of the branch became convinced that Ryan had intended only to put them off guard by appointing, after so much delay, an advisory committee which would surely bring in an adverse recommendation, they revived the plan to organize a committee. Michael Reese, the Hospital Council, a trustee of Michael Reese, and Maremont together gave $5,000. (Although it had been expected to do so, the Welfare Council did not contribute.) Maremont became chairman.

The Committee of 49 reassembled on March 29 to receive the subcommittee's report.

Its recommendations were not much different from Ryan's first proposal. The West Side hospital should be rehabilitated(this had never been a matter of dispute), but less extensively than first proposed. A 500-bed pavilion should be added to the West Side hospital to relieve overcrowding (Ryan had proposed 800 beds). Clinic and outpatient service should be expanded both at the West Side hospital and elsewhere (this acknowledged that the North Side also had a claim to local facilities). Carefully sandwiching encouragement for the branch hospital between two pieces of discouragement, the subcommittee recommended "that no decentralized hospital building program be instituted at this time, but that the Cook County Board of Commissioners give the entire subject of hospital care, in the light of present and future trends, further detailed study before embarking on a program of decentralization."

Farwell, representing the Hospital Council, at once expressed disappointment. He would have to report back to his organization, he said, to discover what action it would take with respect to the

bond proposal. The implication was that he might urge the Council
to fight the proposal.

Underwood, the president of the Welfare Council, had been
invited to attend the meeting, but had decided that nothing would
be gained by doing so. The Council, therefore, was officially un-
represented. However, Mrs. Van der Vries, a board member, was
present, and she observed that "there are going to be some very
unhappy organizations in the community." She did not want to
make any kind of a threat, she said, "but I think you should be
prepared for some expressions of opinion which are not going to
help the entire problem." The subcommittee, she believed, should
at least have recommended that the County Board set aside a sum
for the eventual purchase of a South Side site.

Chaplin, the Republican commissioner who was Maremont's
business associate, found it startling that the subcommittee, meeting informally and in a very rushed manner, had arrived at conclusions radically different from those arrived at by agencies which
had studied the problem for years. He was surprised, too, he said,
that it had postponed any consideration of a South Side branch
to the indefinite future.

Cunningham replied that the problem certainly needed more
study and that he hoped the County Board would not neglect it.
He did not believe that the subcommittee had closed the door on
a South Side branch. That was not its intention.

When the vote was taken, sixteen favored and two (Farwell
and Mrs. Van der Vries) opposed the recommendations. That the
subcommittee's assignment had been to assemble information,
not to suggest a conclusion, and that only eighteen of the Com-
mitte of 49 were present was overlooked or forgotten.

The issue was not settled, however. Ryan knew that the proponents of a South Side branch were likely to campaign against
the bond issue. If they did, they might defeat it. The voters were
in a bad mood, he thought. "People are dissatisfied with every
thing nowadays," he told an interviewer. "They think taxes are
too high and that government isn't doing a good job. I see it by
the letters I get." This was also the view of Duffy, whom Ryan
and others considered a financial wizard. As chairman of the

finance committee, Duffy might have a great deal to say about what bond issues were proposed to the voters.

Voter turnout would be light because only bond proposals and judicial offices were at stake. Moreover, the election was coming just at the wrong time: voters would have the memory of their tax bills fresh in their minds when they went to the polls. Under the circumstances, a few determined opponents might cause a great deal of trouble.

"It is easy to beat a bond issue," Chaplin told an interviewer a few days after the subcommittee made its report. "I could put a full-page ad in our local paper saying, 'This money will not be well spent and as your representative I advise you to vote against it,' and they wouldn't get any votes."

This was well understood by Ryan. What gave him most con-concern was that the proponents of the South Side branch had the newspapers on their side. He attached great importance to the influence of the press in matters of this kind. People who took the trouble to vote on bond issues and minor offices, he had observed, frequently carried newspapers to the polling place with them and followed their recommendations in marking the ballots. This was especially true in the outlying wards and suburbs. Ryan had seen as many as twenty copies of the *Daily News* swept out of a polling place after it closed. The endorsement of any of the papers (except the *Tribune,* which always advised the voters to vote straight Republican) was worth 25,000 to 50,000 votes, he believed. Since they did not crusade, radio and television, although important, did not have to be feared.

The hospital bond proposal would come before the voters to-gether with a number of very important city bond proposals, and a campaign against it might have adverse incidental effects upon the city proposals. Ryan and Duffy had no responsibility for the city bonds, of course. But they did not want to be in any way responsible for their defeat. They had, therefore, a special incentive to placate proponents of the South Side branch.

Even before the subcommittee made its report, Ryan told Meyer that a compromise was necessary. Meyer agreed, and Ryan telephoned Ropchan, whom he regarded as the prime mover in the agitation for a South Side branch. Would the Welfare Council be satisfied if $250,000 were made available for eventual purchase of a South Side site? Ropchan was dubious. A day or two later, the *Tribune* attacked the subcommittee's recommendations editorially. The next day, Ryan telephoned again. Would the Council be satisfied if, in addition, the 500-bed addition to the West Side were dropped from the proposal? That sounded reasonable, Ropchan said, but Ryan would have to talk to Underwood. Underwood said that he could not speak for the Welfare Council and still less for its constituent organizations. However, if the $250,000 figure were raised somewhat and if the proposal to expand on the West Side were dropped, it was not unlikely that the Welfare Council would go along.

Ryan then announced to the County Board and the press that the 500-bed addition to the West Side hospital had been dropped and that $250,000 was being earmarked for purchase of a South Side site; this amount, he said, would be increased later if necessary.

"We got nothing and they got nothing," Meyer remarked sourly after it was all over.

Ryan's office put out a press release announcing with satisfaction that the Welfare Council had pledged vigorous support of the bond proposal. "From your wide experience," Ryan wrote Underwood, in language which was most uncharacteristic, "you have learned, as I have, that governmental work is not an exact science and cannot always follow a set program or blue print in detail. All too frequently broad basic questions of public planning and building compel lengthy deliberations, negotiations and even compromises in the public interest, in order to attain that which is possible for the present and to lay the groundwork for future development and growth."

3

The Welfare Merger

A 64-YEAR-OLD Chicagoan who was out of work applied to the Chicago Welfare Department and received "general assistance." When he turned 65, he went to one of six district offices of a different agency — the Cook County Welfare Department — to apply for "old-age assistance." He had been interviewed at length by caseworkers for the city, but he had to be interviewed again, for the forms and procedures of the two departments were slightly different.

For half a century people had complained that the government of greater Chicago was absurdly complicated. Simplification, everyone supposed, would be a boon both to the taxpayer and to those who did business with government agencies. Here was a case in point. With 876 employees, the County Welfare Department gave assistance to 57,656 cases who were eligible for the four categories of relief that were supported by the federal government — old-age assistance, aid to dependent children, assistance to the blind, and disability assistance. The city department, with 1,123 employees, gave general assistance to 22,822 cases which did not fit any of these categories. That the city's larger staff served fewer cases did not mean that it was less efficient; its cases required closer attention than did the county's. The rationale of the division of labor had been political to begin with — during the Depression it had been possible to induce some states to accept the federally-aided welfare programs only by limiting their scope to politically favored groups: the old, the blind, the disabled, and children; now that the idea of public assistance was well established, there was little to be said for the category system. Professionals in social service administration believed that all welfare needs should be met from a single agency.

On the face of it, it seemed sensible to have the department with the wider jurisdiction — the county — administer all welfare programs. In 1944, the then commissioner of welfare for the city of Chicago had recommended this in the name of economy and efficiency. "Having more than one unit of government responsible for public welfare programs," he had said, "not only involves duplication of administrative costs, but causes confusion in family management where members of the same family receive support from two or three public agencies; each organization has different allowances and different procedures, yet the family must plan as a unit."

The county and city welfare departments had important relationships to the Illinois Public Aid Commission (IPAC), the agency which administered public assistance programs for the state.

The connection between IPAC and the County Welfare Department was particularly close. The federal funds which partly supported the four "categories" were paid to the state, which disbursed them through IPAC in accordance with standards laid down by federal law. Since more than half the case load of the federally-assisted program was in Cook county, IPAC used the county welfare department as its agent. The county department carried on many other activities with which IPAC had no concern (with minor exceptions, it was in charge of all county welfare services), but in the administration of the "categories" it had no other role than as IPAC's agent: IPAC set its policies, regulations, methods of procedure, and standards, and it had no public assistance program of its own.

The relationship between IPAC and the Chicago Welfare Department was somewhat more complicated. There were in Illinois 1,455 local governments which were authorized by law to give general assistance. Any or all of them could qualify for state aid by levying a one-mill tax on property; whatever beyond the yield of the tax might be required for general assistance would be supplied by the state through IPAC. In fact, only 232 local governments did levy the full amount of the tax, and most of these found that the yield from it was enough for their needs. Only 85 to 90 local governments regularly received state aid. Chicago was by far the most important of these; 80 per cent of IPAC's general assistance funds went to Chicago.

Chicago's one-mill tax raised $10 million a year. Whatever its welfare program might cost beyond this would have to be paid by the state. If the city welfare program were to be much enlarged — if, for example, more generous allowances were to be given or the case load much increased — the additional burden would fall entirely upon the state.

IPAC had some legal authority over the local governments which received state aid: it regulated their accounting procedures and set standards of assistance which they could not exceed. So long as they stayed under these ceilings, however, they were free to establish what standards they pleased. One or two actually gave only two dollars a week per person. Others followed recommendations made by IPAC home economists. Still others employed some in-between standard of their own devising.

In some matters, IPAC's authority was unclear: the law said it might approve certain local regulations, but it did not say what was to be done, short of withholding funds altogether, if it failed to approve. Some small places which lacked legal counsel were bluffed by IPAC into accepting regulations which it had no real legal power to impose. But larger places — including, of course, Chicago — were well aware of the limits of IPAC's control and refused to accept its regulations.

In the view of the professional-minded people who administered IPAC, the locally-run assistance programs were mostly bad. The local officials, the professional-minded people thought, were often harsh and money-minded: they were much more sympathetic to the taxpayer than to the welfare applicant. Even when they were well intentioned, the elected officials had faults of amateurism. Not more than fifty localities were doing a good job of administering relief, an IPAC official told an interviewer in 1957. The others were "questionable to bad."

The IPAC administrators believed that general assistance programs should be taken out of local hands and put on a state or at least a county basis. There was no use in proposing such a thing, however, for the local officials who handled relief were determined to retain their control of it and were organized into a powerful lobby. "Locally elected officials," one of their representatives told an interviewer, "take care of emergency needs and then pack them [the indigent] up and make them go back where they came from. Bureaucrats on the merit system would have a tendency to want to build up their own business — to make it look good. They would keep the person on relief forever." Not all of the locally elected officials took this view; some dealt with permanent cases in a very conscientious way. This, however, was the lobby's line.

Under these circumstances, IPAC could not very well propose centralization of all general assistance: to propose this would accomplish nothing and would alienate the township supervisors, whose support IPAC often needed in the legislature. One step might be taken in the desired direction however. The largest of the local welfare programs — that of the city of Chicago — might be brought under the control of the county. The township supervisors would have no objection to this; Chicago, as far as they were concerned, was an alien land.

The fact was, however, that Chicago's was one of the best-run welfare programs in the state — some said in the United States. It was unfortunate to have to apply the principle of centralization only where it was least needed. Besides, although transferring Chicago's welfare functions to the county would bring the overwhelming majority of cases together in one office, even within Greater Chicago there would remain many independent local welfare administrations. And, finally, it was centralization at the level of the state, not of the counties, that the principle of centralization really implied.

The argument for the merger was therefore not as good as might first appear. Yet it was plausible — enough so to appeal to those who wanted the merger for other reasons — reasons that were less easily explained and justified.

The Commission consisted of seven persons appointed on a bipartisan basis by the Governor and subject to removal by him and three state officials who·served ex officio. The chairman was chosen by the Governor. He was George B. McKibbin, a Chicago lawyer who had been state director of finance under Republican Governor Green and had run unsuccessfully for mayor of Chicago in 1943 and for Congress in 1956. The other members were a prominent woman who was the widow of a state senator, a sociologist at a state college in Southern Illinois, the vice-chairman of a Negro insurance company, the dean of the school of social service at the University of Illinois, a leader of the Federation of Jewish Charities, and a former corporation counsel of the city of Chicago. The Commission was unpaid. Usually it met once a month. The meetings, which by law were open to the public, seldom lasted for more than an hour and were devoted mainly to an agenda prepared by the professional staff. The commissioners, however, were in the habit of having a leisurely private lunch together before their meeting, and there was nothing to stop them from settling some matters there.

The Commission did not consider itself a political arm of the Stratton administration, but it tried to be guided by the wishes of the administration. "We never make a purely political decision," McKibbin told an interviewer, "but we recognize that we are part of a current administration and we have to take the policies of that administration into account even when we are opposed to them. If we can see our way to going along with the administration, we do; but if we are definitely opposed, we do not go along." McKibbin saw the Governor every three months to report on IPAC affairs, and on these occasions he usually took some of the other commissioners and the head of the agency's professional staff with him. Their relations with the Governor were always amicable.

The Commission had 2,300 employees who were under the direction of an executive secretary. This position was an important and difficult one, but the legislature had seen fit to prohibit the Commission from paying the secretary more than $11,500, a

salary which McKibbin thought was far too little to enable the
Commission to employ a man of the calibre that was needed. The
incumbent in 1956 was Garrett W. Keaster, who had been a state
employee for many years and, before that, a cashier in a downstate bank. Keaster had no very decided views of his own, but
was much influenced by his chief assistant, Robert Hyde, an
accountant who disapproved of relief in all its forms. McKibbin
kept in fairly close touch with Keaster — he spent three full days
a month on IPAC business, and hardly a day passed that he did
not stop at the IPAC office for a few minutes or talk to Keaster
on the telephone — but he believed very strongly that policy-
makers should operate only through channels and never interfere
in "administration." Because McKibbin leaned over backwards
in carrying these principles into effect, some observers concluded
that IPAC was run by Keaster and Hyde if it was run by anybody
at all. This judgment, however, seems to have been incorrect.
"McKibbin may have straddled the fence and procrastinated," an
insider said later, "but eventually he showed that he and the Commission were running the show."

The director of the County Welfare Department was Raymond
M. Hilliard. In 1934, as a young lawyer just out of DePaul University, his first job had been to prosecute fraud cases for the
Illinois Emergency Relief Administration. Later, he became executive director of IPAC. In 1948, Mayor O'Dwyer of New York was
under pressure from Governor Dewey to clean Communists out
from the city welfare department, and he appointed Hilliard
welfare commissioner. Hilliard went on to become executive director of the Welfare and Health Council of New York, a job which
paid $25,000 a year. In 1954, when the Council's board failed to
sustain him in refusing membership to a birth control organization, he resigned. For a few months he was out of work. Then
McKibbin, who as state director of finance had been on close terms
with him when he was director of IPAC, suggested to the president
of the Cook County Board (at that time a Republican) that he
be brought back to fill a subordinate position in the County Welfare Department, the head of which was about to retire. The
president of the Cook County Board and Daniel Ryan, who was

soon to run against him, agreed privately that, whichever of them won, Hilliard would be retained and promoted.

Hilliard's return had caused apprehension among social workers. Those of them, at least, who were most devoted to the norms of their profession — the "super-professionals — thought of him as a policeman and disliked and distrusted him accordingly. By 1957, however, their fears were allayed. Far from being a "policeman," his professional colleagues now found him a fellow social worker. He never called public assistance "relief," and he was at pains to emphasize in his public statements that it was the fault of circumstances, not laziness or other deficiencies of character, which made people indigent. He advocated more generous standards of assistance, and he said that the way to reduce dependency was to eliminate the social conditions that produced it, especially tuberculosis, alcoholism, rent "gouging," and discrimination against the aged and against racial minorities.

Hilliard's transformation from a "policeman" to a "social worker" provoked much speculation among those who had followed his career. Some said it was to be accounted for by political ambition. It was hard to see, however, how being a "liberal" would help him to be governor. The fact was that he had harmed his political standing by a too soft attitude toward welfare. Governor Stratton, who had once looked to him for advice and had offered him a high post in his administration, was now privately critical of him for being so much of a "spender." Losing the Governor's favor was not a way to success in Republican politics.

Hilliard himself told an interviewer that it had never occurred to him to run for office and that there had been no change in his point of view. He had, he said, always been primarily interested in good administration. Before going to New York, he had done some things for the sake of good administration that were unpopular with many social workers (insisting that people should be financially responsible for their parents was one); afterward, he had merely taken special pains to express his views somewhat before the "super-professionals" expressed theirs.

In the administration of the "categories," Hilliard was subject to Keaster's direction. He was very far from being his subordinate, however. His salary, which was fixed by the Cook County Board, was $18,000 — more than 50 per cent higher than Keaster's.

The Chicago Welfare Department was run by Alvin E. Rose. A newspaperman until 1937, when he was named executive secretary to the Governor's Council on Public Assistance and Employment, he later became an executive of the Chicago Relief Administration. After three years as a combat intelligence officer in the naval air arm, he became commissioner of the city welfare department.

Rose developed a rehabilitation center which was widely regarded as a model of its kind. It was a five-story city-owned former manufacturing plant in which relief recipients were prepared for private employment. Those who for one reason or another could not be rehabilitated were transferred to the County Welfare Department for disability assistance.

As his principal assistants, Rose had two women who were highly respected by the professionals in welfare administration. While giving them virtually a free hand to build what they considered a model program, he frequently identified himself with a "tough" approach to welfare. He was in favor, he said, of doing away with "sympathy-invoking" titles like Old Age Assistance. "Perhaps," he told a legislative committee, "it would be a good idea to call the Welfare Department 'the Poor House.'" Rather than mail welfare checks to able-bodied recipients (as the county did), Rose had them call for them in person; this gave his department a chance to make a partial recheck of their eligibility every month, and it discouraged some of them from taking relief. Work relief for able-bodied recipients, which was carried on at the rehabilitation center, also served to discourage some. "You'd be surprised how many people walk out when we tell them they'll have to work," Rose told a reporter.

Rose had a flair for catching headlines. He was not only an ex-newspaperman but a spare-time writer of mystery stories as well; his own style in public statements was blunt and hard-swinging. It was, naturally, a style that made good copy. The city's welfare rehabilitation center received national and even international attention, his critics said, not because of its intrinsic merits (the cost was excessive, they said) but because he advertised it with such flamboyance.

"He is a damn good salesman," the administrator of another welfare agency remarked somewhat grimly.

Rose's colorful language was frequently taken out of context and misinterpreted. When he warned Puerto Ricans of the hardships of Chicago's slums, he was understood to be telling them to go home. When he observed that 80 per cent of the relief load in Cook County was Negro, that the Negroes had been cotton pickers in the South and knew little else, and that there were no cotton fields in Chicago, he was represented as saying that Negroes as a race were good for nothing but cotton picking.

Social workers, although they knew that the Chicago welfare department was being run by Rose's assistants according to good professional standards, were generally horrified by his public statements, especially when his words were taken out of context. ("Charity should be left to the generous impulses of the private individual and the private agencies.")

"He's always saying the wrong thing as soon as he gets away from those women," a social worker who liked and admired him complained. "He's pretty stupid."

In 1956, the Chicago Junior Chamber of Commerce and Industry cited Rose as the city's outstanding public servant.

Rose's salary was $12,000. This was about the same as Keaster's, but much less than Hilliard's.

Hilliard and Rose had each taken on a coloration likely to insure the maintenance of their organizations in the environment in which they operated. This was an environment in which a variety of interests had to be placated or checked. Hilliard's organization would have been open to attack if, in addition to being a Republican, he had been Protestant, tax-minded, and anti-Negro. As it was, having an Irish grin and being a good Catholic brought him friends in the heavily Irish-Catholic political elite of the central city, and his outspoken advocacy of the "liberal" line in welfare matters got him support from social workers and others who seldom found themselves allied with Republicans. Likewise, Rose, who held a key position in a Democratic administration which was dominated by Irish-Catholics and who was an Irish-Catholic himself, would have been in an exposed position had he been closely identified with the "liberals," race relations reformers, and "spenders" who had been close to the Democratic party since the New Deal. Just as Hilliard needed support from among the natural opponents of a Republican, so Rose needed it from among the natural opponents of a Democrat. What he had to say about "the relief mess . . . commonly referred to as our Welfare State" disarmed the tax-savers in the suburbs who otherwise would have viewed him and his organization with profound distrust. His remarks about Puerto Ricans and Negroes also won him some support from "reactionaries." These remarks were misinterpreted of course — Rose himself was not prejudiced, and he did not like those who were — but if he had seen fit to do so, he could have phrased what he had to say so that there would have been no possibility of misinterpretation.

Since ethnicity, religion, and party affiliation were fixed factors, rhetoric was the one variable which could be manipulated. This, perhaps, explained Hilliard's transformation from "policeman" to "social worker" and Rose's "stupidity." Had the Chicago Welfare Department been run by a fire-in-the-eyes "liberal," Hilliard might have found it advantageous to remain a "policeman." And, in this event, Rose might not have been so "tough."

In the main, Rose and Hilliard did not confront each other directly in policy conflicts. IPAC usually stood between them, and it was up to Keaster, and ultimately to the Commission, to secure what co-ordination was necessary.

In these dealings, Hilliard had the upper hand. He had shown himself able to get a $25,000-a-year job in New York, and his current salary was much more than that of Keaster or Rose. The prestige of this was enough in itself to give him an ascendancy. Keaster, moreover, was a poor administrator, and Hilliard was a very good one. McKibbin, although fond of Keaster, had doubts about his administrative ability. On the other hand, he thought that Hilliard was an unusually good administrator.

Between Hilliard, who had the outlook of a professional social service administrator, and Keaster, who, influenced by Hyde, had that of an accountant, there was an armed truce broken by occasional sniping from the Keaster-Hyde side. Keaster frequently made decisions to which Hilliard strongly objected, but McKibbin, although he had more confidence in Hilliard's judgment than in

Keaster's, never overruled him. Supporting subordinates, someone said later, was part of McKibbin's religion.

Rose and IPAC carried on a running battle. Rose and Keaster were on good terms personally, but relations between their agencies were always strained to the breaking point. IPAC might bluff small towns into adopting regulations which it had no legal right to impose, but it could not bluff the city of Chicago. When IPAC objected to something he did, Rose produced a legal opinion to back himself up. If IPAC got a contrary opinion from the state's attorney general, Rose got one from the corporation counsel of Chicago. "Even on simple matters," an IPAC spokesman said afterward, "there was always a long drawn-out procedure."

The city's rehabilitation program was a particular bone of contention. IPAC believed that it was extravagantly overstaffed and that its full cost had been hidden. When the Commission pointed out that extra costs were being borne by the state (Chicago's contribution being fixed) and demanded a reduction, Rose was indignant at what he considered interference in the city's affairs.

By using a different job classification scheme, Rose managed to pay his employees slightly more than county and IPAC employees were paid for equivalent work. Then, when the city raised its pay scales by 10 to 15 per cent, he raised the pay of the welfare department workers without asking permission of IPAC, which had to bear the added expense and which was clearly entitled by law to pass upon pay scales in the city department. IPAC cut back the pay of the city employees after Rose had raised it, and they, encouraged by Rose, besieged the Commission with indignant letters of protest.

Keaster and Hilliard thought there should be uniformity of pay scales among all three agencies. By taking a step forward out of turn, Rose was, they felt, damaging morale in their agencies. Rose, however, believed that IPAC and, especially, Hilliard (who he supposed was manipulating from behind the scenes) were trying to impair the city welfare program in order to make their own "inferior" programs look good by comparison. He believed that the only way to protect his agency from destruction was to fight hard for its autonomy. As he explained to an interviewer afterward: "They had no business telling us how to wipe our noses.

When they tried to tell me how many employees we should have and what we should pay them, I blew up. I called them stupid, and they got mad."

Sometimes Rose made policy in matters which were clearly outside his jurisdiction. Once, for example, when IPAC, at the Governor's behest, was planning to reduce Aid to Dependent Children, he announced in a public meeting that if ADC payments were reduced he would supplement them in Chicago with enough general assistance to prevent hardship and, incidentally, to offset any savings that might accrue to the state from the reduction. From the Commission's standpoint, this was an intolerable interference with its affairs.

McKibbin and his fellow commissioners, having struggled with Rose on many occasions, came to the conclusion early in 1955 that something had to be done. From their point of view, the best thing would be to give IPAC authority to regulate all local general assistance programs. This, however, was out of the question, for the General Assembly was notoriously sensitive to the wishes of the local township supervisors. The next best thing would be to turn the functions of the Chicago Welfare Department over to Hilliard. That would not give IPAC any greater formal control but it would, presumably, get rid of Rose. And it was the presence of Rose, not the lack of formal control, which IPAC felt was the real difficulty.

Since this was hard to explain publicly in terms that would sound convincing to the legislators, IPAC looked around for more plausible grounds upon which to rest its case. These were easily found. Consolidation would make it easier for welfare applicants to find their way to the right place. McKibbin was a great believer in bringing offices together in one place (as state director of finance, he had negotiated the purchase of an office building in the Loop in which state agencies were centrally located), and he would have favored the merger on that ground alone. Taxpayers, of course, would not be particularly anxious to convenience welfare applicants. They could be assured that the merger would result in economies.

Actually, there was little or no evidence to support the economy argument. The general assistance program would require different treatment from the "categories," no matter who administered it: the "categories" were relatively stable and subject to routinization, whereas general assistance was highly volatile, responding quickly to slight ups and downs in the business cycle. It was true that if the departments were merged, one director, and perhaps as many as ten to fifteen of his top assistants could be spared. All the other employees in both agencies would be needed, however. Indeed, neither agency had been able to hire enough social workers to meet its needs. If there was a real economy in consolidation, it was not that the new agency could drop social workers but that it could make better use of the short supply.

As far as McKibbin could see, there was much to be said in favor of the merger and nothing at all to be said against it. "Everybody is for his own empire," he told an interviewer afterward, "but I can't think of any other possible objection to the merger."

Partisans of the city welfare department thought Hilliard was behind the merger plan and that he was seeking only to increase his own power and prestige. Some thought he and the Governor had struck a bargain: Hilliard would use his influence with the legislature to help the Governor replace IPAC with an executive department if the Governor would merge the city and county departments and put him at the head of the new agency. Eventually, these observers surmised, he would turn up as head of a powerful, centralized state welfare department; this was his chosen route to the governorship.

Actually, Hilliard did not discuss the merger with the Governor, and he objected in the most forthright terms when the Governor proposed replacing IPAC with an executive department. His part in the events that led to the merger was much less than his opponents supposed. He encouraged McKibbin to propose the merger. But neither McKibbin nor the other commissioners required much encouragement: they had all long been dissatisfied with the city department.

When he proposed the merger to him, McKibbin found that the Governor needed no persuasion. He was already fully convinced. For a year or two, his advisers in the legislature — and perhaps Keaster as well — had been telling him that millions of dollars could be saved by changes in the welfare program. The Governor was determined to make a record of economy, and, next to highways, welfare was the largest item in his budget. The IPAC proposal was exactly what he was looking for.

The Governor's advisers made two main suggestions. One was to increase from one to three years the period of residence necessary to establish eligibility for relief. This, they said, would discourage indigents from moving into the state. The other was to centralize control over relief in the Governor's hands. This was to be done in two ways: by bringing the Chicago general assistance program (which took 80 per cent of the state's welfare fund) under state control and by replacing the independent commission, IPAC, with a department responsible directly to the chief executive. With such control, they assured him, millions could be saved.

Rose unwittingly helped them to make this point. By refusing to curtail public aid when IPAC, acting at the Governor's request, sought to do so, Rose made it perfectly clear that if the Governor did not control relief expenditures in Chicago he could not be sure of balancing the state's budget.

The great merit of all these proposals was that they were good politics. Downstaters had been growling about the cost of relief in Chicago for a long time. Anything that would shift more of that cost from the state to the city or reduce it would be popular downstate.

Even in Chicago, however, reductions in relief would be popular with many tax-minded people. Although it was the state, not the city, which would bear any relief costs not met from the one-mill property tax, Chicagoans, who paid about half the taxes raised by the state, would benefit from cuts in relief. Many people could not understand why, in a time of full employment, relief costs were higher than they had been during the Depression.

About three-fourths of the welfare cases in the metropolitan area were Negro. Attacking welfare was a covert way of attacking Negroes, and for this reason it would be popular with some whites in both parties. Negroes were coming to Chicago from Mississippi and other southern states at the rate of several hundred a week. In many cases they were hard to assimilate. Whites could not or would not distinguish between respectable Negroes and "riff-raff";

when Negroes "invaded" a white neighborhood, whites promptly moved away, leaving schools, churches, and other institutions segregated. The transition of a neighborhood from white to Negro was always accompanied by hostility, and often by violence. White politicians were under constant pressure to discourage the spread of Negroes, and they were well aware that when their wards became predominantly Negro their own political careers there would end.

If a residence law would discourage the influx of Negroes from the South, there would be many in Chicago who would favor it. "He has the attitude: 'Let's protect our homes and keep the Negroes out,'" one white legislator said of another, an important Republican whose district was in a transitional area.

There was anti-Negro sentiment among Democratic voters as well as among Republican ones, of course. But the Democratic organization had a strong incentive to hold such sentiment in check and even to suppress it: two-thirds to three-quarters of the Negroes could be depended upon to vote Democratic.

The Republican organization, on the other hand, stood to gain from any measure that would reduce the number of prospective Democrats entering the state. Organization-minded Republicans were not necessarily influenced by racial prejudice: had the incoming Negroes been mostly Republican, the organization would doubtless have welcomed them. As it happened, a residence law and other such anti-welfare measures would keep out of the state many more Democrats than Republicans. The residence law, the Chicago *Defender* (a Negro paper) said, "is a slow but sure way of cutting down the density of the already overpopulated southside wards whose votes have often determined the final outcome of many important elections."

Although organization-minded and tax-minded Republicans had reason to discourage the influx of Negroes, there were some important Republicans who had an opposite interest. The big industrialists of the metropolitan area, most of whom were Republican, depended heavily upon the existence of a large pool of labor. From their standpoint, there were too few Negroes coming from the South; according to the Chicago Association of Commerce and Industry, 400,000 more workers would be needed in the metropolitan area by 1960. Any measures that might reduce the labor supply would be vigorously resisted by the industrialists, some of whom were big contributors to Republican campaigns.

There was, however, another and very much more important group which would oppose anti-welfare measures. This was the Negroes already in Chicago. If the Republicans were to strengthen their weak hold on them, they would have to offer no less generous public assistance than did the Democrats. The measures which would gain the Republican votes downstate and in the anti-Negro districts of the city would surely lose them votes in the Negro wards of the central city.

There were two Republicans in the legislature who were particularly important in welfare matters. Each was, so to speak, one horn of a dilemma the Governor faced.

One was Senator W. Russell Arrington, a corporation lawyer from Evanston, a "silk stocking" suburb of Chicago. He was entirely in accord with the Governor's emphasis on economy, and he believed that the welfare program offered great opportunities for savings. In his district, leading a fight against rising relief costs would be good politics. "Arrington is a clever man who doesn't give a damn about welfare one way or another," one of his opponents said. "He heard Keaster testify ineptly in favor of a deficiency appropriation. I suppose he saw an opportunity. He probably said to himself, 'If this is the kind of leadership the Commission has, I won't have any trouble making it look bad.' "

The other was Representative William H. Robinson, a Negro of Chicago. Robinson was both a professional politician (he was a ward committeeman) and a professional social worker. He was an independent-minded man who had a large following in the Negro community. ("I came up in politics a maverick all the way," he told an interviewer. "I have no Cadillac to wave at the people from. I walk to my office. If someone jumps on me, you'll see the people come to my aid.") To Robinson's constituents, welfare was a matter of first importance.

The Governor had to cast up a balance and make a choice. It was not an easy thing to do. If he took the advice of Arrington, he ran the risk of alienating Robinson and others like him; the Negro wards were extremely important (Mayor Daley had run up one-third of his margin of victory in four of them), and Robinson was the kind of leader who might help him cut into the Democratic strength there. On the other hand, Arrington and others had convinced him that there were millions to be saved by economies in the welfare program. The time was coming when he would be a candidate again — for senator or vice-president, the rumor was — and economy would be the keystone of his campaign.

When Robinson saw him a few months before the legislature convened, the Governor was preoccupied with the need for economy "We must do something about mounting relief costs, Bill," he said, "and we must get rid of the chisellers." To attack welfare would be politically unsound, Robinson told him. A formula for economy should be found, but one which would not hurt people. There was such a thing as false economy.

On one matter the Governor and Robinson fully agreed. If the Chicago Democrats were getting an advantage from the administration of welfare, they wanted to take it away from them and, if possible, get it for themselves.

It was only in the Negro wards that welfare was important, but here it was very important indeed. To a Negro politician, any association with relief — even a nominal one — was a great advantage.

Most downstate politicians supposed that the Chicago welfare department was a rich source of patronage for Mayor Daley. None of the welfare department jobs was under the merit system. There was nothing to stop Rose from giving jobs to people with political connections, and since there were 1,150 jobs to be given, he could have a powerful machine. In fact, Rose had never made any political appointments; he was opposed in principle to doing so, and he had never been asked to do so. "The Mayor didn't have any jobs in the welfare department — not even mine," he said afterward. "I vote a split ticket and the Mayor knows it."

Patronage was not the only way in which the welfare program could have been used politically, however. Caseworkers might have been instructed to give favored treatment to those who were properly introduced, and relief applicants might have been told more or less openly that the Democrats were the source from which all their blessings flowed. As Rose himself explained to an interviewer: "All you had to do was slip an innocuous notice in the envelope along with the checks. For example, when they voted to cut relief 10% rather than go to the legislature for a deficiency appropriation, I could have put an innocent-looking explanation in the envelope saying, "I'm sorry, but Governor Stratton insisted. . . ."

No one who knew anything about the matter believed that Rose countenanced any political use of the welfare program. The newspapers had found a few "payrollers" in IPAC, but none at all in the city department. By common consent, the politicians had left it alone. It was, they apparently thought, too dangerous to be touched.

This did not mean that the Democrats were not getting a political advantage from the welfare program. They were. Rose might do his best to keep welfare and politics apart, but there was nothing to stop a Democratic precinct captain from bringing them together. A captain might give his constituent a card of introduction to carry to the welfare office, or he might make a telephone call in his behalf. The constituent got exactly the same treatment that he would have gotten without the card or the call, or with a card or call from a Republican precinct captain. He did not know that, however, and even if he did, he might feel grateful to the captain for trying to help him.

In the Negro wards, some committeemen maintained an information bureau specializing in welfare matters. "There is a prejudice against social workers in my ward," a Democratic alderman told an interviewer. "Some of them treat their clients as if they were lower than dirt. I have a secretary who explains to people on relief what their rights are, what the law is, and what they're entitled to. She is a sort of social worker. But we don't do anything besides this."

There was nothing to stop a Republican committeeman from giving the same service. Some of them did.

At election time, some Democratic precinct captains in Negro wards threatened voters with loss of relief if they voted Republican. No one ever showed, however, that the welfare department itself gave aid or comfort to this kind of pressure. There might even be some question whether the "threats" were really improper. If a Democratic precinct captain went through a housing project waving a loaf of bread and saying, "If you want it, you've got to vote with us," was he "threatening" or was he merely dramatizing an issue?

There was no doubt that, in certain wards, the Democratic party gained from its long identification with relief and the welfare state. People took it for granted that they were beholden to the Democrats for their relief checks.

From a legalistic standpoint, the merger would not really make any difference. Although Hilliard was a Republican, he was no more likely to do favors for Republican precinct captains than Rose was to do them for Democratic ones. Hilliard, too, believed that relief should be kept out of politics. But even if he had not believed this, there would be little he could do for the Republicans. The County Board, which employed him, was dominated by Democrats and would be for a long time to come.

Even so, the matter was important to the Republican committeemen. Some of them supposed that, after the merger, relief checks would be signed by Governor Stratton rather than Mayor Daley and that this would have a profound psychological effect upon the voters. (In fact, the city comptroller's name, not the Mayor's appeared upon general assistance checks; and after the merger, the county comptroller's, the county treasurer's, and the county president's names — but not the governor's — would appear upon them.) Most voters, the politicians knew, did not identify the county government with the Democratic Party as fully as they did the city government. As long as the voter did not *think* that the Democrats controlled the administration of welfare, it did not matter whether they did or not.

As the committeemen saw it, the merger would have the added psychological advantage of giving the impression that the Republicans were concerned with the problems of the poor. "Ever since the New Deal," Robinson told an interviewer, "people have always associated welfare with the Democratic party. The Democrats were 'the party of the poor man' and so on. They have had a political hey-day on this feeling. This merger represents a change that the Republican party is going through. We're trying to show the people of Chicago that the Republicans care about welfare too."

In his second inaugural address, the Governor stressed the need for economy. Local governments in all states but one, he said, contributed a larger share of the total cost of welfare than they contributed in Illinois. It was evident, then, that Illinois contributed a disproportionate share. (That, elsewhere, local governments may have contributed too much and the state governments too little was a possibility he did not consider.) The time had come for a thorough legislative inquiry into the subject.

Senator Arrington at once introduced a resolution to create a special joint legislative committee to investigate public aid expenditures. The resolution was soon passed and Arrington was made chairman of the committee. On it with him was William E. Pollack of Chicago, the House majority whip. Conspicuously absent was William H. Robinson, the Negro social worker. He was very much discouraged at having been passed over.

The legislature appropriated $5,000 to support the investigations.

The committee, insiders surmised, was intended to discredit IPAC and to recommend measures that would cut relief costs and give the Governor the control he wanted. When IPAC's budget request for the biennium came before him, the Governor cut it from $367 to $317 million. In his budget message, he said he was convinced that the Arrington committee's work would make possible a further cut of at least 10 per cent.

The committee used the whole of its appropriation to employ a firm of management consultants, Stroedel and Associates, to study all aspects of welfare organization and policy. Arrington's agreement with the firm specified that he was to get whatever publicity might result. Stroedel assured him in a letter: "We are not interested in publicity. We work in a highly personalized manner; and we always attempt to become integrated into the functioning of the directing offices that assign work to us. Requests by the press or other interested persons for any information or statements, therefore, will not be handled by us, under any circumstances, but will be referred to you."

The Stroedel report, which was given to the legislature by the committee in the middle of May, recommended almost everything Arrington and other extremists had been advocating: allowances of food, clothing, and shelter should be reduced; three years residence should be required to establish eligibility for relief; the state should take a lien against the property of relief recipients; the localities (Chicago, of course, was by far the most important) should pay a larger, and the state a smaller, share of public aid; IPAC should be reorganized and the salary of its top executives increased (the report did not discuss proposals to replace it with an executive department); and the city welfare department should be merged into the county department.

Since 1949, the report asserted, "there has developed a *unanimous* opinion on the part of the private and public agencies and organizations, as well as on the part of the IPAC Commission and its Central Office Staff, favoring a consolidation; but *nothing* has been done about it. It has been said that the reason for inaction is largely because of the strong personalities of the two persons who direct the separate offices."

Noting that the county department had a staff of 900 and the city one of 1,200, the report asserted, without substantiating evidence, that "a consolidation of the two, just as far as possible, without disturbing essential services, should eliminate a duplication of effort and the attending confusion, as well as provide substantial economies."

The authors of the report estimated — again without presenting evidence — that a merger would save $2 to $4.5 million in the biennium.

The immediate effect of the report was alarming to the supporters of the welfare programs. Newspapers throughout the state carried front-page stories of the economies that could be made. Tax-minded legislators spoke of the report with approval. Some observers felt that the atmosphere in Springfield was unusually hostile to Chicago. The welfare forces soon rallied, however, and counterattacked. McKibbin signed a seventeen-page report, prepared by the IPAC staff, which detailed numerous errors and distortions in the Stroedel report and called it "irresponsible, unscholarly, lacking in perception, and extremely biased." The dean of the School of Social Service Administration at the University of Chicago, Alton A. Linford, said publicly that the report was a waste of the taxpayer's money. A professor at Loyola said it was "both incomprehensible and an insult to the people of Illinois." The executive director of the Welfare Council of Metropolitan Chicago mailed an analysis of it to all members of the legislature in which he said it "represents hasty judgments, a profound lack of knowledge about public assistance programs and an apparent lack of concern for human values."

When the press revealed that the report had been prepared in ten days by two men neither of whom had any prior knowledge of welfare matters, its influence was ended. The welfare forces soon concluded that Arrington's position had been weakened rather than strengthened by his maneuver. He and the report had been taken seriously in early committee sessions, but by the time the welfare bills reached the floor of the House, there were smiles on people's faces whenever Arrington's views on welfare were mentioned. He had gone too far.

The merger bill was introduced at the end of February by four senators. The "first sponsor" (her name appeared first on the bill) was the chairman of the Public Welfare Committee, the second was the majority leader, the third was the majority whip, and the fourth was Arrington. Nothing could have said more plainly that this was an administration bill.

Mayor Daley regarded the merger proposal as a cheap political trick intended to distract public attention from gross mismanagement in IPAC, to give the impression that his administration had been playing politics with relief, and (always a downstate objective) to make Chicago look bad. He had a fierce pride both in his administration and in his city. And his Irish was up. "Why," he demanded angrily of an interviewer, "is Chicago being discriminated against? If the merger is good for Chicago, why isn't it good for Evanston too?" Probably, however, he objected less to the content of the proposal than to the way it was put forward. Had a plan been proposed, after full deliberation, which did not discriminate against Chicago and which was solidly supported by social workers, he might have supported it actively. But he would do everything he could to stop this (as he thought) anti-Daley, anti-Chicago measure, and if it passed he would have it repealed whenever the Democrats had strength enough in Springfield to do so.

Hilliard had expected the merger proposal to be on the agenda for informal discussion between the Governor and the Mayor at the start of the legislative session; that it had not been was due, he thought, only to faulty staff work. In this he seems to have been mistaken. It was almost certainly a part of the Governor's plan to embarrass and annoy the Mayor. They were, after all, political opponents, and in this matter the Governor had nothing to gain and something to lose by co-operation.

The Mayor, however, did not seem to take very seriously the bill's chance of passage. He had had long experience in the legislature (he was in the House briefly and had been for several years majority leader of the Senate), and he knew that as the session advanced there were sure to be occasions when the Republicans would need Democratic support. On one of these occasions, he may have thought, the Republicans would be happy to drop the merger for the sake of something more important to them. That, in fact, might be the reason they had introduced it in the first place.

Since the Mayor seemed unconcerned, Rose was unconcerned. And since Rose was unconcerned, so were the friends and supporters of his agency. For example, Linford, the dean of social service administration at the University of Chicago (to cite only one of several influential social work leaders), seeing that Rose did not think the merger bill had a chance of passage, did nothing to rally his fellow social workers against it. Had he thought the bill had a chance of passage, he and others would have got the Illinois Welfare Association to hold meetings and pass resolutions, and they would have tried to persuade the Metropolitan Welfare Council of Chicago to join them in opposing it.

Ryan, the president of the Cook County Board, made it clear to the Mayor and to the press that the merger proposal was made without his approval. He doubted very much that it would result in savings, he told the newspapers, and, in any case, he was against it.

Ryan called in Hilliard, who he suspected had originated the proposal, and told him he was not to lobby for the merger.

To avoid any misunderstanding, Hilliard stayed away from Springfield while the merger was under consideration. It was, he felt, a misfortune for the cause of welfare that he could not lobby against the other bills on the Stratton-Arrington program.

Keaster was under no such prohibition. He lobbied energetically for the merger and the residence bills and gave no sign of being opposed to the abolition of IPAC and the creation, in its place, of an executive department. His testimony on matters upon which the Commission had refrained from taking a position embarrassed McKibbin, and he was relieved when, at the most critical stage of affairs in Springfield, Keaster had to go to Washington, D.C., to lobby on an important bill. His place in Springfield was taken by Peter W. Cahill, the head of IPAC's Chicago office, who was soon to succeed him as executive secretary. Cahill had a professional point of view, was a capable administrator, and got along well with Hilliard. His appointment, together with the departure of Rose, would meet the need which, so far as the Commission was concerned, had occasioned the merger proposal.

When the merger bill came before the Senate Public Welfare Committee early in May, Keaster was the principal witness in favor of it. He had prepared a statement which claimed that the merger would result in savings of $3 to $5 million in the biennium and which compared the administrative costs of the two agencies. The monthly cost per case in Chicago, according to him, was $14.38, while that in the county was only $4.99.

Senator William J. Lynch, the minority leader, asked Keaster how he had arrived at his estimate of the savings. The savings, Keaster said, would come about in many ways. There would be closer control.

Lynch cut in. How, exactly, had he arrived at the estimate? Had he made a study?

Keaster said, yes, he had made a study.

Lynch wanted to know of what the study consisted.

There would be certain immediate transfers . . ., Keaster began. Lynch interrupted again. What was the process used in making the estimate? What did the committee making the estimate do?

Keaster said it looked at the records.

Lynch asked what formula it used in making its calculations from the records.

There was a formula, Keaster said, but he didn't have it with him.

"You don't actually know," Lynch said. "You say consolidation will result in savings, but you could be $3 million off unless you base your estimate on details. This is an important matter and it shouldn't be left to guesswork. In the past moves of this kind have turned out after a biennium to result in very slight savings or even in losses." He had respect for Keaster and the IPAC staff, he said, but their study of the matter was insufficient.

Cahill, the head of IPAC's Chicago operations, remarked that there were other reasons for favoring the merger. The administrative costs of the city were three times those of the county.

Lynch replied that the services provided by the two departments were not comparable. "Do you contend that consolidation will reduce costs?" he asked Cahill.

"We're not sure," Cahill answered.

Rose took the floor. The figures presented by Keaster and Cahill were new to him, he said, and therefore difficult to refute. He knew they were wrong, however. If the county provided the same services as the city, its costs would be no less. They might even be more because the county's low pay scale caused an extremely high turnover of personnel.

If the Senate hearing proved anything, it was that the decision for or against the merger would have to be made without any reliable information about the possible economies. Both sides were well aware, of course, that the bill would be accepted or rejected on grounds that were both broadly and narrowly political. Neither side could afford to say publicly, however, that these grounds might be as important — perhaps much more important — as a saving in administrative costs.

The fact was, one of Keaster's associates later confided to an interviewer, that IPAC's estimate of savings was pure guesswork. It had been "picked out of the air."

The facts — if there had been any — would have made no difference in the committee vote anyway. The bill was a "must" on the Governor's program, and the Republicans had a majority in the committee.

"This bill is being shoved down Chicago's throat," a Chicago Democrat complained as the vote was counted. "The Chicago members don't want it. It is being forced on us by members not from Chicago."

If the Democrats had any chance of stopping the bill, that chance was in the House. There they lacked only twelve votes for a majority.

Robinson, the Negro social worker, had been appointed vice-chairman of the House welfare committee. This had been done, he surmised, "to shut me up." It did not succeed in shutting him up, however. On the contrary, it gave him power which he used to oppose most — but not all — of the Stratton-Arrington program.

Early in the session, he had introduced a bill to create an interim legislative committee to study welfare. The Governor had gone over the bill with him word by word, suggesting a few changes and agreeing to support it. Robinson had told him that, while he considered himself an administration man in general, in welfare matters he had "a professional commitment to the field" and would feel bound to vote as he thought best. "Okay," the Governor had said. "Do what you can to protect yourself in your district and give me as much support as you can." Although Robinson did not say so, he knew that, far from supporting the Governor's welfare measures, he would fight them as hard as he could.

Before launching his fight, however, Robinson prudently sought to make sure that his own bill was safely passed and that he was elected chairman of the interim committee. When his bill reached the Senate welfare committee, Arrington raised objections to it. With the help of the Senate majority leader, however, Robinson managed to get it by. It was on its way to the Governor for his signature when the administration's welfare program — including the residence bill, the bill abolishing IPAC, and the merger — reached the House welfare committee.

Robinson was in an awkward position. He called the Governor's administrative assistant and complained that the delay in signing his bill was making him look bad in his district. The assistant said he was sorry but the bill had not yet reached the Governor's desk. The next day he called back to say that it had been signed. Robinson breathed a sigh of relief, called on the Governor to thank him, and then gave his full attention to the defeat of all but one of the Stratton-Arrington bills.

When Arrington came before the House committee with an impassioned plea for the residence bill, Robinson took the floor in opposition. Arrington was ingratiating in his references to "his friend, Bill Robinson." Robinson was hostile. He called Arrington "Senator" and said that the residence bill was the product of bigotry.

The residence bill, Robinson thought, was the cornerstone of the administration's welfare program. If it was defeated, the other anti-welfare measures would be defeated too. The Democrats were all opposed to it. Many Republicans were lukewarm. Robinson telephoned McRae, the executive director of the Metropolitan Welfare Council of Chicago, to ask him to find out which Republican legislators had wives active in welfare organization. The ladies, Robinson suggested, might be persuaded to bring pressure on their husbands.

In the committee, Robinson was outspoken in his opposition to the administration bills. ("I've learned," he told an interviewer, "that if you oppose a bill vigorously enough you can stop it. I just said, 'We can't pass this ————.' ") The other two Negro Republicans on the committee stood with him, and so did all of the Democrats. Together they managed to kill two bills: one empowering the courts to declare the mother of more than one illegitimate child unfit and to put her children up for adoption, and another making only one child born out of wedlock eligible for aid as a dependant. The committee approved the residence bill, but only after it was amended to revise from three years to two the period required to establish eligibility.

Robinson did what he could to delay the residence bill. Meanwhile, he encouraged McRae and others to deluge the legislators with letters and telegrams. When some legislators remarked to him on the strong opposition to the bill, he suggested they "lay off" it (refrain from voting); that way they might stay out of the bad books of the administration while assuring the defeat of the bill. When the vote was finally taken, the bill was overwhelmingly defeated. Almost all of the Democrats voted against it. Several Republicans abstained from voting. Several others voted against it. These included the Negroes, two representatives who had Negroes in their districts and who always conferred with Robinson on such issues, a Catholic who was (as Robinson later put it) "amenable to my approach," and a representative who wanted to exchange his vote for one by Robinson against a county planning bill. So strong was the opposition to the bill that the Republican leadership was unable to save face by tabling it.

Seeing what Robinson and other welfare-minded Republicans had accomplished so far, the friends of the Chicago Welfare Department had high hopes that the merger would also be defeated. But Robinson, they soon discovered, intended to support that bill as vigorously as he had fought the others. In their eyes, this was a betrayal. "Robinson sold out," one of them said sadly afterward. "He's a phony. He knew more about what was at stake than did any of the others, but he sold out. He had to do some wrestling with himself first, though. He could have voted against the merger and have said: 'I do this even though I know it will cost me my seat because I know it is right.' But he didn't. He's a phony."

Robinson saw the matter differently. He did not agree with the Governor that a merger would save millions of dollars, but he thought it might make for quicker, smoother handling of applications and for easier transfer of cases from one relief program to another. He would have been satisfied to have either Rose or Hilliard at the head of a consolidated agency; both he thought, were excellent administrators.

In his opinion, however, the real justification for the merger was political. He knew from firsthand experience that Democratic precinct captains were gaining an advantage from their self-asserted connection with relief. As a Republican politician, he naturally wanted this stopped. But he thought the principal political advantage would be psychological. If there were a much-publicized battle between the Governor and Mayor Daley for control of relief, the Governor's victory would impress the voters. Thereafter, they would be less likely to associate relief with the Democrats.

These were reasons enough. But Robinson had an additional one. The Republicans had caucused on the bill, and all but one (this one absented himself from the caucus) had bound himself to vote for it. Nevertheless, the House leadership — according to Robinson's later account — was not certain of its ability to pass the bill. The majority whip, Pollack, therefore asked Robinson, who was more conversant than others with welfare matters and who could not be suspected of being either anti-Negro or anti-welfare, to handle the bill in committee and on the floor.

"I have my price," Robinson told him. "You drag your feet on the rest of this stuff [the anti-welfare bills]. You can talk on the bills and then sit down. That's my price."

Pollack agreed. The residence bill was now as good as dead, and Robinson was pledged to make every effort to get the merger bill passed.

The merger bill, it was soon apparent, was not going to be as fiercely opposed by the welfare forces as the other bills had been.

The Welfare Council of Metropolitan Chicago, which had been very effective against the other bills, said nothing about the merger. In its criticism of the Stroedel report it had limited itself to "items on which we believe we have some competence"; these did not include any of the recommendations dealing with organization. McRae, the executive director of the Council, did not ask his board to take a position on the merger. Personally, he was against it; he thought that the Governor was trying to take control of welfare for purely political purposes. He knew, however, that there were many Republicans on his board who would not share his suspicions. For a time he apparently felt so strongly that he was ready to jeopardize his job by testifying without authorization from his board (McKibbin, among others, was surprised to meet him in Springfield where he had come, he said, to testify against the merger); but if that was his intention, it was never put to test, for the opportunity for him to testify did not arise.

The Chicago industrialists who opposed the residence bill because it might curtail their labor supply took no stand on the merger. Joseph Block, for example, the president of Inland Steel Corporation and of the Chicago Association of Commerce and

Industry, went to Springfield to oppose the residence bill but said nothing of the merger proposal.

Other Negroes agreed with Robinson that the merger was not a "race" issue. The Chicago Urban League and the National Association for the Advancement of Colored People, both of which fought the other welfare bills, were indifferent to the merger. The Chicago *Defender* did not discuss it editorially, but Walter L. Lowe, a Negro insurance broker who was active in welfare matters, endorsed the merger while attacking the other welfare bills in a news column. "Only recently," he said, "the head of the Chicago Welfare Department compared public assistance with the Poor House Over the Hill, and stated 'unfortunately there are no cotton plantations in Chicago in which Negroes might be put to work.' "

Two of the major Chicago newspapers favored the merger for the economies that it was expected to bring. "Let's find Mr. Rose another good job and help the taxpayers by eliminating his department," the *Tribune* proposed. The *Daily News* thought a merger which would save $3 to $5 million was entirely sound. The *Sun-Times,* while admitting that the merger would be more efficient and economical, believed "it is wrong to make politics the controlling factor." The matter should be postponed, the editors said, until all aspects of it could be studied sensibly, apart from the political considerations that dominated it.

Rose's "tough" posture was not serving him well. It did not prevent conservatives like Arrington from destroying his agency. And it alienated many natural allies among the welfare-minded. Leaders of the social service profession who liked and trusted Rose and knew perfectly well that his public statements were not to be taken at their face value found it impossible to support him energetically. To do so would give the impression that they favored the "tough" rather than the "liberal" view. Some were torn between conflicting inclinations and so did nothing. As one social service leader later explained to an interviewer:

> If it had been a matter of principle, the social workers would have taken a position. Downstate people were behind the merger, and we don't trust them. We were sure they didn't mean welfare any good. We saw it as a political move on Stratton's part.

You ask why we didn't fight the merger then. Well, Al Rose prided himself on being hard and tight-fisted. Many of his ways of operating have been severely criticized by social workers. He has done things like publishing articles in the *Police Gazette* describing his methods of getting chisellers. He employed FBI agents to catch deserting fathers.

He tried to find jobs for people with some capacity to work. But if the person doesn't take the job, Rose won't give him any assistance. This is a pretty strong-armed method; social workers feel there is too much coercion involved. There are a lot of borderline case. A person may be physically able but psychologically unable. We didn't like Rose's tough-minded approach.

But on the whole Rose ran one of the best assistance programs in the country. He fought for more adequate standards of assistance. The merger is to make the Chicago department subservient to IPAC.

We were in a funny position. We favor integration, but why begin with the only good department in the state and leave those trashy programs unintegrated? This merger isn't even county-wide; it just takes Chicago.

We were in a spot. We favored integration, but we were suspicious of the people behind it.

I didn't think it had a chance to pass until a week before it did. I thought the Democrats were so strongly against the merger that they would never let it go through. So even if we had wanted to, we really didn't have time to get organized. If we had really felt strongly and unanimously on the issue, maybe we'd have been able to. But you see we didn't.

Besides, social workers don't carry much weight in Springfield. We have been told that if we ever want anything, the best thing is to keep quiet.

By the time the bill reached the House Welfare Committee, Rose could see that his cause was lost.

When Rose went to Springfield to plead his case, he found that there was no room for argument or compromise. In private conversations in the corridors and hotel lobbies, he told legislators that they were acting precipitately; there ought to be a careful study before a merger was effected. "We agree with you," some Republicans told him. "But the word has come down the line. The Governor wants this bill."

Under the circumstances, the only hope was in delay. If the Democrats could keep the bill from coming up for a vote, it might be lost in the last-minute rush. Or, at the last minute, the Governor might agree to trade the merger for something else.

The Democratic leaders had, in fact, already proposed a trade. It was clear that the bill to replace IPAC with an executive department could not be passed without Democratic help; this was because the township supervisors' association had successfully lobbied against it with downstate members. If the Governor would drop the merger, the Democrats told him, they would pass the bill abolishing IPAC. The Governor, however, had refused to make the trade. Probably, he had no hope of passing the executive department bill without Democratic support, but he apparently attached more importance to the merger than to the creation of the executive department. This was easy to understand. Control of the four federal "categories" meant very little, since they operated under rules drawn up by the federal government. It was in the administration of general assistance, where the federal government played no part, that there were opportunities to economize. The Democrats knew that the Governor would not give up the merger for the executive department bill if he could help it, but thought that delay might force him to compromise against his will.

At Rose's suggestion, Mayor Daley asked De La Cour, the minority leader of the House, to have Davis, the leader of the Negro Democratic bloc, handle the bill. Davis learned of his assignment only five minutes before committee hearings were to begin. This was the time, Rose believed, for a passionate, bitter-end defense of his department, and he knew that Davis, a preacher, could rise to dramatic heights if sufficiently aroused. In the few minutes before the hearings began, he took Davis aside and tried to create in him the mood the occasion required.

Rose had brought nine witnesses from Chicago to testify against the bill. If they took an hour or two each, the committee would not be able to act for two or three days.

The Republican chairman of the committee responded by limiting the time for all witnesses to twenty minutes. This brought howls of outrage from the Democrats. It was not uncommon to limit testimony, but the custom was to impose such a stringent limit only with unimportant bills. This was not an unimportant bill, and the Democrats claimed — and seemed actually to feel — that a gross injustice had been done them by the chairman's rule.

The Democrats next demanded that a subcommittee investigate the matter thoroughly, something which would take several days at least. The majority refused. All this took a whole afternoon.

In the evening the committee met again. The witnesses had by now all gone home to Chicago, but the Democrats had found another means of delaying things. When Davis questioned the presence of a quorum, it was found that only thirteen of the committee's thirty-two members were present. "It's post time," De La Cour said to the Republican manager. "Where are your horses?" The Democratic members of the committee, it appeared, had failed to find the committee room. If all of the Republicans had been present, the absence of the Democrats would have made no difference. As it was, however, nothing could be done, and the rules prevented another meeting for at least twenty-four hours. This time it was the Republicans who were angry. The Democrats, some of them said, had "played it dirty."

It was a week before the committee met again. Then the chairman, anticipating more delay (there were now sixteen witnesses to be heard) absented himself, leaving Robinson, the vice-chairman, in charge. After hearing McKibbin, a Republican moved to limit testimony to twenty minutes for each side. The Democrats were in a strong position to oppose this motion, for it had been agreed beforehand that they were to be heard at length. However, De La Cour, the Democratic leader, knowing that Robinson was determined to reach a vote if it took all night, suddenly asked, "Why don't you move that the bill be reported out?" The Republicans quickly accepted the suggestion, and the bill was recommended by a vote of 21 to 10.

Davis, the Negro who had been asked to handle the bill for the Democrats, was furious. Maybe De La Cour thought he could make a big name for himself by opposing the bill when it came to the floor, he remarked to another legislator.

"Who can get away from the fact that this is politics?" De La Cour asked rhetorically as the votes were counted.

Robinson acknowledged that this was politics. "I was never taught this at the school of social service in Chicago," he said.

A few days later, the merger bill was passed by a vote of 96-70. Every Republican but one was in his seat, and every one who was in his seat voted for the bill. Three Democrats joined the Republicans. Two of these had run in the primaries without organization support. The third was an old man who confided that he had four relatives on the Governor's payroll.

4
The Chicago Transit
Authority

S OMETHING had to be done about the Chicago
Transit Authority (CTA). Like mass transit systems everywhere,
it was in financial trouble. Created in 1947 as a municipal corporation after many failures of private enterprises, it had managed
to keep its head above water for nearly ten years; during this
period, it had made principal and interest payments on its bonds
and had invested a huge sum in modernization of equipment. In
1956, however, a deficit was in prospect, and a larger one could
be expected every year thereafter. Improvement of the system
was urgently needed — especially extension of rapid transit lines
and installation of safety devices — but, as matters stood, it was
barely meeting its operating expenses and was accumulating no
reserves against depreciation.

About a million persons rode CTA twice each workday. Forty
per cent of these went from the outlying parts of Chicago to the
central business district to work or to shop. (About half of the
800,000 people who entered the central business district every
day traveled on CTA's trains and busses.) Forty or fifty thousand
were suburbanites who took CTA for the last lap of a longer
journey by railroad or auto. The system served all of Chicago
— hardly anyone in the city was more than a short walk from
a CTA station — and twenty-nine other municipalities as well.
This was by no means all of Cook County; most of its out-

lying parts were served by other lines. A few places were not served at all because they did not have enough traffic to support service.

CTA's revenues came almost entirely from fares. The City of Chicago, with the aid of federal funds, had built subways and turned them over to it for operation, and the city and state had exempted it from certain taxes. Otherwise, it was supported by its passengers.

The number of these had declined steadily. In 1946 the average Chicagoan took 319 rides by mass transportation; in 1956 he took only 163. Traffic on the rapid transit lines (mainly to and from the central city) had held up relatively well; the big loss was in bus traffic. Meanwhile, operating costs had increased. CTA had raised its fares, but it had done so very slowly (it charged twenty cents in 1956 for a ride that cost five cents in 1914) because it feared fare increases would cut traffic further. If the number of passengers held constant, a five-cent increase in 1956 would raise revenues by $28 million, an amount ample to meet the needs. But the number of passengers would almost certainly *not* remain constant: CTA estimated it would drop by 12.5 per cent, leaving a net increase in revenue of not much more than $8 million.

The dilemma was illustrated by a *Sun-Times* cartoonist who drew a half-starved horse (CTA) with an enormous feedbag (rising fares). "The more he eats the skinnier he gets," the caption said.

There were some grounds for supposing that CTA would have little trouble with the legislature.

For one thing, the amount of subsidy needed was not large. Twenty-five million dollars a year for fifteen years would put it in first-class shape. In the second largest city of the United States this was very little. New York gave its rapid transit system $100 million a year.

CTA's million riders — one might expect — would powerfully support a measure to improve the system at the taxpayers' expense. The riders comprised 20 per cent of the population of Cook County and 10 per cent of that of the state: there were enough of them, in other words, to make a difference politically.

Chicago had great weight in the legislature. Of the 177 representatives, 69 came from Chicago and 21 from other places in Cook County (these other places were called "country towns," a very inappropriate term in most cases). Of the 56 senators (there were two vacancies), 16 came from Chicago and 6 from the rest of Cook County.

Forty-nine representatives and 13 senators from Chicago and Cook County were Democrats. These were, to a considerable extent, under the control of the mayor of Chicago, Richard J. Daley. As chairman of the county Democratic committee, Daley had much to say about who might run for office. He was also the dispenser of patronage and other favors in the city. (Daniel Ryan, the president of the County Board, had the county patronage, but he and Daley were one so far as the legislature was concerned.) One-third of the Democratic legislators from Chicago and Cook County held city or county jobs (the minority leader of the House, for example, was a civil service examiner in City Hall), and almost all of the others had relatives or henchmen on the public payroll. (For that matter, several Republicans received patronage from the Democrats in return for support in matters which the Republican leadership did not consider crucial.) If Daley favored a subsidy for CTA, most of the legislators of Cook County would almost have to favor one too.

Actually, Daley was extremely anxious to avert a fare increase. In a purely legal sense, he had no responsibility for CTA other than to appoint four of its seven commissioners (the others were appointed by the Governor). CTA was not political; neither party got patronage from it, and being a commissioner was not a stepping stone in politics. Nevertheless, in the general view, the Mayor of Chicago had some responsibility for the way the system was run. If everything went smoothly, probably no one would give him credit. But if something went wrong — if there were a fare increase, for example — he would be blamed more than anyone else. "Every time a rider pays 25 cents he will think of Daley, not of the legislature," a suburban Republican representative remarked smugly.

The Mayor had other reasons also for wanting to help CTA. He believed that the future of the central city depended to some extent upon the use made of mass transportation. People who gave up riding CTA lines did not stay at home; they switched to automobiles. This meant that city streets and parking places were constantly becoming more congested and the city's budget more burdened with the expense of new expressways, parking places, and traffic control facilities. People would blame the Mayor not only for the higher fares but for unbalanced budgets and traffic congestion as well.

As automobiles replaced mass transportation, it was likely that fewer people would come to the Loop to do their shopping, banking, dining, and movie-going. Once in an auto, one could as easily turn away from the city as toward it. Outlying shopping centers had already sprung up in many places, and there would surely be more of them. The owners and managers of the great banks, department stores, and office buildings of the central district feared that their better customers would turn more and more toward the suburbs, leaving the center of the city, surrounded as it was by slums and blight, very badly off. Cheap and convenient mass transportation, they hoped, would keep the customers coming from the middle-class neighborhoods into the center of the city.

The Mayor was well aware of the great importance these interests placed upon the preservation of the central business district. A few years before, they had formed the Central Area Committee, through which they could work behind the scenes to strengthen and improve the center of the city. In any poll of well-informed persons, the heads of the committee would have been listed among Chicago's "power elite." They were: Joseph L. Block, president, Inland Steel Company; Fairfax M. Cone, president, Foote, Cone and Belding; Newton C. Farr, partner, Farr, Chinnock and Sampson; Wayne A. Johnston, president, Illinois Central Railroad; William V. Kahler, president, Illinois Bell Telephone Company; David N. Kennedy, president, Continental Illinois National Bank; Homer J. Livingston, president, The First National Bank of Chicago; Hughston H. McBain, chairman, Marshall Field and Company; Charles F. Murphy, partner, Naess and Murphy; William A. Patterson, president, United Air Lines, Inc.; John T. Pirie, president, Carson, Pirie, Scott and Company; Robert P. Williford, executive vice-president, Hilton Hotels Corporation; Holman D. Pettibone, chairman of the board, Chicago Title and Trust Company; and Kenneth V. Zwiener, president, Harris Trust and Savings Bank.

All four of the Chicago daily newspapers were very much in favor of subsidizing CTA. Their interest was like that of the other big businesses in the central district; it coincided especially with that of the department stores, upon whose advertising they principally depended. The *Sun-Times'* tie to the group was particularly close; its editor and publisher was Marshall Field, Jr.

Although he had much less reason to be concerned than did the Mayor, Governor Stratton would not be indifferent to an issue which concerned so many voters and such important ones. He could, if he wished, do much to help in the legislature. With a great deal of patronage at his disposal (some said he controlled ten thousand jobs), the Governor could make things very difficult for an unco-operative Republican by opposing him in the primary with a patronage-supported candidate of his own. Such extreme measures were rarely needed, however. Almost every Republican legislator — and many Democratic ones — wanted some favor from the Governor. The Governor could veto any line of an appropriations bill, and a veto was almost impossible to override. It followed from this that he could either check a legislator at every turn, leaving him nothing to point to with pride when he returned home from Springfield, or make him the source of many blessings to his constituents.

It was said that Stratton and Daley had agreed to recognize each other's spheres of influence. Stratton would help Daley in matters essential to him in Chicago if Daley would do the same in matters essential to Stratton downstate. (Daley, his enemies said, had already made a heavy payment on account by slating a weak candidate to run against Stratton at a time when, because of scandals in the Republican administration — the state auditor, an elected Republican who served concurrently with Stratton, had gone to prison in 1956 for embezzlement — Stratton's chances for re-election were very poor.) If the Mayor and the Governor had, indeed, agreed upon spheres of influence, CTA's prospects were good. It was unlikely, however, that they had. As one of the

Mayor's closest associates pointed out to an interviewer, they would have to wait until the session was well advanced and then take the issues one by one, for only in this way could each be sure of making the best use of his bargaining position. To suppose that they could make one big trade before the legislature started was unrealistic. There was no doubt, however, that if they agreed and were determined, the Mayor and Governor together could put almost anything they wanted through the legislature.

Despite all this, there were reasons for taking a dim view of CTA's chances.

For one thing, it could not be taken for granted that the CTA riders would favor a subsidy, even though one would increase their comfort at others' expense. Many riders hated CTA bitterly. The system was a symbol, perhaps, of all that was most wearisome and aggravating in their lives: it stood for the tyranny of routine, the too-intimate contact with fellow men, the indignity of being one of the mass. Whatever the reasons, there seemed to be constantly building up in the riders a charge of emotion that vented itself against the system and its management. CTA, many riders seemed to believe, was run by crooked politicians and incompetent bureaucrats who would only fritter away any subsidy that might be given. It would be better to return the system to private enterprise or at least put it in the hands of competent managers. And so on.

"Except for religion and politics," the *Sun-Times* observed editorially, "no local topic of conversation can arouse more mixed emotional reactions than a mere mention of the Chicago Transit Authority."

In short, there were riders — and probably not a few — who would be pleased to see CTA get its come-uppance, and who might even administer punishment at the polls to any politician who was overly zealous in its behalf.

If the million who rode CTA could not be counted upon to support a subsidy, still less could the much larger number of Chicagoans who did not ride it. These might object vigorously to being taxed for a facility they did not use. As the *Tribune* observed editorially, "Today's politician, who seeks to help the strap-hanger at the expense of the motorist, runs the risk of offending more voters than he pleases."

The attitude of the motorist was, of course, of great importance. Advocates of mass transportation sometimes took it for granted that the motorist had not counted all the costs of his ride to and from the central city. Surely, if he took into account not only the costs of his car and its upkeep, but the cost in taxes of an endlessly elaborate system of expressways and the cost both in higher commodity prices and in taxes of the premature obsolescence of the central business district, he would much prefer to ride in a public vehicle, especially one which was fast and cheap. On this assumption, the practical problem was to find a means to charge the motorist all of the costs which he incurred and, at the same time to offer him the alternative of a cheap and not unpleasant ride by mass transportation.

The problem was certainly a difficult one. How could each motorist be charged his fair share of the costs which his demand for a highway would entail? And how, until this was done, could mass transportation be made attractive enough to compete with the automobile?

There was a possibility that the advocates of mass transportation misjudged the situation and that, rightly posed, the problem was not merely difficult but actually insoluble. The advocates of mass transportation had made the mistake, perhaps, of judging the motorist's tastes and values by their own. It might be that the motorist would (if he had to) pay anything in higher taxes and prices and undergo any inconvenience for the sake of his car. There was even some evidence that people did not switch from autos to mass transportation under the most favorable circumstances. When a suburban line converted a standard 51-passenger bus into a "dream bus" for 44 riders and equipped it with reclining foam rubber seats, carpeting, wallpaper, drapes, television, razors, and a refrigerator for the run from the Loop to Park Forest, it never had more than 12 passengers and sometimes only one or two; the loss on three daily round trips was $1,000 a month.

The Chicagoan, perhaps, was well aware of the cost of his car. He just happened to be constituted differently than some people supposed. Even if public transportation were free and all the costs of the automobile were paid out of his own pocket, he might still prefer to drive his car.

It might be, in other words, that Chicagoans wanted to buy, not transportation merely, but transportation associated with other satisfactions as well — satisfactions which mass transportation was inherently unable to provide. The automobile, as one student of popular culture remarked, was a costume in which the American dressed himself to go upon a stage — the highway — where he played a part in an enthralling drama. To suppose that he would go back to riding trains and busses merely because it was cheaper to do so or that he would allow the automobile to be placed under a handicap showed (if this view was correct) a very fundamental misunderstanding of the popular mind. It was a mistake that the politicians would not be likely to make.

If Chicago motorists had little enthusiasm for CTA, those of the suburbs had even less. Most of the subsidy would be used to bring rapid transit lines closer to the suburbs. It was the suburbanite, therefore, not the Chicagoan, who would be chiefly accommodated. ("Why the CTA should have any concern about people who choose to live outside of the city limits is a mystery to me," Reluctant Rider observed in a letter to a newspaper.) The suburbs would prosper and the city suffer if "the flight from the city" was made easier. But this was not the light in which suburbanites saw the matter. Most of them did not use CTA, and the few who did felt they owed it nothing but their fares. "Let those who use and need this transportation bear the expenses," an Oak Lawn man wrote to a Chicago newspaper. "I'm not an isolationist, but I don't believe that the people of Chicago would be very happy to pay for decent roads in my neighborhood." This, of course, was what downstaters would also say.

Even among the bankers, merchants, and real estate men whose vast properties in the Loop would be served by the extension of rapid transit lines to the suburbs, there was coolness to the subsidy idea and even some outright opposition. Moreover, neither Daley nor Stratton had much to gain by trying to please the businessmen. They controlled no votes, and they would contribute to the Republican Party no matter what.

Some powerful interests stood to gain from the increased use of automobiles. Those who made and sold automobiles, distributed gasoline, operated garages and parking lots, built expressways, or sold materials for the building of them — these, among others, would oppose legislation giving mass transportation an advantage at the expense of the automobile. So would the many people — bankers, merchants, realtors, and even doctors and lawyers — who had a stake in the city's eighty-odd neighborhood or "satellite" shopping centers. These did a sizeable share of Chicago's retail business. Anything which made it easier for the customer to go downtown was bad for them.

The Mayor and the Governor were, of course, well aware of these crosscurrents of interest and opinion. They knew, too, the salient facts of political arithmetic. The central city was heavily Democratic and would remain so, whatever happened to CTA, while the suburbs and downstate were predominantly Republican. No Republican governor in his senses would, without a *quid pro quo,* shift some part of the cost of transportation from the central-city Democrats and place it upon the suburban and downstate Republicans. To do such a thing would be considered downright stupid. The smart thing would be to embarrass the Democratic mayor by letting him take responsibility for a fare increase. And Governor Stratton, whatever else he might be, was, everyone agreed, a smart politician.

Mayor Daley, for his part, would appear to advantage in the eyes of the Chicago voter by making a show of forcing the suburbanite to contribute to the support of CTA. That there were more Republicans than Democrats among the suburbanites made the effort all the easier. If he wished to subsidize CTA from taxes on Chicago residents, a majority of whom were Democrats, it would not be hard to get the approval of the legislature. But, as it must have seemed to the Mayor, this would be unjust — and bad politics besides.

Soon after the legislature convened (January 9, 1957), CTA would be expected to offer recommendations for dealing with its problems. Formulating the recommendations was a task for its board.

The board consisted of seven members — four appointed by the Mayor of Chicago and three by the Governor. Its chairman was Virgil E. Gunlock, an engineer whose professional life had been spent in public service in Chicago. He had been commissioner of subways and superhighways and then commissioner of public works prior to his appointment to the board, in 1954, by Mayor Daley's predecessor. Gunlock had had much experience with politicians, and he got along with them well. He was a Democrat, but not in any sense a politician himself.

The vice-chairman was Werner W. Schroeder, a lawyer (he was president of the Chicago Bar Association in 1957) and former Republican National Committeeman. Schroeder had been a co-author of the legislation which created CTA and was one of the Governor's principal advisers on transportation matters.

The other members appointed by the Mayor were two lawyers who had once been active in Democratic politics (one had been executive assistant to Mayor Kelly, and the other had been an alderman) and the president of a large meat-packing firm, Swift and Company, who was a Republican. The Governor's appointees (in addition to Schroeder) were an insurance broker and a woman who had for many years been a state representative from suburban Cook County.

Gunlock's was a full-time job which paid $35,000. The other board members were less than full-time (the law said only that they might have other business activities); they were paid $15,000 and met eighteen to twenty-five times a year in public formal sessions lasting from one to several hours, as well as in numerous informal, unscheduled conferences. The heads of CTA's operating divisions reported to a general manager, who in turn reported to Gunlock. Gunlock and the general manager together prepared the agenda for board meetings. Although the board played an active part in the determination of general policy, it was Gunlock and the manager who ran the organization.

Gunlock was the only member who had come to the board with the conviction that CTA would have to be subsidized. The others (including Schroeder, who, at the suggestion of the Civic Federation, had written into the law a requirement that CTA pay its way out of fares) had more or less slowly come to believe that it was essential to the welfare of the metropolitan area that mass transportation compete successfully with the automobile and that this could never happen without subsidies.

Gunlock had at once set about making a long-term physical plan for the system. The "physical program" — an inventory of capital improvements needed to bring the system to what was thought an "adequate level" — had to be put together with no idea of the amount of money that might be available. There would be no need at all for such a plan if money were to come only from fares, for there was no possibility of improving the system from them alone. The board had to assume that it would get a subsidy eventually and that it would be a large enough one to justify planning an adequate system.

Early in 1956 Gunlock went to Mayor Daley, then newly elected, to sound out his attitude on CTA's plans for expansion. The Mayor was having his assistants prepare a program of capital improvements for the city as a whole. Gunlock and the others concerned should see to it, the Mayor told him, that the plans for all improvements were fully co-ordinated. How high a level of expenditure by CTA he would favor would depend, in part, upon the competing needs: he would have to see the grand total of what was wanted by all departments and agencies before he could decide. He would, however, take immediate action on one CTA request: that the city require, in all new expressways, a reserved place for a rapid transit line.

At this conference, the Mayor asked Gunlock to have a complete set of CTA estimates ready in the fall. In October, he looked the completed estimates over briefly and said he saw no point in making them public until some thought had been given to how they might be financed.

No plan of financing would have any chance of success in the legislature without the Mayor's backing, but the Mayor did not give Gunlock any indication of his views on how the money should be raised. That was a matter for the board. "We only knew that he wanted to help," Gunlock told an interviewer later. "The rest was up to us."

In less than a month, the board had agreed upon a brief policy statement which it circulated to the Mayor, the Governor, and others.

To meet operating needs without a fare increase, the statement said, $5 million would be required annually. This would offset the deficit and permit purchase of much-needed rolling stock. Long range capital improvements (Chicago, the statement said, was perhaps fifty years behind the needs of the times for off-the-street rapid transit, and there was imperative need for block signals and automatic train-control facilities) would require $20 million a year for at least fifteen years.

The money to offset the deficit, the statement said, should come largely from highway funds. Mass transit exists only to move people and, therefore, in the purest sense, performs a highway service. Highway funds should be used to maintain ways and structures, to clear snow and ice from them, and to repave streets torn up by the removal of trolley tracks. If, in addition, CTA were exempted from city and state taxes on electricity, its annual deficit would be overcome without the need of a fare increase.

The board went on to list — without, however, endorsing — a number of ways in which money for long-range capital improvements might be raised:

1. A tax of one per cent per gallon on motor fuel sales in Chicago would raise $10,500,000 a year. A state-wide tax would yield $26,000,000.

2. An increase of 20 cents per $100 in the Chicago general property tax would raise $18,665,800. The same increase in rate would yield $25,770,200 if applied to the county as a whole and $30,719,200 if applied to the five-county metropolitan area.

3. A payroll tax of 0.4 per cent on the 1,700,000 persons employed in Chicago would yield $20,000,000. If one-third of this were paid by the employer and two-thirds by the employee, the average employee would be taxed $8.00 a year.

4. The legislature might appropriate highway funds for CTA's use, just as in a previous biennium it had appropriated $15,000,000 from general funds for township roads.

Gunlock himself favored a metropolitan-wide tax on both property and motor fuel. It would be fair, he felt, to divide the tax burden equally between property owners and automobile users; in his opinion it was clear that both would be benefited. Schroeder, the vice-chairman, took no definite position. In the past, he had said publicly that CTA (or some similar public corporation) should be empowered to issue bonds and levy general taxes, but it was not clear what he favored at the moment. The others on the board favored a motor fuel tax on the ground that mass transportation was a "highway use." After a meeting in the latter part of January, Gunlock told the press that the board was considering a gasoline tax increase of one cent a gallon and a special levy of 10 cents per $100 on real estate. It would not ask authority to levy the real estate tax itself, he said. That would be done by Chicago and certain suburbs.

His statement brought a frightened stir from the *Sun-Times,* the newspaper most devoted to CTA's cause. Even the mention of an increase in real estate taxes, it said, could generate so much opposition that it would be impossible to win public approval of any kind of subsidy. The Mayor, at the same time, told reporters he hoped a property tax increase could be avoided.

The next week the board dropped the property tax from consideration. It recommended, instead, a state-wide tax of one cent a gallon on gasoline, the receipts to be divided equally between CTA and the state. CTA's share — $13,000,000 — would be about equal to the contribution of Cook County motorists. The advantage of a state-wide tax was that motorists would not be able to cross a county line to avoid it, an action which would both reduce the yield of the tax and invite opposition to it from gas station owners on the Chicago side of the line. By giving half the yield from the tax to the state, the board hoped to gain support from downstate interests.

While these plans were being made, a tragedy occurred which gave dramatic evidence of the need for the improvements CTA was asking. A CTA train crashed into a North Shore train, killing 8 persons and injuring 169. The accident put CTA on front pages, and people began to take its needs more seriously. The climate of opinion, Gunlock felt, was very much changed by the accident. But even so, he did not expect success in Springfield. For most people, the subsidy idea was new. It would take time to get them used to it. A hard fight in the legislature would help prepare opinion, but would probably not do much more than that.

Early in January (it was two days after the legislature convened), Governor Stratton, Mayor Daley, President Ryan of the Cook County Board, Gunlock, and others met in the first of several conferences on metropolitan mass transportation. The occasion for the meeting was not CTA but another railroad, the Chicago, Aurora and Elgin (CA & E), a private line which ran west from Chicago. Half a mile of CA & E's right of way was to be acquired by Cook County to permit the construction of an expressway to the Loop. Unless the railroad and the county came to terms, condemnation proceedings would be necessary, and work on the expressway would be delayed. For some time the railroad had been seeking permission from the state to suspend passenger service. This would leave five thousand Kane and DuPage County commuters without convenient public transportation to Chicago. The commuters and their local officials were up in arms. They had taken their case to the Governor and had gotten a sympathetic hearing. (DuPage was sometimes called the most Republican county in the state, and the chairman of the Illinois Commerce Commission, an adviser upon whom the Governor was said to rely, was a resident of Aurora, a western terminal of CA & E.) The Governor had publicly proposed that the state buy CA & E with highway funds and turn it over to CTA to operate.

Daley, Ryan, and Gunlock were not opposed to taking over CA & E, but they said that before this could be done CTA would have to be guaranteed against losses that might arise from it. After two hours of discussion, the conferees told the press that they had decided to "take another 60 days to see if we cannot come up with a well-rounded program to submit to the legislature."

In the next two months, there were three meetings. Gunlock presented a detailed plan for operation of CA & E by CTA, and the Governor agreed that CTA should be subsidized. The only issue was one of financing. The Mayor and Ryan vigorously supported CTA's recommendation of a one-cent state-wide gasoline tax. "I don't believe I could sell that downstate," the Governor answered. "I just wouldn't have a chance."

In the conference room, the atmosphere was friendly and relaxed. The Governor, the Mayor, and Ryan did not have the manner of antagonists driving a hard bargain. Presumably, they had not forgotten that they were politicians and that this was politics. But there was no mention of the purely political gains and losses that might be involved.

The Governor, Gunlock thought, really wanted to help. Understandably, he was not willing to start a fight within his party which would endanger other, and to him more important, parts of his legislative program. But if a way could be found to deal with CTA's problems without starting a major fight, the Governor would, Gunlock thought, support it.

In the middle of March, the Governor, the Mayor, and the President of the County Board announced agreement on the following points:

1. That CTA be given permission to issue general obligation bonds supported by real estate and personal property levies in Cook County for capital improvements, provided the affected voter approved in a referendum. A tax of five cents per $100 of assessed valuation, it was noted, would produce $6,500,000.

2. That the county board of each county having a population of over 100,000 be permitted, without referendum, to impose a gasoline tax increase not to exceed one cent. In Cook County this would produce $12,000,000. This money might be used to make up operating losses.

3. That city, county, and state governments allot, from current gasoline tax receipts, funds for building improvements such as "open cut" subways in new superhighways. This would provide, in part, for the purchase and subsidized operation of CA & E.

4. That CTA be exempted from payment of various city and state taxes and charges.

The Governor had not yielded much. Except for the purchase of CA & E (which, of course, was wanted by suburbanites, not by Chicago) and the exemption from taxes and charges (a minor matter), CTA was to get no subsidy from state funds. If the people of Cook County wanted to tax themselves for the system's support, they were at liberty to do so. This was not much of a concession from the Governor.

Mayor Daley, however, could claim some advantage from the plan. It might avoid a fare increase. From his standpoint, this was a most important consideration. It was true that a county-wide tax on gasoline would be paid largely by Chicagoans, but some contribution, at least, would come from motorists in the country towns. (That the County Board would actually levy the tax could hardly be doubted: ten of its fifteen members were Democrats from Chicago. The Democratic machine would find transferring part of its gasoline tax revenues· to CTA painful, however, for, as applied to highways, the gas tax money was a source of patronage and an inducement to road builders to make campaign contributions.) Authority to impose a special real estate tax if the voters approved was less likely to be helpful, for the voters would almost certainly not approve. Nevertheless, the authority might come in handy some time.

Gunlock was now very optimistic. At first he had expected little from the conferences. The most that was likely to come from them, he had thought, was greater public understanding. But now that the Governor, the Mayor, and the President of the County Board all seemed seriously to be seeking a solution, something was likely to come of it. He began to think that a fare increase might be averted after all and that a start might even be made on a long-term program of improvements. When he brought the Stratton-Daley-Ryan proposals to the CTA board, it quickly endorsed them.

In other quarters the proposals were both welcomed and opposed. The Chicago daily newspapers agreed that CTA should be helped and that a gasoline tax was the best way of doing so. Stratton and Daley, the *Sun-Times* said, were to be commended for taking a forthright and courageous stand on what was undoubtedly the No. 1 problem confronting metropolitan Chicago. The *Tribune* said that although the idea of a county-wide real estate tax should be examined carefully, the proposed gasoline tax was justified if the receipts were used only for capital improvements. The *American* was "reluctantly convinced that some tax plan will have to be adopted or this community will choke on its traffic." Some kind of county-wide taxation was needed, the *Daily News* said. "Unless adequate mass transportation is provided," it went on, "the so-called 'flight to the suburbs' will be reversed."

The editors agreed that the plan would provoke bitter opposition. Although it would amount to only ten cents a week for a family owning a house assessed at $10,000, the *Sun-Times* said, the proposed property tax would arouse more resistance than the gasoline tax. Initial reaction to the plan was not encouraging, the *Daily News* found. "However, it would be too much to expect that any plan for new taxes would get instantaneous welcome, either from taxpayers or their representatives. The reaction simply indicates the selling job that faces the CTA and the civic and political leadership of city, county, and state."

Opposition came principally from four sources:

1. The "country towns" — that part of Cook County which lay outside of Chicago proper — opposed being taxed to support a transportation system which did not serve them directly. That it eventually would serve them if it were properly financed did not, apparently, impress the suburbanites.

Our village [the president of North Riverside wrote to a Chicago newspaper] has a population of 7,147, but we have no public transportation excepting Bluebird bus as it passes to and from the zoo. In spite of all our efforts we have been unable to get the CTA, the Chicago and West Towns, or any other system to serve our village. To place a tax on our real estate (to subsidize the CTA) would be unjust. To deprive us of our motor fuel tax funds would be unfair and unjust. We have adopted a program for maintaining and improving our streets which is paid for out of this gas tax money. If we are deprived of this money we would have to levy more taxes on our residents or impose special assessments on them.

The CTA is primarily a Chicago transportation system, as its name implies. I believe the city of Chicago should provide the additional funds necessary to sustain the CTA.

Chicago has raised the price of water to the suburbs without justification, and apparently the suburban water purchasers are subsidizing the Chicago water system. It is about time the city of Chicago learned to live within its means and leave the suburban towns alone.

For one reason or another a good many suburban politicians had a grudge against CTA. The Authority, a Republican representative complained later to an interviewer, had talked of extending the elevated service to his area and instead had actually cut it. "They consulted no one. If someone complained, their attitude was, 'if you don't like it, lump it.' They give us nothing and they ask for everything."

At first, the representative said, he had been inclined to help CTA. However, he wanted it to take him and other legislators into its confidence — to give them full information about its salaries, hiring practices, and so on. This it had not done.

It irked him, too, he went on, that the Governor had not consulted him and other suburbanites before coming to the agreement with Mayor Daley. "No one bothered to talk to us at all," he said. Probably, Stratton and Daley had agreed that CTA was to belong to Daley. This (he went on) would account for the Governor's recent appointment of a woman to the CTA board: she was a "ringer" who would never insist upon getting the facts and would easily be dominated by the Democrats on the board.

Besides, he said, he personally didn't like the Governor. It was true that he had an excellent record, but as a person he was cold. When you go to him for something, he sends you off to one of his assistants and you're not sure whether the assistant has orders to help you or not. He liked a man who was warm, and who would do what he could to help you.

He wasn't afraid of the Governor. Why, once, on another matter when he opposed him, the Governor's administrative assistant came around to talk to him. He had told the assistant that the Governor owed *him* something, not he something to the Governor. "If the Governor campaigned in my district," he had said, "he couldn't hurt me, but I could hurt him."

Looking back at the CTA subsidy issue after it had been decided, the legislator was "rather proud" that he and other suburbanites had been able to beat not only CTA and Mayor Daley but the Chicago newspapers and the Governor as well. It was, he felt, quite an accomplishment.

2. Organized highway users were another important class of opponents. They had been trying for years to establish the principle that gasoline tax receipts should never be used for other than highway purposes. Twenty-seven states had constitutional provisions against "diversion," and the highway users hoped Illinois would soon be the twenty-eighth. CTA's claim that rapid transit ways should be regarded as highways was outrageous. If this

idea were accepted, mass transportation systems all over the country would ask for highway funds. The issue was therefore a national one, and there was a fundamental principle at stake.

The most important of the anti-diversion organizations was the Illinois Highway Users Conference. This was an organization of organizations. Its members included associations of truck owners, car dealers, bus operators, rural mail carriers, dairy farmers, oil companies, gas station owners, motel owners, and road building material (asphalt and concrete) suppliers. Occasionally, a member organization, while agreeing with the Conference in general, disagreed with it on a particular issue. In such cases the Conference omitted the objector from the list of those it represented on that particular issue. Thus, for example, the Chicago Association of Industry and Commerce, although remaining one of its strong supporters, was not listed by the Conference as an opponent of the CTA subsidy; many of the Association's members had more at stake in measures to strengthen the central business district than in highways. Similarly, an association of bus owners declined to be listed on the CTA issue because the bus owners hoped that by refraining from opposition to the CTA subsidy they might earn the Governor's approval of a bill to relieve them of certain taxes.

So important was the principle involved in the CTA issue that the National Highway Users Conference sent two workers from Washington to help with the lobbying. Together, the Illinois and Washington lobbyists mapped out a strategy which they later described with the pride of master workmen in a special report to their membership:

. . . a public relations committee was formed, comprising five experts from the Chicago area. The PR committee subsequently held five very successful meetings, culminating in the preparation and distribution of a pamphlet that was issued to most of the groups. In addition a speakers' bureau was named, with two members of the PR committee assigned to write speeches. One member of the PR committee was assigned the exclusive job of personally calling on newspapers throughout the state.

Among the more notable achievements of some of the associations included demonstration meetings and "coffee breaks" within the companies. One such meeting resulted in over 50 persons marching into the Capitol announcing their opposition. One association devoted the entire space of its publication on two different occasions. The presidents of several associations sent action bulletins or letters to their members telling them to contact their legislators. On several occasions the Speakers' Bureau was asked to provide speakers for meetings. Telegrams were dispatched to legislators at critical times. One association clipped stories from a newspaper which denounced the proposed diversion and placed them in the hands of all legislators. Company and association publications almost every week included stories against such diversion.

But the bulk of the fight was carried in the persistence with which bulletins were sent out from IHUC headquarters to the associations where their secretaries, in turn, urged their people to act. This activity paid off in handsome dividends because the mail came in to desks of legislators by the thousands. Several of them announced they had received more mail on this than on anything else. Some said they had received as many as 500 to 600 letters. . . .

Action bulletins continued two or three a week from IHUC headquarters. Some 550,000 of the "Stop Raids on Your Highways" pamphlets were dispatched to the groups by mail and followed up by NHUC representatives. Contact with the newspapers was increased. A man was placed in Springfield, full time, for the purpose of keeping the groups informed on legislation and coordinating the moves of lobbyists. It should be mentioned here that the pinpointed lobbying was carried on by a hard core of 10 to 15 persons.

It had been noted that most of the downstate members of the House were opposed to diversion, while most of those in Chicago were in favor. This left the balance of power, amounting to 22 votes, from the Cook County suburban area. . . . With this in mind, an NHUC representative spent two full weeks in suburban Cook County calling on companies and organizations, where a member of the PR committee had also given considerable attention to the suburban newspapers in this territory. This move, as shown later, proved to be an astounding success.

In addition, various organizations, that had not done so before, moved into Springfield for last minute contacts with legislators. Prepared statements were placed in the hands of legislators who had voiced interest in receiving material.

Another important anti-diversion organization was the Chicago Motor Club. It had about 250,000 members in the northern two-thirds of Illinois and northern one-third of Indiana who paid annual dues of $15 to $20 for emergency road-towing service and similar benefits. The club published an eight-page monthly newsletter, *Motor News,* which advertised its insurance and travel bureaus and kept members posted on legislation. What its members thought about legislative matters the club had no way of knowing; this did not, however, prevent it from "representing" them. Mayor Daley said later that the club was chiefly responsible for the failure of the subsidy proposal.

"Diversion of motor fuel taxes is not only morally wrong," the club president wrote in the *Motor News*, "it could jeopardize the state's highway program." In issue after issue he exhorted club members to write, wire, or call their senators and representatives. For their convenience, the *Motor News* carried in each issue a set of maps showing the House and Senate districts and giving the names of the legislators.

Apparently hundreds of members actually did write. "This was something that people could get excited about," an executive of the club said later. "I can't remember any campaign which aroused so much feeling."

3. The commuters of Kane and DuPage counties, although favoring measures to keep CA & E running, were very much opposed to paying a tax for that purpose. Politicians from those counties met with Governor Stratton one evening in the Executive Mansion to tell him that their constituents "just won't sit still for a tax increase of any kind." The state, they said, would be responsible for suspension of passenger service and, therefore, it should provide any subsidy that might be needed.

The Governor expressed surprise. He had supposed that continuing CA & E service was a matter of great importance to Kane and DuPage counties. If it were so important, he said, surely the local people would be willing to contribute one cent a gallon toward it.

CTA supporters had hoped that Kane and DuPage counties' interest in CA & E would lead them to support a plan for the general improvement of CTA. It was clear now that this was not the case and that, in fact, if it cost them a few dollars, the western suburbs would not support even that part of the plan which would serve only them.

Some observers believed that the Governor had interested himself in CTA only because he wanted to help the CA & E commuters. If this was so, his interest would probably now cease since it was apparent that the commuters were not really vitally concerned.

4. Many weekly newspapers in the more than eighty communities into which Chicago was divided opposed any kind of subsidy for CTA. The community press had been brought into existence by the growth of satellite shopping districts, and it reflected the interests of neighborhood merchants who wanted people to shop close to home. ("We would hate to see our friendly neighborhood gas station owner get caught in the middle," the *Daily Calumet* explained, opposing the gasoline tax increase.) Altogether, the weekly papers had a circulation of about a million. Some of their readers were very much devoted to them. Because they were small (and therefore did not swamp the reader with more news and opinion than he could absorb) and because they stood independently for what they considered the good of the community, their influence on many readers was considerable.

Of course, the readers' opinion would make little difference if the Democratic machine insisted upon regularity from the legislators. The *Southtown Economist,* listing the names and addresses of legislators in its circulation area, acknowledged that they might be reluctant to defy their party leaders. But they should remember, it warned, "that they will have to go back to the voters to win re-election and that public resentment against the tax boosts is so intense that many of them may be defeated." Such huffing and puffing was not likely to frighten senators and representatives who owed their election to the Democratic machine. It might, however, reduce somewhat the energy with which Mayor Daley, the party leader, would press the issue.

That the daily newspapers were right in predicting bitter opposition to the Stratton-Daley-Ryan plan was amply shown within a few days. "Discussion of the proposed CTA subsidies unfortunately has degenerated into denunciations of all taxes, criticism of the CTA management, and assertions by motorists that the CTA is none of their business," the *Tribune* observed at the end of March. "No progress will be made toward a solution until it is understood by both the legislators and the public that transportation in a crowded city must be dealt with as one problem. Motorists and users of public transit are in the same boat, and taxes will have to be collected from both to keep it afloat."

Meanwhile, the business leaders of Chicago made their views known in testimony before legislative committees and in a private talk which Pettibone, the head of the Central Area Committee, had with the Mayor. Suprisingly, in view of their vast stake in the central business district, these leaders opposed the Stratton-Daley-Ryan proposals.

That, at least, was the impression Mayor Daley got from his talk with Pettibone. Actually, the Central Area Committee's position (which was set forth in a public letter from Pettibone to the Governor, the Mayor, and the President of the County Board) was full of if's, and's, and but's. It distinguished, as did the *Chicago Tribune,* between subsidy for operations and subsidy for capital improvements. CTA's riders, it said, should pay its operating expenses in full, even if doing so necessitated a fare increase. An operating subsidy would lessen the incentive for good management and tend to stifle other forms of transportation. On the other hand, "selected" improvements and extensions — for example, construction of rapid transit lines — should be subsidized. The particular improvements to be subsidized, however, should be approved by some agency subject to voter control. Rolling stock should be paid for from income, and the system should continue to pay taxes.

The committee seemed to favor postponing for at least two years (the legislature met biennially) any effort to reach a long-term settlement of CTA's problems. It would be unwise, Pettibone told the Mayor, to adopt a long-range program for one segment of transportation apart from the others. Within a few months the results of an elaborate transportation survey would be available, and from this it would be possible to plan a transportation system "on the basis of demonstrated needs and actual traffic patterns." The implication seemed to be that the legislature should defer any very important action until the next session, two years hence.

On the crucial question of where a subsidy might come from, the committee had nothing at all to say.

The Mayor was exasperated. "Do you mean to tell me," he asked Pettibone, "that your organization is taking this stand?" Pettibone said again that all metropolitan transportation service should be considered before fundamental decisions were reached.

"Fine," the Mayor said, "but if we want to push ahead we've got to get started. We want money to support these expansions." Pettibone, however, was unpersuaded. The Mayor, for his part, was mystified by the attitude of the businessmen. He had supposed that they would enthusiastically favor steps to strengthen the central business district. At the very least, they might have invited him to appear before them with an explanation of his plans. Apparently they were determined to oppose.

The Chicago Association of Commerce and Industry took a stand very similar to that of the Central Area Committee. Joseph Block, its president (he was also president of the Inland Steel Corporation), told a legislative committee that the Association favored relieving CTA of various city and state taxes and charges, but he said nothing of the much more important parts of the Stratton-Daley-Ryan plan. What he failed to say, of course, was more telling than what he said.

Had he been aware of the difficulties under which Pettibone and Block labored, Mayor Daley might have sympathized with them as fellow politicians. For the fact was that, in order to preserve harmony within their organizations, both men had to confine themselves to a highest-common-denominator line which was bound to be equivocal and ineffective.

Pettibone's task required an especially delicate touch. Marshall Field and Company wanted to avoid a fare increase even if this meant subsidizing CTA's operating expenses. On the other hand, Wayne A. Johnston, president of the Illinois Central, was violently opposed to any subsidies. ("I don't get one. Why should they?") If the Committee took a strong stand in favor of a subsidy, Johnston might resign. This would be a hard blow, for, through his control of Illinois Central's real estate, especially the air rights over the railroad tracks on the lake front, and his chairmanship of the site selection committee of the Board of Trustees of the University of Illinois, he would have a great deal to say about certain matters in which the Committee was vitally interested. But if the Committee did not support CTA strongly enough, Marshall Field and Company, and perhaps other department stores as well, might withdraw their support. Field's participation was important because it was playing the leading part in the Fort Dearbon project.

Pettibone had a talent for finding the terms on which conflicting interests could agree. (As a young man he had wanted to become a diplomat. Lack of money for higher education had made him a business man instead, but he had never lost his taste for negotiation and behind-the-scenes manipulation; it was this as much as anything, some of his associates said, which made him a success in business.) Somehow, he managed to draft a statement to which both McBain, the head of Field's and Johnston agreed. (Out of regard for Johnston's sensibilities, it did not use the hated word "subsidy" except to express disapproval; where the idea was endorsed, circumlocution was employed: we believe selected improvements should be paid "from sources other than users of facilities of the Authority.") But Johnston, some said, agreed to "go along" only if it was clearly understood that the Committee would not carry its support of the subsidy proposal one word beyond the terms of the agreed-upon statement.

Block's difficulties were hardly less than Pettibone's. Some members of the Association of Commerce and Industry were outraged at the very suggestion of an increase in the property tax. Others, especially the Standaard Oil Company, would not stand for an increase in the gasoline tax. Standard Oil, as it happened, was one of the Association's principal financial supports.

The Civic Federation, a taxpayer's association, deliberated upon the Stratton-Daley-Ryan plan and decided to take no stand. It was much easier, a former president remarked afterward, for the Federation to take a stand when the issue was one of reducing taxes. When it came to deciding where an additional tax should be placed, it was almost impossible to get agreement.

Organizations like the Chicago Real Estate Board, which represented one interest only, had a comparatively easy time of it. The Stratton-Daley-Ryan suggestion that a property tax be levied if the voters approved was, the Real Estate Board said, "a vicious move that could bring the city close to bankruptcy." The Board's concern was not to solve CTA's problem, but merely to avoid an increase in the property tax.

When the Governor, the Mayor, and the President of the County Board announced their agreement, most people took it for granted that they would press hard for its adoption. If they did, it would almost certainly be adopted no matter what the opposition, for when the three of them acted in concert they were virtually unbeatable.

"Presumably," the *Tribune* remarked, "both men [the reference here was to the Governor and the Mayor only] will use all the influence they command in the legislature to get the program adopted at the present session." This, the Mayor told an interviewer afterward, was certainly his understanding of his agreement with the Governor.

The agreement was hardly reached, however, when it became evident that the Governor was, to say the least, using somewhat less than his full resources to secure its passage. After their regular Monday evening conference with him, the Republican leaders of the Senate and House told the press that they could not, under any circumstances, introduce the bills that he, Daley, and Ryan had had drafted.

Arthur J. Bidwell, the Senate majority leader, said that he had read the draft bills and that "they're awful." "We've got to do something to help the CTA," he said, "but these bills are not the answer. I'll have a thousand letters against them next week." The trouble with the bills was that they contained no clear-cut plan for CTA's use of the subsidy; they were so vague, Bidwell said, that the agency could just dip into the gasoline and property tax revenues with no strings attached.

John W. Lewis, the House majority leader, said that he had not read the draft bills. The implication was that he did not intend to read them.

This was a remarkable development. Technically the majority leaders were officers of their houses: one was elected by the Senate and the other appointed by the Speaker of the House. It was well understood, however, that they were both chosen by the Governor and responsible to him for the management of his program. He could have them replaced if they did not serve to his satisfaction, and — although such a thing was most improbable — if he tried hard enough he might even bring about their defeat in the next primary election.

That they would revolt against the Governor was unlikely. It was especially unlikely that they would revolt against him on an issue which did not affect them vitally. Bidwell was a prosperous businessman who had been in local politics for thirty years and was well entrenched; supporting the Governor on the CTA issue might lose him a few votes, but it could not (as he later acknowledged to an interviewer) jeopardize his position. He was also the elected leader of an association of suburban Republican township organizations and, as such, the vice-chairman of the Cook County Republican Committee. The suburbs were bitterly opposed to being taxed for the support of CTA, and Bidwell had a responsibility to represent their point of view. However, if he had decided that his obligation to the Governor came first, he would not have lost his leadership of the suburban bloc.

Lewis also had no need to fear the electorate. He was a farmer and livestock dealer who was widely known and trusted in the downstate counties he represented. His constituents might be dubious about any measure for the benefit of Chicago — even one which would cost them nothing — but they would not vote him out of office for supporting the Governor. Lewis was determined in his opposition to the subsidy plan. His trade in livestock had brought him close to the trucking business and made him receptive to the arguments of the Highway Users Conference. "I've been able to lean over backwards on lots of things as majority leader," he told an interviewer afterward, "but the CTA subsidy was wrong in principle."

Actually, however, Bidwell and Lewis had not defied the Governor and were in no danger of being disciplined by him. He had made it plain to them that he did not regard the CTA bills as "must" legislation. He thought they were sound and should be passed. He hoped Bidwell and Lewis would see fit to support them. But he was not going to insist upon it. "The Governor," Lewis said later, "never pressured me in any way, shape, or form."

Although there was little doubt that he could have his way in a showdown, the Governor apparently felt that the price of victory would be more than he could afford to pay. Only by deferring to the wishes of the legislators on some occasions could he get them to defer to his on others. In the main he had to rely upon goodwill and respect, rather than upon threats and promises, to get his work done in the legislature.

He had known from the beginning that Bidwell and Lewis would be opposed to subsidizing CTA. It was surprising, then, that he had not brought them into the negotiations with Daley and Ryan, thus insuring that the agreement would have their support. CTA was, in fact, Lewis said later, the only matter during the whole session upon which he and Bidwell were not consulted in advance by the Governor. Why was it that on this matter alone the Governor had deviated from his rule?

Another question might also be asked. Why, knowing that his leaders would not willingly support the agreement and that he could not afford to force them to support it, did the Governor not tell Daley and Ryan that he was not in a position to do more than *recommend* a position to the legislature?

The Democrats were willing to make some guesses on these questions. The Governor, one of them said, used Bidwell and Lewis as a screen to hide behind. For some reason, he had suddenly decided not to carry out his part of the agreement. The opposition of Bidwell and Lewis was a convenient excuse.

As to why the Governor suddenly chose to drop the agreement, the Democrats had two explanations. One was that Pettibone, the leader of the business interests in the central city, had insisted that he do so. The other was that he had entered the negotiations, to begin with, only because of a campaign pledge to maintain CA & E's commuter service; seeing that they could keep CA & E only at the price of contributing to the support of CTA, the suburbanites (according to this theory) asked the Governor to drop the matter entirely.

These explanations were untrue, Bidwell and Lewis later told an interviewer. There was nothing "phony" about their opposition to the subsidy bills, and they did not believe that the Governor privately welcomed it. The Governor, Lewis said, was not that kind of a man; he would say what he meant straight out. Bidwell believed that the Governor had, for a while, been quite irked with him over the CTA matter. He had not said anything to him directly, but he had expressed some dissatisfaction to others.

Later, neither Bidwell nor Lewis could offer any explanation for the Governor's failure to invite them to join the negotiations or to consult them before coming to an agreement. That he had simply forgotten to take them into account was most unlikely; he was far too careful a player for that.

From the beginning of the session, Gunlock and his advisers had hoped to use it to create understanding of CTA's problems so that, if they failed this time, they might have better success the next time. Accordingly, the Democratic leaders supported a Republican-initiated move to create a legislative commission on metropolitan mass transportation. Two days after the Stratton-Daley-Ryan agreement was announced, the legislature, acting against the advice of the Governor, created a ten-man joint study commission. In the House, nineteen Republicans joined the Democrats in a 94 to 59 vote. Not all of these Republicans were on CTA's side. Some wanted a forum before which to oppose a subsidy.

Elroy C. Sandquist, a Republican of Chicago, was named chairman of the commission. Sandquist, in private life an automobile salesman, was beginning his eleventh term in the House. He had helped pilot the legislation establishing CTA through the House, and this gave him, he felt, a particular stake in the agency's future. When the train accident occurred, he had written the Governor that something had to be done about CTA. They had meant to have a talk about it before the session began, but other things had interfered. No doubt Sandquist would have welcomed an invitation to meet with the Governor, the Mayor, Ryan, and Gunlock. None had been extended, and now as chairman of the study commission, he would make his own inquiry and come to his own conclusions. Although the Governor had opposed the creation of the commission, Sandquist did not feel that he was placing himself in opposition to him by heading it. He was, he told an interviewer, "an administration man."

The Sandquist commission held five hearings in Chicago at which those who favored and those who opposed a subsidy repeated arguments that were by this time well known. Mayor Daley

did not testify; instead, he sent a letter reaffirming his support of
the subsidy principle.

Near the end of April the commission was ready to report.
After a half-hour conference with the Governor, Sandquist told
the press that it had decided against any direct subsidy by the
current session of the legislature. It would recommend creation
of a joint interim commission to carry on the study it had begun,
and it would offer bills to relieve CTA of certain city and state
taxes and charges. But this was all. The Democratic members of
the commission wanted a subsidy, Sandquist said, but they would
sign the report, nevertheless.

The next day, however, when Sandquist went to Senator Lynch,
the minority leader, to get his signature on the report, Lynch called
Mayor Daley on the telephone and then said that he could not
sign it. Sandquist was disturbed, for one of the Republicans on
the commission, Granata, the leader of an Italian voting bloc in
Chicago, asked for a further effort to reach agreement on the
report, and this left him without a majority. Lynch made matters
worse by taking the floor to denounce the "say-nothing, do-
nothing" report and to demand to know "why this Commission,
dominated and controlled by the Governor's own Republican
Party, failed to support an agreement on these taxes reached
jointly by the Governor and Mayor Daley."

The Governor was apparently embarrassed either by Lynch's
criticism or Granata's demand for further negotiation. At any
rate, at his suggestion, Sandquist introduced, along with several
bills to implement the commission's report, another which had no
relation to the report. This other bill gave municipalities, counties,
and the state Department of Public Works and Buildings permission to use gasoline taxes to pay for subways and other capital
improvements to rapid transit systems.

Lynch and three other Democratic senators, meanwhile, had
introduced six bills of their own. These not only exempted CTA
from the state and city taxes and charges but also gave the
counties part of the auto license fees collected by the state (most
of the fees were collected in Cook County, of course) and
appropriated from gasoline taxes already collected by the state
$30 million for aid to rapid transit systems during the biennium.

The Lynch bills, insiders said, were intended only to make headlines in Chicago. "I don't think there's a Chinaman's chance of the CTA getting any state money," the Senate majority whip told reporters. "We don't feel they've exhausted their own resources."

Suddenly, however, an event occurred which seemed to change the situation altogether. An administration bill to increase the state police force by five hundred men was before the House. Heavy opposition from the Illinois Sheriff's Association made its passage unlikely. (The Governor, some said, meant to use the additional policemen to raid downstate gambling joints, thus cutting off the income of certain Republican politicians and thereby increasing his own power). Just as the vote was to be taken, the Democratic leader of the House was called to the telephone. He returned to ask for a ten-minute recess. The Cook County Democrats caucused. Afterward, all of them voted for the Governor's bill.

Daley, it was said, had made a trade to get the Governor's support of the Lynch bills. That Daley had indeed engineered the sudden shift of the Democratic votes was obvious. That he would not have done so except for something in return was also obvious.

But it did not follow that support for the Lynch bills was the promised return. There were other things which were more important to the Mayor (later in the session, in fact, he had Republican help in defeating a bill to impose a tax rate limit on Chicago; the tax limit would have hamstrung his administration). That the Lynch bills were not an object of the trade became clear when Lewis, the House majority leader, said he would never vote for the diversion of gasoline tax revenues. A few days later, all of the Lynch bills were killed in committee.

The Sandquist bills were now CTA's only hope. When hearings were held on them, a state highway engineer appeared in opposition. Sandquist was surprised. "These bills were handed to us by the Governor's office," he said; he had himself talked recently to the head of the Public Works and Buildings Department. Had the engineer talked with his boss recently? The majority whip of the House, however, said that he had no reason to believe that these were administration bills, and he proceeded to testify vigorously against them. In another administration, the confusion might have been attributable to carelessness or incompetence. The Stratton administration, however, had proved itself extremely efficient in such matters. Evidently the Governor was not adverse to confusion in this matter.

While the highway engineer was giving his testimony, the Governor, the Mayor, Gunlock, and others were once again discussing the possibility of CTA's acquiring CA & E. Gunlock, with the Mayor's backing, said that CTA could not operate the suburban line without a subsidy of at least $20 million a year. Stratton turned to members of the DuPage County board of supervisors and to legislators from DuPage County who were present. They were willing to use their gasoline tax funds to make up losses incurred by CTA in operating CA & E within the borders of DuPage County, provided Cook County would do the same, they said. But they would not pay one penny toward subsidizing CTA's Chicago operations. The meeting ended in failure.

Chicago, the Governor told reporters, should face up to a fare increase. A 25-cent ride would be reasonable, and "people would pay 30 or 35 cents." At this Daley bristled. A fare increase, he said, would cause a reduction in the number of riders and clog the streets with autos.

Why had he not pushed the plan agreed upon by him and Daley? a reporter asked the Governor.

"It failed to win public acceptance," the Governor replied.

After a five-minute discussion, the House, on June 18, passed the largest appropriation in its history — $644,999,013 (about half of which was to come from federal aid), to be spent in the biennium on highways. This done, it turned to the Sandquist bills.

Gunlock, meanwhile, had been working hard to put CTA's case before the legislators. CTA kept an able part-time lobbyist in Springfield as a matter of routine: there were always a number of bills which would affect it in one way or another and which, therefore, had to be watched. Gunlock himself now spent as much time as he could in Springfield. At breakfast, lunch, and in the corridors of the capitol and of the hotels, he buttonholed whatever legislators were willing to hear his story. There were at least fifty, he estimated later, with whom he talked for at least a few minutes. A few of these, he thought, changed their minds because of what he said. Mrs. VanderVries, a Republican member of the CTA board who had served for many years in the legislature, talked to others. Three or four lawyers who often defended CTA against accident suits were members of the legislature; these did what they could to be helpful.

Sandquist had arranged to have the least important of his bills acted upon first. The House made little objection to exempting CTA from the state utility tax, from city snow-removal charges, and from charges for operating on Chicago park boulevards. The strongest opposition was to the first of these measures (the only one which was at the expense of the state), and on this the vote was 103 to 41 in favor. Lewis, the majority leader, abstained from voting. The majority whip voted against all of the bills.

That evening, when the most important of the Sandquist bills came to the floor, Lewis said that in his entire legislative career he had never encountered a worse bill. "Monstrosity and sabotage," he called it. Under the bill, every bit of motor fuel tax revenue could be used for the CTA. It would even be possible to use the money to buy taxicabs in Springfield and turn them over to CTA. There was nothing to stop the Governor from taking money away from township road repairs and farm-to-market roads. "When a bill is presented of this nature," he said, "they must think we're mighty ignorant."

De La Cour, the minority leader, pled with him:

DE LA COUR: All during this session we from Chicago have been more equitable in our thinking for your downstate needs.

LEWIS: Do you want all the state gas funds? It's in the bill.

DE LA COUR: No, we're just asking for equity. We go along with you fellows. We're having growing pains. At the moment we have a particular need. John, consider our immediate needs.

The majority whip also spoke in opposition, although he did so, he said, "personally" and not for the administration. He was against diversion of motor fuel taxes as a matter of principle, and this was diversion plain and simple.

Dolezal, a Republican from the Cook County suburbs, urged all suburban legislators to vote against the bill. Instead of demanding a subsidy for it, he said, the newspapers would do better to demand that CTA extend its service to the suburbs. CTA, he went on, was closely allied to the Morrison Hotel (Chicago headquarters of the Democratic Party); the fine names on its board were a "cloak of respectability" which should not deceive the legislature.

Erlenborn, a young Republican from DuPage County (he was one who had breakfasted with Gunlock), wanted to know what was so sacred about the gas tax fund. A rapid transit line in the median strip of an expressway would carry ten times as many people as a six-lane highway. "We in our county," he said, "see this bill as meaning that the CA & E will run. Our County Board has asked us to work for the bill." (This did not represent a change in DuPage County thinking; if the Sandquist bill passed, DuPage might still demand that CTA be subsidized exclusively from state funds.) A Kane County representative who had attended the last conference in the Governor's office opposed the bill. "No one asked me to support this bill," he said. "I'm voting 'No.' "

A Logan County man spoke "as a person from downstate." If this bill was passed, he said, there would be a continual clamor from Cook County for a larger share of the gas tax fund. The Chicago newspapers were already saying that Chicago and Cook County were getting too little of it. He was ready to recognize that Chicago had a problem. Let's grant Chicago an increase on their sales tax," he suggested. "Let retail sales in the Loop carry the cost."

As the speechmaking drew to a close, the electric scoreboard showed 57 in favor of the bill and 96 opposed. Sandquist hurriedly asked permission to postpone action, and no vote was officially recorded.

Some Democrats now began to talk of a filibuster. It would be easy to stage one. The constitution virtually required that the session end on June 30, and there were still hundreds of bills, including several of great importance to the Governor, to be acted upon. If the Democrats insisted that every bill be read in full the required three times and that all other forms be observed to the letter, they could bring the session to a sudden end.

Mayor Daley and his principal legislative leader, Senator Lynch, decided against a filibuster. They believed public opinion would not stand for one. On another issue — aid to education, perhaps — a filibuster might be popular. But to take such an extreme stand in favor of higher taxes and the unpopular CTA would play directly into the hands of the Republicans. The filibuster was a weapon which could be used only under the right circumstances.

Sandquist, at the suggestion of southern Illinois leaders, revised his bill to provide that only in the five counties of the metropolitan area would gasoline tax revenues be diverted. This change, he was told, would make the bill acceptable elsewhere in the state. He took the revised bill to the Governor and got him to call in Lewis, the majority leader, and persuade him not to oppose it.

Sandquist took the microphone, on June 22, to ask the Speaker for recognition. Instead of recognizing him, the Speaker called him to the rostrum to ask what he intended. When Sandquist explained that he meant to call up his bill, the Speaker was dismayed. To do so, he said, would create havoc with the timetable. There were still several "must" bills to be passed and only six days left. Sandquist insisted, and the Speaker turned to Lewis, the majority leader, for advice. Lewis shrugged. The Governor was willing to have the bill taken up, he said, and he himself had agreed not to oppose it.

Alerted perhaps by the lobbyists of the Illinois Hightway Users Conference, several representatives from suburban Cook County had followed Sandquist to the rostrum. Now that the subsidy was to come altogether from the metropolitan area and not even in part from the state, they were more than ever opposed to it. If the bill were called up, they told the Speaker, they would filibuster. Sandquist argued. Finally, he looked for De La Cour, the Democratic leader, to whom he had confided his plans and from whom he had had a promise of help. De La Cour, however, was nowhere to be found. Neither De La Cour nor Sandquist wanted to risk being accused of starting a filibuster. And even if the bill could somehow be got past the House, it would surely be defeated in the Senate. The case was hopeless, and Sandquist returned to his seat.

5

The Fort Dearborn
Project

THE central business district of Chicago, like those of most other large cities, was in danger. Its heart was the "Loop" — an area of stores, theatres, office buildings, banks, public buildings, enclosed by a loop of elevated tracks. Beyond the Loop was a mixture of factories, warehouses, and slum housing. Further out from it were residential districts: the Black Belt to the south; Irish, Polish, and Italian working-class districts to the west, and the white middle and upper-middle class to the north. The Loop's danger was in-growing decay. The industrial warehouse and slum district around it cut it off from the outlying residential areas and the suburbs. Mass transportation was unpopular. People with cars — especially middle and upper-class people — were doing more and more of their shopping in neighborhood and suburban shopping centers. While these were springing up on all sides, there was very little building in the Loop and many of the older properties on the fringe of it were deteriorating badly.

"We need people — we've got plenty of business space," a realtor told an interviewer. The people needed were not the low-income whites and Negroes who lived closest to the Loop (the number of these had in fact increased) but people with purchasing power to support the great stores, banks, and entertainment places that were the heart of Chicago. Unless something drastic

126

was done to bring the better customers closer to the Loop, blight would spread inward. As the realtor said, "Unless something drastic is done, you will write off State Street in fifteen years. And the minority groups will take over and then, no matter what the white people do, it can never be brought back, no matter what is done. And the whole damn town will go to hell." The Chicago Plan Commission took much the same view. In 1952 it published a policy statement encouraging construction of high-rise apartments near the central business district. People who could afford to live in such places would be good customers for the downtown stores. But the Commission could only recommend, and anyone with money to invest would pay more attention to market factors than to its recommendations. The fact was that land costs close to the central city were so high that very few could afford to live in apartments built there.

This was the situation in 1949 when Arthur Rubloff had his "fabulous idea" (the adjective was his) — the Fort Dearborn Project. Rubloff might have been a character out of an Horatio Alger story. (He had in fact received the Horatio Alger Award from the American Schools and Colleges Association in 1955). Starting from nothing, he had made himself one of the biggest real estate operators in Chicago and in the United States; his gross business (in 1958) was $120 million. Extraordinary talents as an idea man, speculator, and promoter had brought him to the top of his profession and had given him a name for leadership. He had invented the "Magnificent Mile," a plan which had enhanced real estate values along Michigan Avenue just north of Chicago's downtown Loop district, and he had pioneered in the development of new shopping centers and new plans for neighborhood redevelopment. The Fort Dearborn Project was one of many of his ideas for the improvement of the city.

In brief, his plan was to clear out a hundred acres of unsightly warehouses, small industries, and slum housing across the Chicago River to the north of the Loop and to rebuild it with high-rise apartments and public buildings in a "garden" setting. This would bring customers close to the Loop and prevent the spread of Negroes and poor whites — and consequently of "decay" — from the periphery into the central city. The cost would be at least $450,000,000, according to the first estimate.

For Rubloff this was a mere beginning, hardly more than a gesture in the right direction. "It is impossible to maintain the central city on a block by block basis," he told an interviewer. "We must look at Chicago as a whole. I had it in mind that Van Buren and State streets should be completely demolished and we should build high-rise apartments in a garden setting to accommodate perhaps 100,000 families downtown." Others were not likely to follow so bold a flight of imagination, however, so Rubloff held himself in check and prepared a more modest scheme. "It would be," he said, "a step in the right direction but not a panacea."

He selected the Fort Dearborn area because he lived near it and passed by it every day on his way to the office. That it was on the Chicago River and thus formed part of the impression one got of the city from the Lake Front was in his opinion a reason for making it the starting place.

If Rubloff had not had to take account of realities, his plan might have called for nothing but high-rise apartments: that, at least, would have been the way to bring the largest number of good customers to the Loop. But being a practical man, he knew that a vast public subsidy would be needed. Public housing would defeat the purpose of the Project entirely; it would, in his opinion, lower property values rather than increase them. He favored instead a magnificent civic center along the northern bank of the river where land costs were highest. Around the civic center there would be middle-income housing. If necessary some light manufacturing might be put in the background. The apartments, Rubloff thought, should rent for $50 per room. One-third of them should be "efficiency" apartments; the rest should be one- and two-bedroom units. It would be necessary, of course, to displace the people who lived in the area, but there were few of them — 9,469 in 1950. It was one of the big advantages of the Fort Dearborn site that less relocation would be required there than almost anywhere in the city.

Rubloff conceived his fabulous idea November 16, 1949. To develop it and illustrate it with perspective drawings, he needed thc hclp of some able architects. He said he had spent $100,000 of his own money for such work in connection with the Magnificent Mile. This new project, he decided, would have to be financed by others. One after another, he tried to persuade several architectural firms to contribute their services. Doing so, he argued, would be a public service and quite likely a good investment as well, since a firm which made the first sketches at its own expense would not be overlooked when there were multimillion dollar contracts to be let. None, however, was persuaded.

Finally, he called Nathaniel Owings, a partner in Skidmore, Owings and Merrill, one of the largest architectural firms in the United States and one which had done a great deal of public work in other cities. Owings had been chairman of the Chicago Plan Commission and active in many civic improvement undertakings. The reason Rubloff had not approached him to begin with was that Owings, while chairman of the Plan Commission, had advocated a somewhat similar project immediately west of the Loop which had come to nothing. Since his own idea had not taken hold, he would be unwilling, Rubloff supposed, to invest in someone else's.

Owings, however, turned out to be very much interested. When Rubloff told him that he could get a group of "top civic leaders" to back his idea, Owings agreed to put his staff to work on the idea.

Rubloff went to Hughston McBain, chairman of Marshall Field and Company. Field's was not only the largest retailer in the central area, but was on the north side of the Loop on the site which would benefit most from the Project. Field's had been building branch stores in the suburbs, but it was deeply concerned with the future of the central area. Considerations of profit and loss were enough to justify this concern, but Field's was one of the oldest Chicago businesses and as such it felt it had a special responsibility to give leadership in civic affairs. McBain had been interested in Rubloff's schemes for civic betterment on other occasions and had urged him to come to him when he needed co-operation.

McBain liked the Fort Dearborn idea. Here was a public service which would be good for business. After he had made some inquiries he was enthusiastic. Several insurance companies (the most plausible source of financing for such a large venture) thought well of it, as did Chesser Campbell, an old friend (they had been roommates at the University of Michigan) who was publisher of the *Tribune*. "After McBain became thoroughly indoctrinated," Rubloff said later, "he realized that the Project would be fabulous."

McBain was one of the highest paid (over $100,000 a year) and most prestigious businessmen in Chicago. He was therefore in an excellent position to recruit others to support the Project. In fact, other matters interfered, but Field's vice president helped Owings recruit a select group of Sponsors. These included Holman Pettibone, chairman of the Chicago Title and Trust Company; Gilbert Scribner, Sr., senior partner in the real estate firm which managed the Wrigley Building, among other properties; a utilities executive; and the chief officers of Chicago's third, fourth, and fifth largest banks.

These arrangements took a great deal of time, but in March, 1954, the Project was ready for a public launching. McBain and the other Sponsors invited twenty-one business leaders to a meeting. These were the bankers, manufacturers, utility executives, and merchants who headed the biggest businesses in the city. The invitation said only that the meeting "importantly concerned all good Chicagoans." Secrecy helped create an atmosphere of drama, the Sponsors felt, and a dramatic Project deserved a dramatic presentation.

All those who were invited came. Rubloff flew in from Honolulu to make the main speech ("Do you feel you have a stake in Chicago?" was his theme) and to display the elaborate perspective drawings and the model which Owings' firm had prepared for the occasion.

"There were some compliments and some were skeptical," Rubloff said later. The head of Carson, Pirie, Scott and Company, one of Field's competitors, was noticeably cold to the Project. He had been quietly making plans for a prize contest on Loop rehabilitation and the Project was sure to compete with his contest for public attention. Merchants on the south side of the Loop were less than enthusiastic: they were too far from the

Project to benefit and they depended upon working-class rather than middle-class customers.

Although they did not see fit to say so at the time, some of those who came to the meeting thought that the Project was only a way of buying time for the major merchants to arrange an orderly retreat to the suburbs. One businessman told an interviewer: "The merchants have a large investment and it is frozen. And you know what the trend is in the central districts of all big cities — they are on the toboggan. Well, these fellows are fighting a delaying action. They are smart enough to know that they can't reverse it, but they are trying to slow it down."

Chicago's four major newspapers, which of course were concerned with the future of the central business district and with department store advertising in particular, greeted the Project with enthusiasm. It was "breathtaking," one of them said, and its backers were men of "soaring imagination." The *Tribune,* which almost always favored building and development projects, said that the planners were doing the city a service "whether or not the dream came true" by showing what was possible.

The Project was just next door to the *Tribune,* and for that reason the newspaper was reluctant to campaign as vigorously for it as for some other issues. As the editors explained later, "Our ownership of property on Michigan Avenue might seem to make us prejudiced in favor of Fort Dearborn." The *Sun-Times,* which was owned by Field Enterprises Inc. (which, in turn, was *not* the owner of the department store) and was preparing to build a new plant on the north bank of the Chicago River in what was to be the commercial part of the Project, welcomed the Project and did not hesitate to plug hard for it whenever occasion arose. It acknowledged its own stake in the matter without embarrassment but maintained that its editorial view nevertheless took account only of what was good for the city as a whole. Once the *Sun-Times* prefaced its endorsement of one phase of the plan by remarking, "To the extent that we are disinterested — and we feel we are to a considerable extent — we believe . . ."

A few days after the businessmen's meeting, the plan was officially presented to Mayor Martin Kennelly, who, after warm congratulations to the Sponsors, referred it to the city agencies for detailed study.

There was reason to believe that the plan would be well received by the officials in these agencies. F. T. Aschman, executive director of the Plan Commission from 1950 to 1956 and later a private planning consultant, had developed what was called the "anchor concept." His idea was to "compress" the central business district of Chicago between residential areas and thus to prevent it from spreading itself out and dissipating itself; compression, Aschman maintained, would preserve the high property values of the central district whereas lack of compression would encourage a gradual shift of valuable store and office properties out of the Loop and to the north. Aschman's ideas were popular, and the Project obviously fitted them nicely. It would be the northern "anchor."

The civic center which was a prominent feature of the Project also had its supporters among the officials and planners. A civic center (but in another location) had been part of Burnham's famous 1909 Plan of Chicago and the idea had cropped up now and then ever since. The Plan Commission had recently made studies of possible locations of new public buildings and had concluded that the north bank of the Chicago River would be "acceptable." The river bank needed improvement and it was what the architects called a "dramatic" site for a civic center. There were, however, other acceptable locations, and the Commission made no promises. The idea of putting apartment buildings near the river had not occurred to the Commission. It had unofficially classed the whole tract as commercial and industrial.

To make the Project a reality would take a good deal more than the approval of the Mayor and the Plan Commission, however. The civic center would include county, state, and federal offices; consequently, the Sponsors would have to get the agreement of County Board President Ryan, Governor Stratton, and the head of the federal government's General Services Administration. Getting the agreement of so many would not be easy; even so, it would be only a small part of the whole task. The residential and commercial parts of the Project would require an enormous block of valuable real estate which could only be acquired with public authority and public money. It might be possible for the Chicago Land Clearance Commission to acquire the land under the redevelopment powers of the Federal Housing Act and to re-sell it below cost to private developers on condition that they adhere to an approved plan. On this basis the federal government might pay as much as two thirds of the net acquisition cost and the city and state might pay a good deal of the rest. But first the Land Clearance Commission would have to survey the area and designate it as eligible for slum clearance, then the City Council, the Illinois State Housing Board, and the Urban Renewal Ad-ministration of the Federal Housing and Home Finance Agency would all have to approve the Project plan.

These were not the only hurdles. Unless private investors were ready to take the land at reduced prices from the Land Clearance Commission and build on it according to plan, the whole under-taking would come to nothing. The amount of private capital that would be needed was very large. Only an insurance company would be likely to have it, but insurance companies, as experience in Chicago and many other cities had shown, were not easily convinced of the practicality of such projects.

Leading the Project to success would obviously require the whole attention of a very capable executive. Accordingly, in the summer of 1954 the Sponsors borrowed the services of one of Marshall Field's vice-presidents, Earl Kribben, whose normal job (his title was actually "vice president for civic affairs") was to represent his company on the boards of a dozen or so civic asso-ciations whose activities it wanted to further as a public service or for business reasons. His proven ability in these connections had made him widely known and liked and had given him an un-usual acquaintance with the political and administrative in's and out's through which such projects as this had to pass.

Kribben, some said, did not have the influence of McBain or Pettibone. He was, according to this view, a vice president, whereas they were chairmen of the board. When it came to dealing with other businessmen or with politicians, he could not carry their weight, even though it was well understood that he spoke for them. Another vice president told an interviewer: "Chairmen talk to chairmen. Presidents talk to presidents. Vice presidents talk to vice presidents. Undoubtedly McBain can talk on levels that Kribben can't. It is an interesting phenomenon: these men take each other on faith. One chairman can call another and ask for $10,000 and get it easily. But that is not true at the vice-president level."

Kribben himself later ridiculed this estimate. He could, he told an interviewer, talk to anyone without any difficulty, and he could get money from chairmen when other chairmen couldn't get $1.98. "I have a unique *entree,*" he explained. "They all know my position is *pro bono publico.*"

His experience, if not his position in the status hierarchy, inclined him to treat his problem as one of merchandising. "I'm really a salesman, and what I'm selling is an idea," he told a reporter. He kept the press supplied with architect's drawings and news of impending developments. He was a tireless after-luncheon speaker before every civic association willing to hear about the Project. By 1957 he had made about eighty presentations, describing plans, showing models, and explaining finances.

He was more than a salesman, however. He charted a course through the sea of obstacles which continually threatened to swamp the Project. One of his first problems was the financing of the local government portion of the civic center. The voters could be asked to approve general obligation bonds, but there was danger of their refusing and, in so doing, dealing the Project a fatal blow. To avoid this danger, Kribben and the Sponsors devised an ingenious plan of financing. They asked the legislature to create a Public Buildings Commission with power to sell forty-year revenue bonds, buy land and erect buildings, and liquidate its bond from rents paid by the public bodies. With the backing of Governor Stratton and the new mayor of Chicago, Richard J. Daley, the legislature passed the necessary legislation in 1955. The Illinois Supreme Court, however, ruled that the bonds must be paid off in twenty rather than in forty years. This meant that the Public Buildings Commission would have to charge higher rents than had been anticipated. It might, therefore, be difficult to find underwriters to market its bonds, and in the end the State of Illinois might have to be persuaded to buy them. All this was but a part of Kribben's problem.

With the federal agency, the General Services Administration, Kribben's task at first seemed easy. Edmund F. Mansure, the head of it, was a Chicago man whom Kribben had known for some time and whom McBain had met once. At Mansure's direction the General Services Administration supplied Kribben with estimates of probable federal space requirements in Chicago. Unfortunately, however, Mansure resigned. His successor was not a Chicago man and not particularly interested in the Project. Both Governor Stratton and the Republican president of the Cook County Sanitary District were enthusiastic supporters of the Project, but, compared to the federal and city governments, neither the state nor the Sanitary District was an important consumer of office space. The state, moreover, had recently bought an office building and the Sanitary District had just built one.

The key figures on the scene were two Democrats, Richard J. Daley, Mayor of Chicago, and Daniel Ryan, the President of the Cook County Board. McBain, Pettibone, Kribben, and others came to Daley shortly after he took office. Daley was impressed with their glowing accounts of the Project, and he was given to understand that all of the principal public agencies — the federal government, the state, the Sanitary District, the Park District, and the Board of Education — were ready to take space in a "Government Center" in the Project. This being so, there was, he felt, much to be said for having the city hall there too. When Owings, the architect, asked him to be photographed with a model of the Project for a *Life* magazine story, he readily consented. While the photographers were making ready, his press secretary asked if he realized that he was being identified with the Project. Did he really wish to be? The Project was basically a real estate promotion, the Mayor told him, but there was a lot of good in it. Some weeks later, on a flight to Pittsburgh to view the Golden Triangle, Kribben asked the Mayor for a few lines that could be quoted in a brochure about the Project. The press secretary drafted a weakly approving statement and passed it to the Mayor. The Mayor handed it back. "Make it stronger," he said.

That the Project was intended in part to make money the Mayor considered obvious. He had no objection to it on this ground, provided that it benefitted the city without placing an undue burden on the taxpayer. That the benefits to the city would be great he was assured on every side and so it seemed to him. In his opinion, the steady drift to the suburbs was a disaster that somehow had to be stopped. The city had to be made attractive to middle-class residents. Any plan for doing this was likely to have his cordial support, no matter who proposed it or why.

This much was on the level of policy. But the Mayor was also by temperament a booster. He liked to do things and to do them in a big way. He liked to encourage others to do things. No matter how he might feel personally, he always tried to take a positive, optimistic, enthusiastic tone. This was a sensible tactic, of course, for everyone felt that a Mayor ought to be a booster and not a knocker. But with Daley it was not simply a matter of tactics — it came naturally to him. Even in private he found it hard to throw cold water. When he called the Project "imaginative and big," some assumed that he favored it. Those who knew him better realized that this was his normal way of responding.

In any case, the Mayor would probably have kept his doubts and reservations, if he had any, to himself. When he took office, everyone seemed to be agreed that the Project was a great thing. If he had quickly cast doubt upon a scheme which certain of the most prominent business leaders of Chicago had matured with so much effort and expense and which seemed to have won such general approval, he would have incurred much criticism and have gained nothing.

No one knew for sure where Ryan, the President of the County Board stood. He was said to have called the Project "nonsense" in private. But Rubloff and he were good friends (Rubloff was said to have given him some sound advice in business matters in times past), and Rubloff was sure of his support. When Kribben arranged for a *Tribune* man to sound him out, he seemed to be enthusiastic.

As the affairs of the Project became increasingly complicated, they were left more and more in Kribben's hands. The supporters were busy with other things and some of them, as time went on, began to lose enthusiasm. Kribben sent around mimeographed memoranda to keep the Sponsors informed, and on infrequent occasions he called a meeting of them. He was no longer merely the salesman of the Project. "Kribben," an observer said, *"is* the Fort Dearborn Project."

Whether he had the qualities that were needed to bring the Project to success (assuming, of course, that success was possible) was a question on which opinions differed. "The main reason we've got anywhere is Kribben," said one Sponsor to an interviewer. "He's a hard plugging, relentless guy. He won't let go of anything." Others thought his very energy and persistence might be a handicap. "Kribben is selling too hard," one said. "He is not giving the feeling of participation to the people he tries to interest. He should try to draw others in and make them feel a part of it. He should get the Mayor to feel that *he* had located the city hall so that he could say 'I put the city hall there.'"

Rubloff's identification with the Project was now less close. For a while he had employed a public relations man who put out press releases referring to him as the "creator" of the Project, but when Kribben pointed out that it could have only one spokesman, he at once desisted. He attended meetings regularly, but was not one of the Sponsors. "The silk stockings got in and Rubloff is not there any more," someone observed in 1957. The fact was that the Sponsors admired Rubloff and were fond of him; they were certain, too, that his motives in proposing the Project were entirely public-spirited. Nevertheless, they felt that his connection with it might be misconstrued. "There never was the slightest suspicion that he was using the Project to make a fast buck," one of them explained later. "In fact, he was trying to pay the community back for the opportunities it had given him. But he *had been* in big money-making propositions in the past, and so it was entirely reasonable that others might think that in this case." Apart from this, there was another reason why his role was less prominent. Men like McBain, Pettibone, and Kribben, whose ideas the business community thought "sound," who had the resources of great corporations at their disposal, and who were used to the discipline of teamwork, were needed now. Conceiving a fabulous idea like the Fort Dearborn Project took one kind of talent. Realizing the conception took other kinds. "The chief credit for the Fort Dearborn planning," the *Tribune* remarked editorially in 1957, "belongs to Hughston McBain, chairman of Marshall Field & Company, whose firm has invested a large sum in the enterprise. . . ."

At first blush it was logical to suppose that the city and county courts would go into the proposed civic center. They were now inadequately housed in the city-county building in the heart of the Loop, together with offices of the mayor, the Cook County Board, the sheriff, the coroner, and a good many other local agencies.

It very soon became plain that moving the courts would provoke opposition — enough of it, perhaps, to doom the whole Project. Ten thousand lawyers had offices within easy walking distance of the city-county buildings. Courts and lawyers had to be close to each other, even if there were a place in the Project to which they could move, the lawyers would resist a change.

The banks were in a similar position. They did frequent business in the courts and with the lawyers who had offices near the courts. To move the banks was of course entirely out of the question.

The Chicago Title and Trust Company, Pettibone's firm, was one of those that would be injured by movement of the courts. Its big office building, directly across the street from the city-county building, was in a location that was presently ideal, and neither its officials nor its many tenants would be willing to journey back and forth from courts located on the north bank of the Chicago River. The building was managed by Leo Sheridan, who managed about one-fifth of Chicago's private office space. He and Pettibone would certainly oppose movement of the courts, and they would make tough antagonists.

It was not surprising, then, that within thirty days of their first public announcement, the Sponsors revised the plan to exclude the courts. The courts, they thought, had best stay in the Loop; indeed they had best stay in the existing city-county building, for if a new building were proposed for them elsewhere, it would compete for funds with the Project and some people might even argue that if the courts could not follow the civic center, the civic center should follow the courts. Considering all this, the Sponsors concluded that there should be a thorough study of the possibility of turning the city-county building into a courthouse when the other agencies left it.

However, this possibility did not appeal to the judges. Chicago had one of the biggest back-logs of court cases in the nation; it would be four years before some of the cases reached trial. Inadequate courtroom facilities were alleged to be a main cause of the delay. When it became known that the Sponsors of the Project were proposing to turn the old city-county building over to the courts, some judges and attorneys were very much dissatisfied. If the old building were to be used, nothing could be done to relieve overcrowding until the Project was completed; even then there would be years of confusion and upset while the old building was being converted for additional courtrooms. By the time the courts were settled in the remodelled building the backlog of cases would be even larger than at present. The only way to break the bottleneck, the judges and attorneys thought, was to begin construction of a wholly new courthouse immediately; to press this view they formed the Committee for a New Courthouse.

When the Committee for a New Courthouse announced its aims to the press, Pettibone called one of its leaders to say that the situation was "very delicate" and that the Sponsors of the Fort Dearborn Project hoped to avoid a controversy. "They wanted us to keep our big mouths shut," an advocate of the new courthouse said later.

Among the managers of Loop office property there were several who were delighted with the thought that a new court building might be located near their buildings. They were therefore anxious to enter into an active alliance with the Committee for a New Courthouse. The Committee, however, was unwilling. "We are lawyers, not real estate men," one of its members said. "What we were trying to do was look at it objectively. But we found that we were in the middle, between two real estate groups who were using the courthouse as a kind of bait."

An ally whom the Committee did accept was the elected sheriff of Cook County, Joseph D. Lohman, a Democrat. Lohman was crusading for a new and larger jail, and the Committee agreed to devote the top floors of its proposed new courthouse to maximum-security cells. Through Lohman the Committee got the county architect to make a study showing the infeasibility of converting the existing city-county building. A study of this kind by a technical expert was an indispensable preparation for a decision which in the end would have to be taken on non-technical grounds.

Lohman's support did not carry with it the power of the Democratic machine, however; he was on less than cordial terms with Mayor Daley and County President Ryan. Moreover, although he said nothing publicly, Daley was much opposed to having the criminal courts and the jail as a part of a civic center. A civic center, he reasoned, should be the showplace of the city: the criminal courts and the jails were visited mainly by the dregs of the city — narcotic addicts, prostitutes, and worse. There was no sense bringing these undesirable types into the very center of the city and into an edifice symbolizing the dignity of civic life.

There was an outcry from still another quarter when the Sponsors proposed moving the public library to the civic center. The library occupied one of the most valuable blocks in Chicago (it was on Michigan Avenue between Field's and the lake) and its trustees and staff were determined to keep it where it was. The Sponsors soon dropped their proposal. The reason they dropped it, some supposed, was that McBain feared Field's would be charged with moving the library in order that its location might be taken by some use — an office building, perhaps — that would bring more customers to Field's. The truth was, however, that the cost of moving the library's vast stock of books was found to be so high as to make any move infeasible.

These controversies left a good many people disenchanted with the idea of a civic center. In his after-luncheon speeches Kribben continued to expand on the beauty and convenience of the plan, but privately some of the Sponsors began to tell each other that it might be well to give less emphasis to that aspect of the Project. A few had even become converts to the view of the Commitee for a New Courthouse and were willing to build in the Loop at the risk of competing with the Project.

The Building Managers' Association of Chicago was an old

organization, the membership of which included the managers of practically all the hundred-odd office buildings in the Loop. It represented its members in labor negotiations, looked after their interests in zoning and building ordinances, and in general kept a watchful eye open on their behalf. When the Fort Dearborn Project was proposed, it found itself divided and accordingly took no stand. However, some of its leading members — among them Graham Aldis, Carroll H. Sudler, Jr., and others who managed properties in the Loop — went ahead on their own to oppose the Project as best they could. The scope of their influence was not as wide as that of some businessmen — Pettibone, for example — but they had long been active in real estate organizations and taxpayers' associations and their views carried weight within these circles. Aldis, in particular, had given thought to the problems of the central area. He had been the real estate member of a team which placed third in the Carson, Pirie, Scott & Company competition. (The first and second prizes went to out-of-town contestants.)

At first the opposing building managers tried to reach a compromise with the Sponsors. They talked to Kribben and Pettibone about dropping not only the courts but various other public agencies from the civic center. For a time it seemed that agreement might be possible. "Hold your fire. We're revamping the Project," Pettibone would tell Aldis. Then Kribben, anxious to maintain public interest in the Project, would make another speech emphasizing the advantage of bringing all agencies together on the north side of the river and Aldis and his friends would conclude that nothing short of outright opposition would do.

Aldis, Sudler, and their friends were in a difficult position. They seemed to be representing only their own private interests. It was desirable to put up a broader front — one which could speak in the name of something more than the "selfish interest of a few individuals." They therefore organized the Committee for Government Buildings Downtown. The Committee was recruited as opportunity arose from among the friends and acquaintances of three or four building managers who were very much concerned. "All of us had our businesses to attend to and it was largely a matter of people whom we could contact readily," one of the

organizers said later. "Frankly, it was a hell of a job. It wasn't
a matter of sufficient urgency in their minds. I understand this.
There are dozens of things that sound good but there just isn't
time for them all. There is pressure for innumerable things and
every businessman is participating in good causes and just can't
take on any more. Some said, 'There are good people on both
sides of this issue. I guess I'll just stay neutral on it.'"

Others refused for business reasons. That one man was another's friend of long standing did not mean that he would come
into the Committee as a favor. As one of the participants explained later to an interviewer: "In the big league operations —
and that's what you're talking about here — it doesn't work that
way. Men are moved by interests, not friendship." "Friends can
argue on other matters and still remain friends," another said.
"But they are often afraid to argue if it would involve the loss
of a tremendous amount of business."

As it was finally constituted, the Committee consisted of
twenty-eight business, professional, and real estate men. In addition to Aldis and Sudler, there were Lester Armour, chairman of
the Chicago National Bank; Morton Bodfish, chairman and president of the First Federal Savings and Loan Association; James E.
Day, president of the Midwest Stock Exchange; and John T.
Pirie, Jr., president of the Carson, Pirie, Scott & Company department store, Field's principal competitor. Twenty-eight such
names made an impressive array on the Committee's letterhead.

In competing with the Sponsors of the Project for public support, the Committee was at a disadvantage. It was "defending the
status quo," whereas the Sponsors were "advancing a bold and
imaginative plan for the development of Chicago." In actual
fact, Aldis's conception, which he had developed in the Carson,
Pirie, Scott & Company competition, was as general and defensible as that of the Fort Dearborn Sponsors: the growth in
merchandising, he thought, would be in the outlying areas no
matter what was done; the future of the Loop lay in office
buildings — the Loop would continue to grow as a financial, legal,
and management center; it would be disastrous, therefore, to dilute
the concentration of office buildings — the Loop's real strength —
by moving the government buildings away.

This view of the public interest, however, could not be advanced vigorously without alienating some merchants whose support the Committee needed. For the sake of unity among the Project's opponents, a good argument against it could not be used. Under the circumstances, the Committee tended to be on the defensive. "Going against public improvements is like being for sin," one of its members remarked sadly.

The Committee was casting about for ways to take the offensive when by chance some of its members encountered Tibor J. Haring, a city planner who had worked with Le Corbusier and who had independently developed ideas for Chicago which coincided with those of the Committee. The Committee published and distributed a brochure with illustrations based on Haring's ideas. These showed three groups of new public buildings, each group in the Loop not far from the existing government buildings and all located to replace "blighted" or unsightly structures. On the question of a new courthouse the Committee was equivocal: a new one might be needed, but, on the other hand, the old one might be made to do.

These efforts to strike a positive note were not entirely successful. The Sponsors believed that the alternative plan was nothing but an effort to mask private interests behind the phrase "civic improvement." Only one of the newspapers found the Committee and its plan newsworthy. Some of the Committee's leaders were well acquainted with the publishers of the newspapers; they did not, however, ask for support. Apparently it was good manners that prevented them from doing so. "I hesitated to push it," one of the Committee told an interviewer. "I thought that if he [the publisher] wanted to talk about it, he would." Good manners did not prevent the employment of a press agent, however, and the Committee used one to get its story before the public as best it could.

With the politicians the building managers were also at a disadvantage. Most of the managers contributed to the Republican party and some of them were interested in national issues to the exclusion of local ones. The politicians, on the other hand, were mostly Democrats who had risen by their own efforts from working-class families, many of them attending Catholic colleges; they were entirely concerned with local affairs, especially the struggle for power in the local machine. None of the Committee was on close terms with a politician and the politicians were not likely to regard the Committee members with special interest or sympathy.

The Committee nevertheless had two meetings with Mayor Daley and argued that the proposed Fort Dearborn civic center would be extravagant and inconvenient. The Loop, it said, should be improved first. The Mayor gave the Committee a good hearing, but he seemed to grow less sympathetic to its position as the meetings went on. "We are convinced that others got to him after the first meeting," a Committee member told an interviewer. "He was much more formal. We found him repeating things Kribben had said elsewhere."

The Building Managers' Association was not the only organization too divided to take a stand. Others — notably the Chicago Association of Commerce and Industry, the Real Estate Board, the Civic Federation, and the State Street Council — were in exactly the same position. Each had leading men on both sides of the issue and each was bound to be disrupted by any effort to commit it one way or another. Staying aloof was better, the organizations all decided, than to lose support. As one staff man remarked to an interviewer, "It is better to let controversial things solve themselves. . . ."

Even the Greater North Michigan Avenue Association, which Rubloff himself had headed in 1955, was divided and unable to act. Some of its members owned or managed extensive properties in the area to be cleared for the Project. Those who opposed the Fort Dearborn Project formed an *ad hoc* committee — the Near Northside Land Use Committee — which soon claimed to represent $50 million worth of property.

Even within the ranks of the opponents there was disagreement. Loop building managers like Aldis and others of the Committee for Government Buildings Downtown had no objection to northside residential development if it did not include a civic center. The Near Northside Land Use Committee, on the other hand, did not object to a civic center and certain commercial and industrial features of the Project, but was dead set against the use of public powers to take property from its members for residential development.

Some of the Northside Committee were realtors who depended upon turnover of property. If the area as a whole were redeveloped, there would be little turnover for many years to come. This, however, was not the reason the Committee used to justify its position. Publicly some of its members said that constant talk about the Project prevented the area from being redeveloped by venture capital. If investors could be sure that they would be left undisturbed, there would be plenty of new building there. By creating uncertainty, the Sponsors (so the opponents argued) had depreciated values in the Project area and prevented its normal development and improvement.

Privately, however, some of the Committee said that a Project would sooner or later bring Negroes into the area. Federal funds could be obtained only if guarantees were given against racial discrimination. To be sure, only the highest income Negroes could afford to live in the Project as it was planned. But within a few years values would drop and rents would be lowered; Negroes would then appear in large numbers. This, the opponents argued, would reduce the real estate values in the surrounding area. All in all, they concluded, it might be better to keep the district blighted.

The Central Area Committee was also divided by the Fort Dearborn question. Organized around an executive committee of fourteen, the Central Area Committee included the chief executives of the largest firms in Chicago. The interests of these firms were by no means confined to the central business district (some — the Illinois Central Railroad, for example — were national in scope); the executive committee, which alone could speak for the organization, had been carefully selected to minimize conflicts of interest; and the chairman of the executive committee, Pettibone, was a skillful negotiator who was widely respected in the business community and who, as chairman of the Chicago Title and Trust Company, occupied a highly strategic position in real estate affairs. Despite all this, the Central Area Committee could not agree on the Fort Dearborn Project. Pettibone had been one of the Sponsors from the first. But some contributors

to the Central Area Committee were very much opposed to the
Project and one was even a member of the Committee for Government Buildings Downtown.

Pettibone was in a delicate position. He was one of the Sponsors of the Project; if he withdrew active support, it would suffer
a loss of prestige that might be fatal. On the other hand, if he
used his position as chairman of the Central Area Committee
to advance the Project, he would surely wreck the Committee.
He was carrying water on both shoulders, his critics said. That,
his friends replied, was something he did extraordinarily well;
given half a chance he would work out a compromise acceptable
to all.

Before the Project could become a reality decisions would have
to be taken by various authorities both public and private. Each
would make its decisions in the light of those made by the others,
and so, of course, could not decide until after they had decided.
Like the mythical trains at the crossing, none could pass until
all the others had passed. In a situation so exasperatingly circular,
where there was no "next step" which an opponent could prevent
or a proponent encourage, it was hard to know just where or how
to use one's influence.

In December, 1955, the Sponsors asked the Chicago Land
Clearance Commission to designate the Project an urban renewal
area; this would start the way toward clearing land for resale to
private developers. When he received the application, the executive
director of the Commission reasoned that any decision regarding clearance for private development should await one regarding
the civic center. Residential development would depend upon
what was done along the river bank; unless the warehouses there
were removed, insurance companies would not invest in middle-
income apartment buildings, for the buildings would be cut off from
the river and the Loop by a row of unsightly warehouses.

The civic center was to extend three blocks from the river.
If there was no civic center, housing would have to be extended
all the way to the river's edge. But the property along the river
was very expensive — in some places $54 a square foot —, and
it was hard to see how the purchase of it for subsidized housing

could be justified. (The civic center would be on land assembled under condemnation powers, but it would not be subsidized by a "write-down.") Office buildings would be a suitable use for the valuable land on the river bank, but putting them there would increase opposition to the Project by the downtown building managers.

It was by no means certain that the Land Clearance Commission would approve the application when it got around to considering it. To qualify for a subsidy under the urban renewal law, an area had to be at least 55 per cent residential and at least 50 per cent of the buildings in it had to be "sub-standard." Judged by 1950 census data, both these criteria could probably be met. But the Land Clearance Commission would make its own survey of the area, using its own definitions of "residential" and "substandard" and collecting its own statistics, and there was no way of knowing for sure what conclusion it would reach.

The circularity of the decision process would be interrupted if one or two life insurance companies decided to invest in the Project. In this case the Land Clearance Commission would come under heavy pressure to approve the application and the public authorities would be encouraged to move to the Project area. When the Project was first announced, the New York Life Insurance Company had expressed interest in it, but the Sponsors had not been ready to make commitments. They had been confident that when the time was ripe they could get insurance investment (Scribner was a director of Mutual Life; Pettibone had close relationships with Prudential; and George Dovenmuehle, a Project backer who was the head of a large mortgage banking firm, had many connections). As it turned out, however, insurance companies seemed to have the same doubts that the Land Clearance Commission had. Until it was perfectly clear that the high land costs would be absorbed by public subsidy through the construction of a civic center or otherwise, they would not commit themselves. There were, after all, many opportunities for such investment in other cities and nowhere was much capital moving into housing and redevelopment projects.

The commercial and institutional part of the Project might possibly be got underway without waiting for an insurance company to invest in housing. If one big organization agreed to build its headquarters in the Project area, others would follow. Kribben talked to officials of the American Medical Association and the Portland Cement Association: both were mildly interested. "If they would go in, others would follow damn fast," a Sponsor said. "They're all waiting for some big deal to kick it off. . . . Somebody has got to get the ball rolling."

No one was willing to go first, however, for there was a chance that others would not follow and the one who went first would be left in splendid isolation. If the Sponsors had been able to guarantee that a civic center would be built, organizations like the Medical Association might have been willing to go ahead. And if they had been able to guarantee that the Medical Association and two or three other such bodies would locate there, the Sponsors would probably have had an easier time getting the civic center. But since neither could be had without a prior guarantee of the other, nothing could be done.

Had he seen fit to do so, Mayor Daley could have broken the circle of indecision. He had no formal control over the Land Clearance Commission, but he appointed its members and they would respect his wishes.

The Mayor, however, had lost much of his interest in the Project. He had been keen on it at first, even though he considered it essentially a real estate promotion, because he wanted to encourage families to live in the inner city. When he discovered that the rents would be $50 to $60 a room, he was doubtful. There were few families who could afford so much. That meant that the residential part of the Project would have to be mainly high-rise "economy" apartments for elderly people and childless couples. Influenced perhaps by his Catholic upbringing, he was against development of a kind that might discourage people from having children or interfere with family life. The Sponsors, he soon realized, did not care much about this aspect of the matter: they wanted residents who would make good customers for the downtown stores, and well-to-do childless people were better from this standpoint than not-so-well-to-do families. Moreover the Sponsors felt that the relocation of the Negroes and Filipinos who would be displaced by the Project was not an important matter. The Mayor, however, had to consider their votes.

These considerations were enough to make him dubious. He became even more so when, in reply to a letter of inquiry from him, the Governor and the heads of the other public agencies concerned — the General Services Administration, the Sanitary District, the Park District and the Board of Education — all said that they could not promise to take space in a government center. He had believed (although Kribben later denied having given him reason to believe so) that the agreement of these others was virtually assured. Now it seemed to him that he was being asked to take on behalf of the taxpayers of Chicago a risk that no one else — least of all the Sponsors, who (as it seemed to him) hoped to gain so much from the Project — was willing to take. It irked him that he should be thought such a simple-minded fellow. He told an interviewer:

They claim this entire Project hangs on the city hall. That's childish, idiotic, juvenile. Who can believe that? They took the city hall out of one place in Los Angeles and put it in another place and there's no development around it. What I want to know is: where's the best location for the people of Chicago? Are we going to discommode the people of Chicago for a real estate promotion? I think what we should do is have all kinds of housing up there — high-class, low-class, middle-class. And why shouldn't the entire rebuilding be for houses? Some of them want shopping up there. I think my first responsibility is to the people. I'm for it *if* these gentlemen will come in and show me their money and where they want it. . . . The problem is whether we have just talk or definite commitments.

Whether the Mayor made it clear to the Sponsors that he would require a definite commitment from others before taking action was later a matter of disagreement. The Mayor told an interviewer that he had made his position clear to McBain, Pettibone, and Kribben. But these three later denied that they had received the impression he sought to convey. On the contrary, Kribben told an interviewer, they had been careful to explain to him that they were not a redevelopment group, that they were only trying to pave the way for someone who might form one, and that the best way to get one formed was to locate government buildings on the river bank, thus stabilizing the area. They were surprised

and pained to learn later that he has regarded them as profit-
seeking businessmen trying to entice him into a venture that would
enrich them at the public's expense. In their own eyes they were
public-spirited citizens trying to initiate a project for the good of
the city and thus incidentally — but only incidentally — for the
good of the institutions they represented.

The misunderstanding, some of the Sponsors later surmised,
might be due to the fact that the Mayor had no close friends in
the business world. He had the wrong idea about businessmen
because he was not well enough acquainted with them.

Others less charitable said that there was no misunderstanding.
The Mayor, they said, was opposed to the Fort Dearborn Project
because he wanted a "Daley Plan" as a monument to himself.

The Public Buildings Commission was also in a position to break
the stalemate. It had six members appointed by the Mayor of
Chicago and five appointed by the heads of the other local agencies.
The Mayor himself appointed five businessmen: Henry Crown,
chairman of the Material Service Corporation (suppliers for large
construction projects); Willis Gale, head of Commonwealth
Edison, a utility company; Stuart List, publisher of the *Chicago-
American*; John Sevcik, a manufacturer; and Philip K. Wrigley,
one of the owners of a big office building on the north side of the
central business district. Cook County was represented by President Daniel Ryan; the Forest Preserve District by James A.
Cunningham, an investment banker who was Ryan's friend and
adviser; and the Sanitary District, the Park District, and the Board
of Education by their presidents and vice-presidents.

In making these appointments the Mayor paid no special heed
to the Fort Dearborn Project. In securing the legislation which
authorized a Commission and the sale of revenue bonds the
Sponsors had of course intended to promote the Project. But the
legislation did not restrict the Commission to the Fort Dearborn
site, and the Mayor saw in it a convenient way of getting something done — perhaps something different from what the Sponsors had intended. Accordingly, in his appointments he looked for
persons who would have the support and respect of the business

community and of the press. How they stood on the Project made little difference.

If the Commission had any bias, it was in favor of the Project. Gale had been one of the original Sponsors. The Wrigley Building stood to benefit from development on the north bank of the river. (Wrigley thought there might be a conflict of interest between his public and private roles and offered to resign; he was persuaded to stay, however.) Crown's company did an enormous business in Chicago. None of those appointed was an opponent of the Project.

Some opponents of the Project feared that the Commission, having been created at the behest of the Sponsors, would feel bound to support the Project. The Commissioners, however, felt free to do as they thought best. "As far as I'm concerned," one of them told an interviewer, "there is no relation between the Sponsors and the Public Buildings Commission. They are as separate as chalk from cheese. I understand that the Sponsors urged the passing of the legislation, but that has nothing to do with what I believe to be right or wrong. Daley did a wise thing in choosing men who will do what is best for Chicago, disregarding any selfish or unselfish interest. I won't say that Fort Dearborn won't come into being, but if it does, it will only because there is a consensus that that is the proper thing to do."

Some people suspected that Mayor Daley and County Board President Ryan would use the Commission to ratify a decision made privately by them. However, the Mayor at once told the Commission that he expected it to reach its own decision in its own way.

The Commission was to elect its own chairman. Some Sponsors thought it would be better to have a businessman as chairman than to have the Mayor, who was the obvious alternative. "The nature of a politician is to compromise," one Sponsor explained afterward, ". . . and if the north side and the west side and downtown get roaring, there's a damn good chance of nothing being done. If Henry Crown was chairman, he might be willing to offend some of them. But the Mayor's business — politics — prevents that. If a fellow like McBain were chairman he wouldn't be sensitive to hurting two-thirds of the Loop to help one-third.

So I said, 'To hell with the politicians. Let's get a fellow who doesn't give a damn what people think of him.' There is where a fellow like Moses [Robert Moses of New York] would be a good thing. Moses doesn't give a damn."

It was possible to argue along the same line to an opposite conclusion, and some did. The Mayor, a Commissioner said, would be less sensitive than a businessman to pressures from the business community. Businessmen couldn't defeat the Mayor in election if they tried: "What does it matter [to the Mayor]? Does he give a damn whether Hughston McBain or Graham Aldis are for him? I would think that Dick [the Mayor] has less to lose than any other individual on the committee. There are other individuals on it who might even depend on Mr. A or Mr. B in business. Dick can say, 'To hell with it.' "

Kribben and Pettibone were among those who wanted the Mayor to be chairman. They thought he favored a civic center and that it was best to put the reins in his hands and let him move at his own pace. Otherwise he might lose patience and create difficulties. When the Mayor assumed the chairmanship, they supposed that they had persuaded him. In fact (one of his associates explained later) he took the chairmanship because he had decided that the Commission and its revenue bond powers offered a convenient mechanism for getting certain things done, among which things the Project might or might not be one.

As chairman, the Mayor's first act was to have the Real Estate Research Corporation make a study of the present and future space requirements for public buildings. Real Estate Research reported that public agencies presently required 1,000,000 square feet of office space in the central area and that by 1970 another 2,300,000 square feet would be needed. The courts, it said, should be kept in the Loop (this had already been decided upon informally), and there was no need for a single city-county government center. "There is no indication," the report said, "that either public convenience or functional necessity requires the concentration of all central area government offices in a single 'Government Center.' A single 'Government Center' . . . would appear to afford only intangible benefits in the way of satisfaction of civic pride and the creation of government prestige and opportunity for dramatic architectural accomplishments."

The possibilities open to the Commission were various. It could build a complete civic center in the Fort Dearborn area or it could build nothing at all. It could build according to the plan of the Downtown Committee or it could put a court house at some other place in or out of the Loop. Or, still another possibility, it could put some public buildings at Fort Dearborn and some downtown.

On what basis was the Commission to decide? "Businessmen think pretty much alike," one of the commissioners told an interviewer. "They are measuring cost in every instance and are making decisions that will exonerate their judgment in the future." "I work for good government," said another, "— economy and efficiency."

The mere measurement of cost could not, however, provide a solution to the problem. The least costly thing might be to build nothing at all. Cost had to be considered in relation to benefits, and in this case the benefits were impossible to measure because they depended upon circumstances that were highly unpredictable (did the future of the Loop lie with office buildings or with department stores?) and because the values in question were mostly intangible (was the esthetic value of a civic center on the river greater than the convenience of scattered buildings downtown?). Even if it had been possible to foresee the future and to measure in money all of the values involved, an insuperable obstacle to purely objective judgment would have remained: some interests would suffer by any choice that might be made; who was to say that, whatever the net advantage, the loss to the sufferers was justified?

The businessmen on the Commission were used to making important decisions, but in their businesses they had the profit criterion to guide them. Here it did not apply, for there was no way of measuring in dollars the values that would be created by one plan or another.

Having no satisfactory basis for deciding one way or another, the businessmen-commissioners squirmed in indecision. "This is a goddamned complicated thing," one of them told an interviewer. In such a situation it was natural to call for more facts. The Commission asked the Chicago Plan Commission to make an "objective" recommendation on land use and central area renewal. It awaited the results of a million-dollar study of metropolitan transportation that had long been underway. It re-employed the Real Estate Research Corporation to make new studies of convenience, access, and functional relationships between offices. Noting that there were "powerful material interests" on each side of the government buildings debate, the Chicago *Daily News* piously suggested that the decision be left to planning technicians. "The public will be best served," it said, "if the Mayor's commission accepts the best judgment of the city's own planners as to what is most desirable."

Some businessmen, watching the proceedings from a distance and seeing the futility of all the fact gathering, became impatient with the Commission. One told an interviewer: "A big man phoned and asked, 'What are they doing on this Fort Dearborn thing? These are big men on the Public Buildings Commission. Don't they know the city? They can make decisions in their own businesses without a lot of reports.' Some of the strongest men don't want to make a decision."

A decade after Rubloff conceived his fabulous idea it was dealt a blow that might be fatal. This came not as an adverse report by the Public Building Commission (the Commission never did make a report) but as a recommendation of the City Planning Department. The Mayor, dissatisfied with what was put before the Public Building Commission, ordered the Planning Department to prepare a "practical" and "sensible" plan treating all of the major problems of the central city together. Ira Bach, the head of the Planning Department, was told to work closely with James C. Downs, an old associate who was chairman of the Real Estate Research Corporation and the Mayor's principal adviser on housing and planning matters.

In 1958 the Planning Department's report, which took the form of an illustrated brochure entitled "Development Plan for the Central Area of Chicago," was unveiled at a large and well-publicized meeting in the Mayor's office.

The Central Area Plan rejected the Fort Dearbon concept of

the civic center and by so doing dealt the Project a blow from which opponents said it probably could not recover. The Plan did call for residential development of the Fort Dearborn tract; and this had been part of the original proposal. The Sponsors could — and did — insist that the Project was feasible without the civic center. But this, the opponents said, was merely face-saving on their part. The Project, they thought, was crippled because without a civic center, insurance companies and other big investors would not invest. To be sure, syndicates planned to build one or two apartment hotels. But this was far from the acres of high-rise apartments originally envisioned.

The Sponsors, however, were satisfied that their time and effort had not been wasted. Even if the Project were never built (they did not concede that building it was out of the question), it had been worthwhile because of two developments that had grown out of it. One of these was the Central Area Committee. The other was the City Planning Department's Central Area Plan. Since these by-products were of such importance in their eyes, it is appropriate to trace their history a very short way further.

Holman Pettibone and the Central Area Committee denied that they had a part in preparing the Plan. The newspapers gave the credit to Mayor Daley and the Planning Department. The general view was that the Mayor, having grown tired of the bickering between business groups, had instructed Bach and Downs to package several proposals as a single Plan. It was certainly true that many of the decisions included in the Plan had been made long before. For example, the Plan put the Exhibition Hall at 23rd Street and showed the south Loop railroad terminals consolidated and the land they vacated redeveloped; these decisions had already been made before Bach and Downs went to work. It had been obvious for some time that the Mayor did not want to build a civic center on the north bank of the river.

However, there were reasons to believe that Pettibone had fashioned some compromises among major Loop interests and that those had been included in the Plan. It was even probable that without these compromises the Plan would not have appeared. It seemed likely that these compromises of Pettibone's had been communicated to the planning technicians and that the technicians had included them in the Plan as if they were their own.

The Mayor could not very well launch a plan of his own without taking into account the views of Pettibone and the other businessmen. The Fort Dearborn experience had shown him, if he needed to be shown, that unless the big Loop interests agreed among themselves, no' private investment would be forthcoming and there would be opposition to any public action that might be proposed. The only way to bring a "Daley Plan" to fruition was to incorporate in it the compromises that would bring agreement among the private interests.

Pettibone was probably the only man with enough time, interest, and prestige to secure the agreement that was needed. Daley himself would not go to the businessmen to negotiate an agreement among them: that was not his way. Bach, the head of the Planning Department, did not have prestige enough to go in the Mayor's place, and even Downs, who was much respected by the businessmen, probably did not have weight enough to bring some of the disagreeing interests (for example, Field's department store and the south Loop realtors) together.

Moreover, Pettibone was almost the only leader whose business interest coincided with the idea of a general plan. Each of the Loop interests wanted something for its own particular part of the Loop. Of the prestigious central area leaders, only Pettibone did not care *precisely* where improvements went. His firm, the Chicago Title and Trust Company, would make money wherever there was rebuilding. He was also chairman of the Central Area Committee, and in the long run his success in that capacity would be judged by what was done for the Loop as a whole and not for some section of it. The important thing from his standpoint was to stop the argument and get construction underway.

It is impossible to describe the precise part played by each of the principal architects of the Plan — Bach and Downs, Pettibone, and the Mayor. It is known, however, that a Fort Dearborn Sponsor proposed dividing the public buildings between the Project and the Loop and that Bach was attracted to this idea. In the end, however, no public buildings went to the Project. This, some said, was because the south Loop interests, who contributed heavily to the Central Area Committee, brought pressure to bear upon Pettibone.

The Mayor, it was said, participated actively in the planning. Once or twice he went to see a model of the central area that had been built with detachable parts, so that he could move key buildings around into alternative locations. The model was not the work of the City Planning Department but of the Central Area Committee, and it was kept not in the City Hall but in a private office Pettibone had rented for the purpose.

That Pettibone denied playing an important part in the making of the Plan was not surprising. He knew that the Mayor, who after all was under the necessity of going before the voters every four years, wanted credit for it. He knew also that some people would say that city plans ought to be made by official planners and not by interested businessmen. In fact, his strategy had all been publicly acknowledged in advance: the Central Area Committee, the *Tribune* had said the year before, would unveil its ideas "perhaps under the auspices of public officials"; it was "willing to let the credit go elsewhere if it can promote the sound growth of Chicago."

As it turned out, the Plan — or, as it perhaps should be called, the List and Prediction (for, as has been said, it was partly a listing of decisions that had long since been arrived at and partly a prediction of the outcomes expected in various controversies then underway — miscarried in one particular within a few weeks of its presentation. The General Services Administration announced early in 1959 that it would acquire a site for a federal building about half a block east of the existing courthouse on the south side of the Loop. This was a site that no one had recommended. The Plan, looking ahead for twenty-two years and seeking to deconcentrate the area somewhat, had called for an open plaza and a new federal building in the block that was then occupied by the old federal building. The decisions of the General Services Administration allowed for no plaza and they increased concentration with a structure of about twenty-two stories. Downs, asked on a television program if the Plan had not miscarried in its first application, acknowledged that it had. The federal government, he said, was a law unto itself.

Although Chicago interests had been in frequent communication with Senator Dirksen and others (an important businessman was said to have called a friend in the White House to demand that the General Services Administration be "straightened out"), the federal decision seems to have resulted not from any exercise of influence but from a regional administrator's judgment of what was best for the federal agencies. The amount of money available to General Services Administration for land purchases in Chicago was too small to permit putting federal buildings in two places, as the Plan proposed. Furthermore, the interference with federal business that might be occasioned by tearing down the old federal building before a new one was ready for use was too important to permit re-building on the present site. These were elements of the situation which, however they might be evaluated by the city and its planners, were decisive for the federal government and *its* planners.

Whether all major business interests would be able to agree upon on the Central Area Plan, or upon any plan at all, remained to be seen. Early in 1959, one of the Central Area Committee's members, Newton Farr, acting for the Greater North Michigan Avenue Association, presented to the Mayor and the public a "General Development Plan for the Near Northside of Chicago." This challenged the Central Area Plan on the very issue which had begun the whole affair. The Association disagreed with all of those who had so far played principal parts in the Fort Dearborn struggle — with the Sponsors, the south Loop interests, the Central Area Committee, and the official planners — by asserting that the Fort Dearborn area should be developed not for residential, but for commercial use. If it could be taken seriously, this proposal was the beginning of a new round.

6

The Chicago Campus

For several years there had been agitation to establish a branch of the University of Illinois in Chicago. The main campus was at Urbana-Champaign, in the central part of the state, 130 miles south of Chicago. It had been placed there, in 1868, on the assumption that its students (there were fifty of them then) would come mainly from nearby farms and villages to study agriculture and the mechanic arts. When the veterans flooded in at the end of the Second World War, however, the University was offering 3,000 courses, and half of its 25,000 students came from Chicago and other parts of Cook County. In 1946 it established a temporary branch at Navy Pier, a decommissioned naval training center on Lake Michigan about half a mile from Chicago's central business district, which was attended by 3,800 students. The Navy Pier branch would have to be temporary (the University had only a three-year lease), and its facilities were so limited that only the first two years of the four-year curriculum could be offered. Before very long, students and faculty began a lively campaign to persuade the state legislature to make the branch permanent and to give it a four-year curriculum and a suitable campus.

It was an uphill fight. The private colleges and universities in and around Chicago were, to say the least, cool to the idea. Actually, an expanded curriculum at a University of Illinois branch would not have seriously hurt most of them. (Northwestern University and the University of Chicago were in a different price class and took relatively few of their students from Chicago anyway. DePaul and Loyola, the Catholic colleges, were somewhat more vulnerable. Roosevelt College, the only one which depended entirely upon commuters, was most vulnerable, but it was also of little consequence politically.) Nevertheless, for a time they opposed the establishment of any permanent branch of the University of Illinois in Chicago, and they finally agreed to it only on condition that it give a two-year, not a four-year, course.

The most powerful opponent of the branch, however, was the University of Illinois itself. The administrators at Urbana-Champaign believed that the parent campus would always be the principal one and that, unless the resources for expansion were virtually unlimited, the best thing would be to maintain Urbana-Champaign at a high level rather than divide the resources in such a way that neither campus would be first-rate. As it looked to some Chicago eyes, however, Urbana-Champaign was simply selfish, jealous, and fearful that it would eventually be overpowered by competition from the branch. The dean of the Navy Pier branch, Charles C. Caveny, an ardent advocate of a permanent, four-year branch, found himself a minority of one at meetings of the University administration. "From top to bottom," he told an interviewer, "the administrators at Urbana-Champaign were afraid they would become a whistle-stop. I was poison ivy."

Some alumni, having perhaps a sentimental attachment to the campus they had known, were opposed to a "skyscraper" campus in downtown Chicago. A few leading spirits among them were very much against anything that might give the University the reputation of being a "poor boy's college" or, above all, a "Negro's college." A city campus, they may have thought, would be too near the Black Belt.

Merchants and other business interests in Urbana and Champaign were also much opposed to a Chicago branch. They had long benefited from the University's presence and its constant expansion, and they were in the habit of using their influence to further its development: for many years they had blocked construction of dormitories in Urbana-Champaign (renting rooms was profitable), they had delayed organization of a co-operative bookstore and of co-operative restaurants (selling books and meals was also profitable), and they had been instrumental, some said, in getting the University to raise its fees $20 a semester in order to build facilities, including a $7,500,000 basketball arena, for high school basketball tournaments and other events that attracted business to Urbana-Champaign.

A four-year branch in Chicago, some people thought, would pose a fundamental threat to Urbana-Champaign. The Chicago metropolitan area was growing fast, and a recent reapportionment had given it control of the House of Representatives. The metropolitan area representatives would probably not be solid in their support of the Chicago branch, but, even so, Urbana-Champaign would have to compete with Chicago for appropriations. And if Chicago joined forces with Southern Illinois University, at Carbondale, which had its own small but dependable bloc of votes in the General Assembly, Urbana-Champaign might find itself third in line when the appropriations were handed out. Some prophets gleefully said that eventually the Chicago branch would have a better football team than the old alma mater. This, they playfully affected to believe, was what worried Urbana-Champaign most.

Against this view, it could be argued that the Board of Trustees of the University, not the legislature, would allocate funds between the campuses and that, consequently, there was no danger of competition. It was true that the legislature had always accepted the recommendations of the trustees. There was, however, no way of knowing that it would always do so in the future. And, of course, a split along Chicago-downstate lines might appear within the Board of Trustees itself. The board consisted of nine persons elected on the major party tickets, and two who were ex officio. Its members were unsalaried, but the position offered good opportunities for public service and for self-advertisement, and there were always prominent people who wanted it. Nominations were made in the party conventions rather than in primaries, and the parties almost always accepted the recommendations of the Alumni Association. As a rule the Republicans controlled the board, as they did the rest of the state government, but there was always the possibility (realized in 1958) that the Democrats would win a majority. If that happened, Chicago might have a good deal to say in the affairs of the University.

In 1948 the University prepared an "inventory of needs" which totaled $100 million without providing anything for Chicago. In 1953, however, there was a change in the University's administration. An interim president, Lloyd Morey, who had been on the staff of the University for forty years, most recently as comptroller, made energetic efforts to get something built in Chicago. His successor, David Dodds Henry, who became permanent president in 1955, although believing that the Urbana-Champaign's essential needs should be met first, favored expansion at both Urbana-Champaign and Chicago. The 1960 potential enrollment would be 38,000, he estimated soon after taking office; students should be allowed to go to whichever campus they preferred, and it was likely that 23,000 would want to go to Urbana-Champaign and 15,000 to Chicago.

By 1955 the administrators at Urbana-Champaign seemed to have become reconciled to the inevitability of a four-year Chicago branch. The proponents of the branch, however, felt that the University's intentions could not be trusted. Public promises did not necessarily mean that action was seriously intended. On the contrary (the proponents thought), the University was likely to postpone the evil day as long as possible. "The development of opinion in Urbana-Champaign," Dean Caveny told an interviewer in 1958, "has been from apathy to resentment to acceptance. But they still don't put me on the budget committee although I am the senior academic officer of the Chicago campus."

The University, together with the allied local interests of Champaign and Urbana, was a powerful force in the legislature. Three of the most powerful legislators came from its district. These — all Republicans — were: Senator Everett R. Peters, chairman of the Illinois Budgetary Commission and chairman of the Senate Committee on Committees; Representative Ora D. Dillavou, chairman of the House Appropriations Committee and, therefore, a member of the Budgetary Commission; and Representative Charles W. Clabaugh, chairman of the Illinois School Problems Commission. All three depended in some ways upon the University and were often its spokesmen. But the University was also dependent upon them. Senator Peters, the most powerful of the three, was said to regard President Henry as a "carpetbagger." "Who the hell is he to tell me how to run the University," he once said to a fellow senator. His remark may have been made in a moment of pique and perhaps should not be taken seriously. One close and reliable observer, at any rate, was of the opinion that Peters generally accepted the policy line of the University. There was no doubt, however, that he could exercise a great deal of influence upon the administration of the University if he chose to do so.

Although it depended greatly upon these three, the University was not unmindful of the other legislators. It gave each of them four season passes to football games, and every two years it wined and dined them lavishly on a two-day "tour" of the University in May, the season when important bills were coming out of the committees. According to a Chicago legislator, the University used these occasions to extol its Urbana-Champaign campus and to lobby against the proposed Chicago branch — "brainwashing," this ingrate called his entertainment. Under the title of Assistant to the President, the University kept a lobbyist whom Peters amiably called his "errand boy."

Despite all the opposition, the proposal for a permanent campus and a four-year curriculum gained ground. This was largely due to the efforts of a few Chicago legislators who worked hard to get it accepted by the others. One of these was Representative Paul J. Randolph, in whose district Navy Pier was located. Very few of Randolph's constituents cared one way or another about the branch campus. His interest in the issue, one who knew him well surmised, could be explained by the fact that the Chicago *Tribune* warmly favored a Chicago branch. Randolph, it was said, was generally very responsive to the wishes of the *Tribune*.

At any rate, Randolph had, in 1949, introduced a bill requiring construction of a permanent campus in Chicago. When it came up for passage, Governor Adlai Stevenson called him in and told him that he would be obliged to veto the bill unless it were amended by the addition of the words "as soon as feasible." With this change, it passed with only two contrary votes in the House and with none in the Senate. In 1953, Randolph tried again. He introduced a resolution to establish a legislative commission to study the need for a permanent branch. In 1955, the commission reported: a permanent branch should be established at once. Randolph then introduced a bill to appropriate $4 million to get it under way. His bill was beaten because Cook County Democrats, acting on orders from above, failed to vote for it. The private colleges in Chicago, insiders said, had beaten the bill.

Randolph's efforts were somewhat handicapped because the University had not selected a site for the proposed campus. Why make an appropriation, some legislators asked, before the University was ready to spend the money? The next move was up to the University. If it wanted to go ahead without delay, it would have to find a site before the legislature met again.

From a formal standpoint at least, the site would be chosen by the Board of Trustees. Of the elected members, one was a big businessman, one a wealthy Chicago lawyer, one a Chicago milk company executive, two were downstate lawyers, one was a Peoria insurance agent, one was a well-to-do Chicago housewife, and one was a farmer's wife. The board worked harmoniously and without factionalism. Its decisions were always unanimous.

The most influential member of the board, and the chairman of the site selection committee, was the big businessman. This was Wayne A. Johnston, president of the Illinois Central Railroad, a blustering, assertive man whose word carried much weight with the other trustees partly, perhaps, because of his manner but partly also because of his experience in the management of large affairs. The Illinois Central line passed through Champaign on its way between Chicago and New Orleans (it was an Illinois Central agent, in fact, who had fixed the location of the campus in the first place), and the railroad profited from the traffic the University created. At first, Johnston had opposed the establishment of a four-year campus in Chicago. He was, a former trustee who knew him well told an interviewer, incapable of seeing merit in anything that might adversely affect his railroad. (Once, when the Illinois football team was to play in the Rose Bowl, he insisted that it go there by Illinois Central, although doing so meant a tiresome detour via New Orleans.) Johnston, many thought, would be unwilling to lose the fares of the thousands of students and visitors who had to travel between Chicago and Urbana-Champaign. Difficult as it may have been for him, he had, however, come to believe that a four-year branch should be built in Chicago. Even so, he was not an easy man for the proponents to deal with. He was single-minded, stubborn, and autocratic. "There is only one monarch left — the railroad president," a University official remarked to an interviewer early in 1958. "Johnston's resigned now to the idea that there is need of a Chicago campus, but he thinks the Board of Trustees should do as it damn pleases."

The second most influential member of the board was probably Cushman Bissell, the wealthy Chicago lawyer. He was also a member of the site selection committee.

The other member of the site selection committee was the Chicago housewife, Mrs. Frances B. Watkins. Being a woman and having no special knowledge of business matters, particular weight was not attached to her views. Unlike most of the other trustees, she was a Democrat.

Bissell and Mrs. Watkins were Catholics. They might, therefore, be expected to take a sympathetic view of the problems of De Paul and Loyola, the Catholic colleges that would have to compete with a Chicago branch of the University.

Although not technically a member of the site selection committee, the chairman of the board, Park Livingston, played a part in its deliberations. He was the vice-president of a Chicago milk distributing company and was serving his ninth one-year term as chairman of the board. A resident of a western suburb of Chicago, he had always enjoyed politics. In college he had been president of his senior class; afterward, he had been state director of the Young Republicans of Illinois and an unsuccessful candidate for the Republican nomination for governor and then for United States senator. Those who knew him said that being a trustee was a step on the political ladder for him.

Although the selection of a site, like all important matters, would be discussed at length by the full board, it was likely that the board would accept any recommendation made by the site selection committee and Livingston.

Such a recommendation, however, would have to take into account the views of President Henry. This was so because the

President was liked and respected by the board members and because they felt that he was in a better position than they to decide what was good for the University. There was, however, an additional reason why his influence was great. A few years earlier the University had been rocked to its foundations by a struggle between Livingston and a former president which had ended in the president's resignation. It had taken two years to find a suitable replacement, and in this time the University's prestige had been at a low ebb. If Henry, the new president, were also to leave after a row with the trustees, the loss of standing to the University might be irreparable. He, therefore, had the upper hand in dealing with the trustees; if his wishes were disregarded he might leave, and he was, for all practical purposes, irreplaceable.

When he came on the scene in 1955, President Henry found that some beginnings had been made toward the selection of a site. The interim president, Morey, had appointed a faculty-administration Committee on Future Development to advise him — and, through him, the trustees — with regard to the proposed Chicago branch. The Committee soon recommended establishing a four-year campus and suggested five possible sites. Its preferred site was adjacent to the West Side Medical Center, a vast development which included the Cook County Hospital, the University of Illinois Medical School, and in which Dr. Karl A. Meyer played a prominent part. Meyer, a former president of the University's Board of Trustees, had gone to some trouble to persuade the Committee to recommend this site. From his standpoint, there were great advantages in having the University adjacent to the Medical Center: for one thing, it would be a barrier against the surrounding slum.

Another possibility suggested by the Committee was Thatcher Woods, one of the many public forest preserves in the western suburbs. Announcement that Thatcher Woods was under consideration brought an immediate protest from the superintendent of the County Forest Preserve District. Thatcher Woods, this official told the press, would not be available under any circumstances: it was one of the most beautiful of the preserves; besides, it was the policy of the district, and indeed its legal obligation, to retain all lands in its possession.

A little later, the Committee was reorganized and Dean Caveny made its chairman. The reorganized Committee decided on a new and more thorough survey of site possibilities. For this it recommended, and the President and Board of Trustees approved, employment of a firm of consultants, the Real Estate Research Corporation. One of the biggest and best known firms of its kind in the United States, the Real Estate Research Corporation was run by James C. Downs, an economic analyst and businessman whose technical and public relations skills were much admired and whose judgment was much respected by the Chicago business community and by Mayor Daley. Downs was one of the University's most prominent alumni.

Downs had little to do personally with the site selection process. One of his employees, John Ducey, a former director of planning for the Chicago Housing Authority, did most of the work. Ducey met frequently with the Committee to discuss its requirements and to formulate a long list of criteria that would have to be taken into account in the selection of a site. Five of the criteria were "minima": a site which did not meet all of these would be rejected out of hand. The others were of "general desirability": sites which met the minima would then be rated on the basis of these other criteria.

The minima had to do with availability, size, and accessibility. At least half of a site would have to be "buildable" by July, 1959. A site would have to be large enough for efficient operation — 140 acres was the lower limit — and there would have to be the possibility of expansion later if necessary. A site would have to be within ten miles of the estimated future student potential in Cook and DuPage counties. More precisely, it would have to be accessible by public transportation from the homes of at least 50 per cent of the student potential, with a maximum fare of fifty cents for a one-way trip.

This last criterion — accessibility — in effect excluded both the northern and the southern sides of the city from consideration. Neither Northwestern nor the University of Chicago would have to be provoked by the prospect of a too-near neighbor. Had they seen fit to do so, the planners could have framed this criterion so as to exclude the western suburbs as well: to do this it would only have been necessary to require that two-thirds of the student body be no more than three-quarters of an hour away by public transportation.

From a political standpoint, it was probably good strategy to exclude the northern and southern sides of the city and to include the western suburbs, but political judgments did not enter into the criteria. The Real Estate Research Corporation viewed the problem as a purely technical one. "We had no initial bias," Downs told an interviewer afterward. "We didn't know anything about the University, which I think was the ideal situation. The only attitude we had was that convenience is a major factor in American life." In location studies for shopping centers, banks, and other businesses, the Corporation had often used attitude surveys and various statistical indices of convenience. The problem in locating a campus was essentially the same as that in locating a shopping center, the only difference being that the "customer" was a student. The student's convenience was to be the determining factor. As Downs explained:

Convenience means a lot of things. It means cost out of pocket, or cost in time, anxiety or transportation. It means physical fatigue. The cost of driving three blocks downtown is greater than the cost of driving three blocks in the country. All costs are constantly being appraised by people who are doing something: your wife will estimate the cost of a shopping sortie in relation to the rewards. If she is going after a dress the rewards will be greater and she will expend more. And if she is going after hose she will not expend as much.

For the students, the cost is the same every day. For them there are two cost elements — money and time.

Given any area — the city of Chicago, Greater Chicago, or Illinois — it was possible, Downs believed, for his organization to find by purely technical means the precise location at which convenience (the ratio of rewards to costs) would be maximized. This, in Downs' terminology, was the "idealized" location. There might be a political reason against using the idealized location after it was found, but that was another matter and one entirely beyond his concern as a technician. But even if there was a strong likelihood that the idealized location could not be used, there was, Downs believed, much justification for finding it anyway, for without it one could not estimate the value of what was being sacrificed to political considerations. As he told an interviewer:

If we wanted to locate a bank, we'd establish an idealized location. If we couldn't locate it there, *we'd know it*. Now you may not be able to locate the University at the best site but you ought to know where it should be so that you can estimate the costs.

I think that is the reason the University engaged us. They wanted an idealized site.

As I look at it, the ultimate decision is a political decision. This decision will in practical essence be arrived at by the Mayor and Governor. I think the study is valuable to them. That's the reason I don't say, "Why do you bother to hire us?" When the Mayor and Governor sit down to resolve the question the study will be just as valuable to them as a study for a bank is to the bankers.

The process by which the planners established the technical criteria for an "idealized" location of the University campus was essentially as follows: They plotted on a map the residences of all Navy Pier students and of all Chicago-area undergraduates at Urbana-Champaign. It appeared from the map that most of those who lived less than 55 minutes away from Navy Pier went there, whereas most of those who lived more than 65 minutes from Navy Pier went to Urbana-Champaign. Sixty minutes, therefore, seemed to be a reasonable and workable standard. About 25 per cent of the Navy Pier students drove cars to school. In the normal course of events this proportion would probably increase to 40 per cent by 1970. Students with cars could travel greater distances in 60 minutes than students who used public transportation. Adding the number who would have cars to the number who would be willing to spend abnormal amounts of time in travel, the planners concluded that a campus would serve its purpose satisfactorily even if only half of the potential student body could reach it in less than an hour by public transportation.

When the criteria had been established to everyone's satisfaction, the Real Estate Research Corporation was asked to recommend the site which met them best. After an examination of fifty possibilities, the planners concluded that the best was an artificial island to be built in Lake Michigan opposite the central business district. It would be expensive to build ($3.25 a foot), and it might not be completed before the deadline. However, it had an advantage which Ducey (whose background, incidentally, was in real estate, not architecture or city planning) seemed to find decisive: it would provide the greatest "dramatic potentiality." Indeed, a campus there, his report said, "could very easily become the most famous in the nation."

When Downs, the chairman of the board of Real Estate Research, learned that his staff recommended the island site, he was skeptical. Before there could be any construction in the Lake, it would be necessary, he pointed out, to get permission from the Army Corps of Engineers; this would not be easy and might be impossible. Moreover, the Lake Front was sacred by tradition. Any proposal to build anything there was sure to provoke controversy. The staff, however, insisted that the island would make the best site for the University and that it was feasible. Downs, although still doubtful, decided not to overrule the staff.

That the branch campus might become the most famous in the nation — or even in the state of Illinois — was exactly what would arouse the fiercest opposition in Urbana-Champaign. When the Board of Trustees met to consider the site recommendation, some of its downstate members were critical. The island would cost about $20 million. Surely, some of them said, it should be possible to find a site for much less than that. ("That is $20 million less for us," the Urbana-Champaign people were saying to each other, according to one of the proponents of the Chicago branch.) At the initiative of the trustees, the Real Estate Research Corporation was asked to suggest three or four alternative possibilities.

According to his later recollection, Dean Caveny suggested to Ducey that he take a look at Miller Meadows, a county forest preserve in a western suburb. Ducey could not remember any such suggestion from the Dean. Miller Meadows, he thought, came to his attention in the course of a systematic survey of all site possibilities within the area indicated by the criteria. It would not have been necessary to call it to his attention, he said; he would have considered it as a matter of routine.

In any case, when the Real Estate Research Corporation made its alternative recommendations, Miller Meadows was at the top of the list. The great advantages of the site, the new report said, were two. It lay in the path of the future growth of metropolitan population, and it was relatively cheap — 29 cents a foot, or $3 million dollars. It was reasonably accessible (55.4 per cent of the student potential were within one hour's travel by public transportation), although not as accessible as certain central city sites. The Cook County Forest Preserve District had rented part of it to local farmers in order to prepare the land for eventual development for recreation. Another part was occupied by the District's central garage, shops, and warehouses; these facilities, the District said, could not be moved and would have to be replaced. According to the District, the area had unique value because of its great spaciousness and its accessibility to the west side of Chicago and to the most populous suburbs. For these reasons, the District considered it irreplaceable.

Miller Meadows had one defect which, if the minimal criteria were rigidly applied, might have excluded it from consideration altogether: it was not easily available and it might not be available at all. "The Forest Preserve District," the Real Estate Research Corporation said in its report, "has been historically hostile to such requests. The fact that its attitude has not changed is evident from the District's refusal to furnish us even with factual information relative to sites analyzed in this study." Open opposition from the District, the report said, must be anticipated and counted as a disadvantage of the site.

In order for the site to be considered at least 50 per cent "buildable" by July, 1959, it had to be assumed that the University would be extraordinarily successful in influencing the District or that it could readily persuade the General Assembly to let it take the land in condemnation proceedings. Neither assumption was very plausible.

Organized in 1915, the District was one of the accomplishments of the "city beautiful" movement in which Daniel Burnham and others were pioneers. Early in the century, prominent bankers, merchants, and professional people — most of them ardent conservationists who took walks in the woods on Saturdays — persuaded the politicians to put twenty thousand acres on the western edge of the city into preserves which would be kept in their natural state. The Commercial Club's famous Plan of Chicago anticipated the eventual sale of tracts, here and there, to rich men whose estates, protected by the remaining preserves from encroachments, would form an elegant and aristocratic greenbelt around the city.

After the District was organized, the civic leaders turned their attention to other things. Soon a strong smell of corruption arose. Politicians and their friends were buying up land for resale to the District. Organizations with political pull — American Legion posts, Polish-American clubs, volunteer firemen — were demanding and getting special privileges in the use of the land. When the *Tribune* threatened an exposé, Anton Cermak, the Democratic boss, promised to give control of the District to the civic leaders themselves.

Under a plan of reorganization adopted in 1926, an Advisory Committee of nine prominent citizens was created. It had no legal powers, but Cermak agreed that it was to recommend policies and plans for land acquisition and management. From a formal standpoint, control of the District remained in the hands of a Board of Forest Preserve Commissioners. These were to be the elected commissioners of Cook County wearing, so to speak, other hats. Having a set of politicians act at one moment as Commisioners of Cook County and at the next as Commissioners of a legally separate Forest Preserve District might seem like a needless complication to some, but Cermak and the civic leaders agreed that it would be well to keep the affairs of the District, which were to be under the watchful eyes of the civic leaders, separate from the affairs of the County, which were to be left with the politicians.

The arrangement worked well. On the nomination of the Advisory Committee, the commissioners employed Charles G. Sauers, a professional park administrator, as general superintendent of the District. In 1957 Sauers had been on the job twenty-eight years, and the District comprised 44,000 acres. In all those years the commissioners never once overruled the Advisory Committee, and, of scores of attempts to take land from the District, the committee had successfully resisted all but two. In these cases it did not oppose the taking of twenty acres by a high school district.

The Advisory Committee had its way because it was useful to

the politicians and because it consisted of powerful and determined men. In 1957 the chairman was Edward Eagle Brown, a benign but stubborn old gentleman who was chairman of the board of the First National Bank of Chicago. Others on the committee were prominent businessmen (including Chester R. Davis, senior vice-president of the Chicago Title and Trust Company, and Gilbert H. Scribner, Jr., the realtor who was president of the Civic Federation) and conservationists. In theory, the Advisory Committee was chosen by the commissioners. In practice, it was self-selected, for the commissioners never failed to take its advice.

Brown, the chairman of the Advisory Committee, was kept advised by Sauers, the professional manager, and nothing of importance was done without his knowledge and consent. About four times a year, the full Committee met for lunch at the Midday Club in Chicago to pass on plans for land acquisition and to consider other policy matters. Between meetings, the Committee's affairs were managed by its chairman and those he chose to consult.

Brown and Sauers managed the District in a pre-emptory, perhaps sometimes even a waspish, manner. They had no patience with special pleaders. As one of their published reports said: "All employees are thoroughly inoculated with policy standards. Any suggested change or deviation is carefully analyzed. That which is deemed inimical to public interest is resisted with firmness and resolution."

In 1957 the president of the elected board of commissioners was Daniel Ryan. The relationship between him and Brown was symbiotic. Since the District was fated not to be a source of political patronage or "gravy," Ryan, like Cermak before him, was happy to let the civic leaders run it and to take responsibility for it. "The politicians welcome us as a help to relieve pressure," Brown once told an interviewer. "The Advisory Committee is of such stature that no one can attack it. It does what it wants. That way the heat is taken off the politicians." But if Brown and the civic leaders were useful to Ryan, he was indispensable to them, for he and he alone could get money from the taxpayers and authority from the legislature.

The banker-civic leader, the politician, and the professional administrator, having worked together intimately and successfully for many years, understood each other well enough so that they acted as one. Ryan, Sauers thought, had a deep and sincere attachment to the forest preserves (one preserve was named for his father, an immigrant who became president of the County Board) and could be depended upon to fight for them, come what might. Whether he felt such an attachment or not, Ryan had good reason to rely upon the advice of Brown and Sauers and to give them strong backing. Doing so would mean trouble-free tenure for him. Not doing so would mean a hornet's nest of protest, some loss of confidence in him by good government-minded voters, and perhaps, eventually, embarrassment.

Johnston, the railroad president who headed the trustee's site selection committee, was oblivious to the Real Estate Research Corporation's warning that Miller Meadows would be hard to get. (He later insisted to an interviewer that no such warning had ever been given, but he added that he would have ignored it if it had.) He was used to getting what was hard to get. "Johnston thinks that if you know the right fellow and swing the right club, that's it," one who worked with him in the site selection matter said afterward.

In this case "the right fellow" was Ryan, the president of the County Forest Preserve Board. Ryan blandly assured Johnston that he had no objection to selling Miller Meadows to the University — provided that the Advisory Committee agreed. Johnston then talked to Brown, the Advisory Committee chairman, and got a flat and unqualified "no." But Johnston did not take that for an answer. "You old ———," he told Brown good-humoredly, "you're on the wrong side of the fence."

Livingston, the president of the Board of Trustees, then tried his hand with Brown. Brown's bank, the First National, was one of the main depositories of the University, and one of its officers was the University treasurer. This was the kind of a connection which might be expected to produce co-operation. But Brown was quite indifferent to the University's business claims upon him.

Johnston supposed that it was only Brown's stubbornness that stood in the University's way. However, Chester R. Davis, who was both a former trustee and a member of the Advisory Committee, assured Johnston that this was not the case. The Advisory Committee was unanimous, Davis told him, and if Ryan overruled it, all of the committee members would resign in protest.

Despite these warnings, the trustees, the president, and the faculty-administration Committee on Future Development unanimously agreed to try for Miller Meadows. In May, 1955, the University took the press on a tour of Miller Meadows and announced that this was the site it favored. The Advisory Committee at once made a formal recommendation against the University's request, and this recommendation was unanimously accepted by Ryan and the other commissioners of the Forest Preserve District.

It was Sauers, the administrator of the District, who wrote and signed the letter setting forth the grounds for its refusal. However, he consulted Brown about the line to be taken and even about the details of wording.

Sauers and Brown ignored the fact that the University was offering to pay the District the market value of the land and so, in effect, to replace Miller Meadows with another equally valuable tract. They took the position that the University's was just one more in a long series of attempts to encroach upon public resources. That the University's purpose was also a public one and that it was at least as important as conservation and recreation made no difference. Any attempt to take "the people's land" was "morally reprehensible," especially an attempt by another public agency.

Sauers wrote: "The proposal to seize Miller Meadows area for the University of Illinois is opportunistic and an easy out at the expense of all Cook County people. If a Chicago Branch is needed, also there is needed on the part of the University the courage and principle to achieve the purpose without resort to destruction of existing and hard won values."

Yielding to the request, Sauers went on to say, would establish a precedent which would endanger all forest preserve holdings. (This was not quite true; a precedent already existed in the few acres which a high school district had been allowed to take.) It would cost the District $1,500,000 to provide warehouses and machinery sheds to replace those at Miller Meadows. And, in any case, Miller Meadows was irreplaceable because of its strategic location and great size. "There is not the ethical right to take this area, that through hundreds of years will be needed and enjoyed by our country-starved people. The purpose of the proponents for conversion is one of opportunism — in hope of securing a site cheaply and easily at the expense of the foresightedness and courage of the Forest Preserve District and at the sacrifice of accessibility, so important to a Chicago campus."

In private, Sauers conceded that Miller Meadows would make a very good site for the University. But that, he added, was beside the point. "We're very conservative here. It's not our business to give land to the University. It would be just like selling our land for gas stations. There isn't an inch of land we hold that isn't valuable for public purposes. Even if nobody ever sets foot on the land, we must still hold it."

Sauers and Brown expected the trustees to take their case to the legislature. Accordingly, Sauers wrote to all of the Cook County legislative leaders, warning them to be on guard against a surprise attempt to amend a routine bill so as to give Miller Meadows to the University.

No such attempt was made, however. Johnston and Livingston did not even discuss their plans with Representative Randolph, who had done so much to promote a Chicago branch, or, apparently, with any of the other legislators who were interested in the matter. Without the help of Randolph and the other sponsors of the branch campus, there was not the slightest possibility that the legislature would take Miller Meadows from the District and give it to the University or, indeed, that any provision at all would be made for a Chicago campus.

The trustees' failure to press the matter in the legislature was particularly surprising because the Forest Preserve District happened at that time to be asking the legislature to authorize it to enlarge its holdings. That the District wanted something from the legislature gave the trustees a strategic advantage: they could have the University's friends in the legislature hold up the District's bill until the District came to terms with Johnston and Livingston. The trustees failed to take advantage of their opportunity, however, and the session ended with Miller Meadows never having been discussed.

After the legislative session, the trustees reiterated their desire for Miller Meadows, and Sauers and Brown, speaking sometimes through Ryan, reiterated their opposition. Finally, the secretary of the trustees wrote Brown, asking for a joint meeting of the trustees and the Advisory Committee members. Brown flatly refused. The trustees renewed their request. They were disappointed, their secretary wrote, that representatives of one public body should refuse to meet with those of another. Brown had the secretary of the Advisory Committee write an indignant refusal. "We question the propriety and ethics of the proposal . . .," the letter said.

When the legislature met again, in the winter of 1957, it was plain that if the University was to get Miller Meadows, it would have to be by action of the legislature. Randolph and other legislators who had been trying for years to get a branch campus established expected that the trustees would come to them early in the session for advice and assistance. The trustees had asked the Budgetary Commission for $3 million to start the Chicago branch, but the Governor, acting on the advice of the Commission chairman, Senator Peters (whose district, it will be remembered, included Urbana-Champaign), reduced the amount to $1 million on the grounds that the trustees, not having fixed upon a site, were unready to spend more. Randolph intended to introduce a bill to appropriate $4 million. When he did not hear from the trustees, he took the initiative by telephoning Livingston to tell him what he planned to do. Livingston asked him to hold off for a week and said he would call him back then. However, he did not call back. Randolph called Livingston twice and left his number, but Livingston did not return the call.

At the end of March, Randolph introduced a bill to appropriate $4 million for a permanent, centrally located campus "in the city of Chicago." The bill had 93 sponsors — 4 more than the number of votes needed to pass it in the House. Robert E. Cherry, a Democrat, introduced a bill in the Senate which in effect called for quick action somewhere, and another Chicago Democrat, Representative James P. Loukas, introduced a resolution to establish a House committee to consult the trustees and assist them in finding a site. Loukas, who was a newcomer to the legislature, took the advice of old-timers who said that the resolution would have a better chance if he "dealt the Senate in" by making the committee a joint one. He did so, but although his resolution was quickly passed in the House, 95 to 27, it never reached the committee stage in the Senate. Senator Peters, acting, some thought, for the trustees, had it killed.

Randolph, Cherry, and Loukas all preferred downtown Chicago to Miller Meadows as a location for the branch. Their bills were not intended to rule out Miller Meadows or to override the trustees, however. The important thing, in their eyes, was to get the permanent branch established promptly. If action could be had faster by building in the suburbs than by building in Chicago, they were willing, as their subsequent behavior proved, to accept a suburban site.

The trustees, however, seemed to think that the Chicago legislators were their natural enemies. Before the session had advanced very far, the feeling was mutual. The trustees, a Chicago representative told a newspaper reporter, were "arrogant and smug — too powerful."

The trustees had chosen Miller Meadows precisely because it would be hard to get, Randolph and some other Chicago legislators finally concluded. They had chosen it because they were secretly determined to prevent the establishment of any branch at all, or at least to delay it as long as possible, and because they wanted to create a prolonged and finally fruitless controversy as a delaying tactic. Randolph and others publicly charged the trustees with "stalling." A parent-teacher association at Navy Pier passed a resolution accusing them of insincerity and bad faith.

This theory was plausible. It would explain why the trustees had not pressed their advantage in the last legislature and why they did not take Randolph or other leading legislators into their confidence in this one. It would explain, too, their failure to ask for an adequate appropriation and to propose legislation enabling them to take Miller Meadows from the Forest Preserve District.

One could offer various "explanations" of why this or that member of the board wanted to delay — Johnston because he wanted the traffic between Champaign and Chicago for his railroad, Bissell and Mrs. Watkins because they wanted to protect the Catholic colleges from competition, Livingston because he wanted to make political capital downstate while seeming to promote the welfare of the western suburb in which he lived, the downstate trustees because they were jealous of Chicago, and so on. But these explanations were, at best, no more than plausible, and many well-informed people put no stock in them at all. "The trustees and the administration," a former high official of the university commented privately, "have been faced with very great problems in this matter, internally and externally. Whether they faced those as aggressively and courageously as they might have done is of course a matter of opinion. Whether they moved as rapidly as they might may be questioned. But that does not necessarily mean lack of interest or presence of dubious motives."

The "dubious motive" theory derived its plausibility — such plausibility as it had — partly from the difficulty of explaining the trustees' behavior on other grounds. If they were sincere in wanting a site in the western suburbs near Maywood, why had they not chosen a privately owned tract which could be quickly acquired under the power of eminent domain? Very early in the site selection process an alumni committee headed by Chester R. Davis had unofficially recommended such a site, one which, it happened, almost adjoined Miller Meadows. Moreover, the Real Estate Research Corporation had listed as one of several recommended sites the Riverside Golf Course, only two hundred yards from Miller Meadows. The golf course would cost about the same as Miller Meadows, and it was virtually as accessible (50.3 per cent of the potential students would be within an hour's distance of it by public transportation, as against 55.4 per cent for Miller Meadows — an insignificant difference, considering the margin of error in the population projections), but it had the great advantage (an advantage only if the trustees were sincere, of course!) of being readily available.

There were other theories privately offered to explain the trustees' behavior. One was they wanted to locate the branch so that it would not become a Negro or a "poor boys" college.

When an interviewer asked a trustee about this, he replied: "Miller would not bring in Negroes. My dear man, they just don't go to college. There are only a few large Negro colleges. They haven't got the desire, ambition, intelligence, the capacity. Why, look at how few there are out there at your University of Chicago. . . ."

Some suspected that the trustees' real reason for insisting upon a suburban site was to avoid opposition from the private colleges, which (according to this theory) were up in arms against any threat of competition for night-school students. The trouble with this explanation was that the University of Illinois had never offered night classes, and, besides, none of the private colleges or universities regarded that kind of business as anything but a nuisance.

Neither the anti-Negro theory nor the night-school theory explained why the trustees did not take the Riverside golf course when they found that they could not get Miller Meadow without a fight. The golf course would have served either of these purposes just as well as Miller Meadows would.

Another explantion would account for the trustees' insistence upon Miller Meadows. It was an ugly one, and there was nothing to support it, but this did not prevent it from being offered in private. The Illinois Central had a railroad siding at Miller Meadows. Johnston, some said, was insisting upon Miller Meadows to get business for his railroad and to appreciate the value of its land. Even darker possibilities were suggested. "Why don't you check the options that certain trustees hold in the Miller Meadows area?" some Republican representatives asked a Chicago newspaper man. One representative was said to have evidence of something amiss and to have been dissuaded at the last minute from bringing it to the floor of the House. No one who knew how things had sometimes been done in Chicago could rule out these possibilities entirely. Such gossip, however, was always spreading through the corridors, the hotel lobbies, and the bars of Springfield. The legislature produced it as a by-product, as a sawmill produces sawdust, and no one attached much importance to it.

There was an explanation which would fit the known facts better and which was inherently more plausible. This was that the University president, Henry, having had previous experience in the administration of two downtown campuses, Wayne, in Detroit, and New York University, strongly believed that the atmosphere of a big city would not be conducive to the best undergraduate life. Henry, consequently, favored a suburban site, and the trustees backed him because they agreed with him and because they felt that in such a matter he should have a free hand.

This would not explain the University's failure to accept the Riverside Golf Course. But for that, too, a plausible explanation could be offered. Miller Meadows was a more desirable site than Riverside Golf Course because it was larger. That was enough for Johnston, who was a railroad president and used to having his own way. If it was the better site, he wanted it for his University. And he expected to get it, no matter what.

With the full support of Brown and the other members of the Advisory Committee, Sauers, the administrator of the Forest Preserve District, led a lively campaign to arouse public opinion against the University's plan to take Miller Meadows.

Ryan, the president of the Forest Preserve Commissioners, was a powerful first line of defense. The University could not possibly put him under such pressure as to compel him to yield. Nevertheless, it would make it easier for him to resist if he could claim that public opinion favored the Forest Preserve. Sauers and an assistant, Roland Eisenbeis, accordingly went to work to generate expressions of public support that would strengthen Ryan's hand and — if that should prove necessary — his resolution.

There was no danger that the Board of Commissioners would overrule Ryan, but there was danger that the legislature might overrule the Board. This could only happen with the consent of Governor Stratton. Sauers and Eisenbeis therefore bombarded the Governor and key members of the legislature, as well as Ryan himself, with appeals to save Miller Meadows from the University.

Sauers and Eisenbeis made speeches to Rotary clubs, garden clubs, Izaak Walton leagues, YMCA's, Boy and Girl Scouts, and community-improvement associations throughout the suburbs. They sent out mimeographed letters on the official letterhead of the District to conservationists, to the many assocations which held their annual picnics in the preserves, to school teachers, and to many others. They inspired editorials in the Chicago and suburban press; a Chicago *Tribune* editorial writer was particularly close to them, and the *Tribune* carried four editorials in support of the District. When a newspaper said anything favorable to the University's proposal, Sauers and Eisenbeis saw to it that the editor received a volley of protests.

Sauers' letters, the phrasing of which was approved by Brown, went right to the point. A typical one, addressed to "Dear Citizen and Group Member," read:

These recreational lands should remain in the hands of the people. They should not be allowed to be broken up for the benefit of a few at the expense of the public. If this should take place, none of your park systems would be safe from unwarranted grabs. You must protect what is yours.

Will you bring this matter before your organization and consider it in the light of public good? We ask that you formally resolve against the taking of forest preserve lands by the University of Illinois or any other body. We also ask that you advise President Daniel Ryan of the Board of Forest Preserve Commissioners, County Building, Chicago, and Governor William Stratton at the State Capitol in Springfield.

Sauers and Eisenbeis gave special attention to the towns near Miller Meadows. If the people of these places could be convinced that the University would be an undesirable neighbor, the forest preserve would win some powerful allies, for the legislature was not likely to put the campus in the suburbs if the suburban representatives did not want it there. In a letter to the president and trustees of the village of Riverside, Sauers wrote:

For ninety percent of the village residents nothing is to be gained by more congested streets or by increased populations. Inherent in an increase in population are incessant demands to meet the needs for more apartment houses, traffic control, schools and adequate law enforcement. To meet these demands will require each village to assume a larger financial burden and with this will go the loss of those values that make suburban life so pleasant and desirable.

Some village people were fearful that a campus would bring Negroes. Sauers did not allude to this possibility in so many words, but he came very close to it: "Demands for residential facilities for the large corps of service employees necessary to maintain and clean buildings and grounds would be expensive. Then, too, in the future, nearby housing developments might be sought by or for attending students."

In its controversy with the trustees, the District labored under a handicap. Whereas the trustees were fortified with the "impartial" and "expert" report of the Real Estate Research Corporation, the District had nothing of the kind. Without a "purely factual" report of its own, the District's case might seem like special pleading. At this juncture, Charles DeLeuw, of DeLeuw Cather Company, a large firm of management engineers, telephoned Sauers and offered to make a site selection study as a public service at the nominal fee of $1,000. Sauers quickly accepted. The DeLeuw Cather report found, not surprisingly, that a site near the West Side Medical Center was much to be preferred over Miller Meadows. It would be nearer to the potential students and to cultural institutions, would afford greater opportunities for part-time employment for students, and would facilitate urban re-development. "Chlorophyll and running water are important to college students," the Chicago *Tribune* remarked approvingly, "but time, money, educational opportunities, and civic realism are more important."

The District's effort to arouse public opinion seemed to be highly successful. Hundreds of people sent Sauers copies of letters they had written to Ryan, the Governor, and others. "We have them licked," Sauers wrote Ryan in March, 1957. "Hold fast to your present position . . . that you have no alternative except to abide by the recommendation of the Advisory Committee. I fervently hope that you will maintain this stand."

Some forces in the suburbs, however, were mustering in the University's behalf. Louis Nelson, an official of a Maywood bank, got the suburban chambers of commerce to organize in support of the Miller Meadows site. Several high school principals and other public officials spoke out in favor of it. Although certain localities, fearing Negroes, were set against having a campus nearby, it was clear, in the spring of 1957, that most suburban politicians favored one. Sauers and Eisenbeis, although they had done their cause much good, had not succeeded in arousing the suburbs against the University.

In the spring of 1957, the legislature had before it two bills —
Randolph's in the House and Cherry's in the Senate — which
required the trustees to establish a branch campus *in the city of
Chicago.*

Cherry knew that his bill could not be passed without the help
of the suburban senators, and when one of them, Senator Ozinga,
told him that unless it were amended to substitute "Cook County"
for "the city of Chicago" not a single suburbanite would vote for
it, he accepted the change. He was confident that the bill would
be amended in the House; accepting Ozinga's amendment was
merely a maneuver to get it under way.

Senator Peters, the tough and powerful spokesman of the
Urbana-Champaign interests, opposed Cherry's bill. There was,
he said, no need of a four-year branch in the Chicago area. There
were already six colleges and universities there, and not one of
them was operating at capacity. To duplicate in Chicago the
Urbana-Champaign facilities would cost $275 million. Eventually,
there would be need for this expenditure, but at present the
existing two-year branch at Navy Pier should suffice.

Korshak, a Chicago Democrat, took the floor to assure Peters
and other downstaters, half seriously, that a Chicago branch "would
not jeopardize the integrity of the football team at Urbana."

Cherry's bill passed the Senate, 35 to 18.

A few days later, Peters approached Korshak to ask him to vote
against a proposal by Southern Illinois University to establish an
engineering school. If Korshak changed his vote, Southern Illinois'
bill would come out of committee. Peters wanted to prevent that
because an engineering school at Carbondale would compete with
the one at Urbana-Champaign. Korshak, who had independently
come to the conclusion that an engineering school was not needed
at Carbondale, told Peters he could be counted upon. In return, he
said, he hoped that when the Chicago branch campus came before
the Senate again, Peters would "forget the football team." Peters
promised he would.

In the House, meanwhile, something similar had happened.
When Randolph's bill came before the Appropriations Committee, a member from a western suburb offered an amendment directing the trustees to build a branch in Chicago "or in the environs

thereof." Randolph much preferred a downtown site, but he needed the support of the suburbanites and therefore agreed to the amendment. In his opinion, the most important thing was to get the branch under way; the question of location was secondary, and, anyway, the amendment did not exclude Chicago as a possibility.

Another leading Chicago Republican, Pollack, vigorously opposed the amendment to Randolph's bill. Pollack had introduced a bill in the previous session to locate the branch on a particular site in his ward. His bill had never got out of committee. Pollack emphasized that this time he was not recommending any particular site but that he was determined the branch should be in Chicago.

Pollack's views were especially important because he was the majority whip. Randolph's bill was not an administration measure; consequently, as Pollack himself explained to the House, he was not acting in his official capacity. Even so, his position was not exactly that of an ordinary member.

Livingston and Johnston, the trustees, came before the appropriations committee to justify their choice of Miller Meadows. A downtown site, Johnston explained, would take valuable property from the tax rolls and would increase traffic congestion. It would be hard to expand on a downtown site if the need arose; the necessity of finding relocation housing for the people displaced from the site would mean delay; and high-rise construction would be expensive. On the other hand, a suburban location would offer pleasant living conditions for faculty members and would be easily accessible to students. If the branch were at Miller Meadows, there would be no encroaching land uses in the future. The University, Johnston said, expected to pay the Forest Preserve District a fair price for the land or to find it another tract as good or better for its purposes.

Randolph, Pollack, and other Chicago representatives who had expected to be consulted had an opportunity now to tell the trustees what they thought of them.

"You have been stalling on this," Randolph told Johnston. "Unless something happens soon there's going to be a separate four-year state university in Chicago with a separate board of trustees."

Elroy C. Sandquist, also a Republican of Chicago, asked Livingston:

"You found out eight months ago that you couldn't have Miller Meadows and you're still stuck with it. Is that right?"

"That's one way of putting it," Livingston replied.

"It'll be another two years before anything is done for a Chicago campus," Sandquist shouted. "Don't try to kid this committee."

Sauers also appeared before the committee. He said that the trustees' proposal to take Miller Meadows was "an unethical encroachment on another public body."

A downstate Republican, acting on his own initiative and without consultation with the trustees, then introduced an amendment which would empower the trustees to take Miller Meadows by right of eminent domain. A Chicago Republican said that if this amendment were accepted the bill would surely be defeated by Chicago votes; he moved that the amendment be tabled. His motion lost, but when the amendment was put to a vote, it also lost. Finally, the Committee accepted an amendment requiring construction in the city of Chicago "or the environs thereof."

The next week, when the bill came to the floor of the House, the debate centered on the amendment. Pollack and others argued that the word "environs" was much too indefinite and that the trustees were likely to use it as an excuse for insisting on Miller Meadows and, thereby, to delay matters further. Randolph, on the other hand, was willing to accept the amendment. "All we want is action," he told the House.

Representative Harewood, a Negro Democrat from Chicago, wanted the branch to be in Chicago. It should not be a country club, he said. Students should be able to ride a streetcar to school; poor boys and girls couldn't afford automobiles. But another Negro from Chicago, Robinson, a Republican, took a contrary view. The experts, he said, referring to the University authorities, should be free to do what they thought best. A Chicago alderman, Vito Marzullo, who was present to lobby in behalf of the City Council, came on the floor and told Robinson — somewhat irately, Robinson thought — that he was betraying the Negroes by not insisting upon a downtown site. (Marzullo was one of several lobbyists who, being former representatives, had the privilege of the floor.)

Robinson begged to differ. "The South Side Negro," he told an interviewer afterward, "doesn't go to college just to prepare for a job; going is part of the status pattern. The middle-class Negro is the one who goes to college, and he goes as an expression of his drive upward in the status pattern. Most Negroes who would go to the University probably have their own cars and would go regardless of location."

Downstaters sat back in amusement while the Chicago area representatives quarreled. It was the downstaters who would finally decide, for they held the balance of power. "You downstaters should be suspicious of a suburban site," a Chicagoan warned them. "There would be marching bands and football teams at a suburban branch."

When the vote was taken, the amendment adding the words "or in the environs thereof" lost, 55 to 100. The bill then passed the House, 116 to 18.

Now that the Senate had passed a bill directing the trustees to establish a branch in Cook County and the House had passed one directing them to establish it in the city of Chicago, a conference committee consisting of two members of each house was appointed to recommend a settlement of the difference. The House conferees were both prepared to insist upon "the city of Chicago." Senator Cherry, who was one of the Senate conferees, preferred that wording also. But the other Senate conferee, Ozinga, would not agree to a unanimous report unless the crucial words read "Cook County." If it were not unanimous, the report would probably not be accepted and both bills would die. It was only a day or two until adjournment, and controversial matters were likely to be dropped by the wayside.

Randolph urged Cherry to withdraw his Senate bill. If Randolph's bill were the only one in the field, the conference problem would not arise.

Cherry refused. He thought there was a good chance of getting his bill adopted.

Finally, the conferees yielded to Ozinga and reported in favor of "Cook County." However, the House, energetically led by Pollack, refused to accept the report. The conferees met again and, this time, produced a "city of Chicago" report which was immediately and overwhelmingly accepted in the House. The bill reached the Senate only ten minutes before adjournment *sine die*. When the roll was called, Senator Peters, the Urbana-Champaign leader who had promised Korshak that he could forget the football team if Korshak would vote against Southern Illinois University's engineering school, did not vote. Instead, he signaled Ozinga and a number of other Republican friends, who left the floor as the vote was being taken. The report failed to get enough votes for passage, and a minute or two later the legislature adjourned.

Supporters of the Randolph bill felt that Cherry was responsible for what had happened. Cherry, they said, hated to see Randolph get the credit for the bill: that was the real reason why he had refused to withdraw his own bill.

Nonsense, Cherry told an interviewer later. The reason he had not withdrawn his bill was that he had expected it to pass. It was Peters who killed it, and those who had taken up so much time discussing it had given him the opportunity. "Frankly," Cherry said, "I don't think the amendment made any difference at all. I don't think Senator Peters wanted a branch in Chicago, in Cook County, or anywhere else."

It was Pollack, others said, who was responsible for the bill's failure: if he had really wanted to get the branch under way, he would have agreed, as did Randolph and Cherry, to a wording that the suburbanites would support. Not so, Pollack told an interviewer. The Senate leaders had agreed to accept the House's wording, and it was only because of an oversight in the last-minute rush that it failed to pass. Cherry was amused at this interpretation. It was not by oversight, he said, that Peters, although remaining on the floor, failed to vote or that Ozinga and his friends left the floor when the voting began.

The downstaters were amused. John W. Lewis, the genial farmer who was majority leader in the House, chuckled, some weeks later, when he recalled what had happened. "The Chicago people were like the dog that saw his bone reflected in the water when he crossed a bridge," Lewis said. "He dropped it by trying to get more. It just shows about human nature."

If the trustees really meant to "stall," they had been entirely successful. It would be two years before the legislature met again. And then the same thing was likely to happen all over again; with downstate help the suburbanites would always be strong enough to check the Chicagoans, without, however, being strong enough to get the branch for themselves. Those who wanted delay — if, indeed, there were any who did — had reason to hope that if the suburbanites eventually retired from the fray, two sets of Chicagoans would enter the lists and fight each other to a draw. One set of Chicagoans wanted the campus located near the West Side Medical Center. These included Dr. Karl A. Meyer, head of the Cook County Hospital; the Sears-Roebuck Company, whose main plant was affected by the deterioration of the neighborhood; and Raymond Hilliard, head of the County Welfare Department, who believed the campus should be situated so as to eliminate the city's worst skid-row district and who, with an architect friend, had gone to the trouble of preparing perspective drawings and supporting statements in the hope that his boss, Ryan, the president of the County Board, would enter the controversy.

Another group favored a near-South Side site. This was a railway yard which would be made available through the consolidation of several terminals. Many businessmen thought that to interpose the University campus between the South Side slum and the central business district would be a great boon to real estate values: it would give the downtown area a southern "anchor" comparable to the northern one that the Fort Dearborn Project was intended to provide. Holman Pettibone, the head of the Central Area Committee, began to take an interest in the University's site selection problem when it became clear that the railroad terminal consolidation would be consummated.

Unless Governor Stratton and Mayor Daley intervened, the struggles between Chicago and the suburbs and between the west and the south sides of Chicago might go on indefinitely. Anticipating the argument to come, the trustees, early in 1958, employed the Real Estate Research Corporation to make another study of site possibilities. "I want someone to back up the recommendations I am going to make," Johnston told the press. "I want an unbiased viewpoint."

7

The Exhibition Hall

WHEN Colonel Robert R. McCormick built a Gothic skyscraper on Michigan Avenue to house the Chicago *Tribune,* he had these words of his cut into the wall of the lobby:

THE NEWSPAPER
IS AN INSTITUTION
DEVELOPED BY MODERN CIVILIZATION
TO PRESENT THE NEWS OF THE DAY,
TO FOSTER COMMERCE AND INDUSTRY,
TO INFORM AND LEAD PUBLIC OPINION
AND TO FURNISH
THAT CHECK UPON GOVERNMENT
WHICH NO CONSTITUTION
HAS EVER BEEN ABLE TO PROVIDE

This being his credo, the Colonel enthusiastically supported projects to boost Chicago. The Century of Progress Exhibition, which was held on the shore of Lake Michigan at 23rd Street, in 1933-34, and which made a million dollars for its sponsors, struck him as exactly the kind of thing that was needed. When the Association of American Railroads sponsored an exhibition at the same site in 1948 and 1949, he ordered the *Tribune's* city desk to give it "the full treatment." The railroad fair brought hundreds of thousands of visitors to Chicago and, to the amazement of its sponsors, netted $500,000. Fairs, the Colonel decided, were a great thing for Chicago.

When the Association of Railroads decided not to continue its fair another year, the *Tribune* put up $50,000 and collected another $950,000 from downtown stores, hotels, restaurants, and other businesses in order to run the fair a third year. Partly because of bad weather, the venture was a financial failure. A bonding company which had guaranteed that the Burnham Park would be restored to its original condition after the fair had to make good on its pledge.

After the unsuccessful season, a meeting of the leading backers was held. The Colonel, who rarely descended from the Tribune Tower into the ordinary world, attended in person. What he heard was discouraging. According to Major Lenox R. Lohr, who managed the Century of Progress Exposition and the Railroad Fairs, the buildings on the Lake Front site, which had been meant to last only one year, were falling apart. To put the fair on a permanent basis, as the Colonel wanted, would require a large capital investment and a continuing subsidy. When they heard this, the downtown businessmen sat around glumly. They had, of course, listed their subscriptions to the fair as tax losses. Even so, it was obvious that they could not support a permanent fair. "It was an unsatisfactory meeting," one who was there recalled later. "Nothing definite happened. They talked in circles, except for the Colonel. Sometimes there were long silences."

The Colonel, however, was determined. He told W. Don Maxwell, his managing editor, to work the problem out one way or another.

Maxwell had no doubt about where the needed subsidy should come from. For more than half a century, Illinois had subsidized about a hundred county agricultural fairs. A large part of the money came from taxes on parimutuel betting at horse races. Cook County betters paid 80 per cent of these taxes, but, there being no fairs in the city, Chicago got nothing back in subsidies. In 1951 the *Tribune* got legislators of both parties, from Chicago and downstate, to introduce a bill to even things up by imposing an additional tax. One cent of each dollar received by the parimutuel race tracks was to be put into a special fund to aid "industrial, scientific, educational, and cultural" fairs and exhibits. Without taking anything away from the county agricultural fairs, the new tax would allow Chicago to put the lake front fair on a permanent basis.

The race-track owners, fearing the additional tax would hurt their business, opposed the bill vigorously. (The price for voting against the bill was said to be $500 to $1,000.) Nevertheless, the bill passed, largely because of the efforts of a *Tribune* reporter, George Tagge, who was assigned to see it through. Tagge had covered the legislature for fifteen years, and he knew more about its inside workings than did most of its members. Many legislators were his friends of long standing. Others wanted to get on his good side or to stay there.

Governor Stevenson was inclined to veto the bill. He was opposed to state aid for fairs of any kind, and he was under pressure from a Chicago publisher, John S. Knight of the *Daily News,* who had had an interest in a race track. However, at the urging of Richard J. Daley, who had been his director of revenue and had since been elected Cook County Clerk, and of Joel Goldblatt, a Chicago merchant, he let the bill become law without his signature.

Early in 1952, the Chicago Park Fair, a non-profit corporation, was organized under the new law as the official agency to run a permanent Lake Fair.

Maxwell and two other interested citizens, James L. Palmer, president of Marshall Field and Company, and Kent Chandler, a manufacturer, traveled to Toronto to inspect a municipally-run fair there. All three were very much impressed, especially by the fine set of exhibition buildings. In the club car on the way home, Palmer observed that if Chicago was to have an outstanding fair it would first have to build a fine exhibition hall. "That," he said, "is the first thing to shout for." The others agreed.

For this, new legislation was required. In the 1953 legislature, accordingly, Tagge pushed through another *Tribune* bill, this one to permit construction of a hall in Burnham Park at 23rd Street, the site of the former fairs.

Opposition was even fiercer than before. This time it came from three privately owned Chicago halls whose business would be threatened by the construction of a fourth. By far the largest and most important of the privately owned halls was the International Amphitheatre. Located near the stockyards, it had been built primarily to house the International Livestock Exposition but had been widely used for large gatherings of many kinds. The Republican and Democratic national conventions, for example, were held there in 1952.

The Amphitheatre was managed by William Wood Prince, one of the trustees of an estate which held a large block of stock in it and in the Armour meat-packing company. He soon became the leading opponent of the proposed exhibition hall and, therefore, an object of attack by the *Tribune*. "The easterner who under term of his uncle's will operates the amphitheatre . . .," Tagge called him.

The race tracks, however, no longer opposed the hall. Maxwell, who had once been the *Tribune*'s sports editor, called his old acquaintance, Ben Lindheimer, an owner of two of the largest tracks. Lindheimer, Maxwell thought, had reached a stage in his career when he would be susceptible to appeals to public service. Instead of giving the race tracks a reputation for being grasping, he suggested to him, why not give them one for disinterested statesmanship? Supporting a great public improvement for Chicago would be good public relations. Besides, of the hundreds of thousands of people who would come to the exhibition hall, many would find their way to the nearby tracks. Lindheimer quickly agreed.

This time the *Tribune* had the support of the newly elected Republican governor, William G. Stratton. Stratton owed the *Tribune* a great deal and was on close terms with it. He and Maxwell conferred almost weekly.

"I didn't have to 'sell' him or make any kind of a deal with him," Maxwell told an interviewer later. "When he heard what we had in mind, he said, 'That's a great thing for Chicago.' "

But although he supported the *Tribune*'s bill, the Governor did not include it in his "must" legislation. Maxwell had no doubt that if he insisted, the Governor would make the bill a "must" item: the *Tribune*'s support was vital to him, and in a showdown he would sacrifice almost anything to keep it. But Maxwell did not think of insisting. The Governor's influence with the legislature was not unlimited. If the Governor exerted himself to pass the exhibition hall bill, he would have to drop something else. It would not be fair to the Governor or to the Republican Party to insist that the exhibition hall get absolute priority.

The consequence was that, despite the Governor's support, the bill barely squeaked through the legislature. Without Tagge's efforts, it would surely have been defeated.

Meanwhile, the basic conception of the project changed. The Colonel's idea had been to operate an annual summer fair to attract tourists and "keep things lively." Later, he and others saw that tourism would be better promoted by attracting trade shows and conventions than by running a fair. This led to the conclusion that a fine exhibition hall was the thing to shout for.

Chicago had always been an important convention city, but since the war the number of out-of-town convention visitors had gone up at an impressive rate:

1946	522,000
1947	675,000
1948	882,000
1949	704,000
1950	996,000
1951	995,000
1952	1,011,000
1953	1,027,000

The average visitor was thought to spend about $160 in Chicago. Obviously, the city — or at least the part of it that catered to tourists — would profit much from an increase in the number of conventions. This was particularly true of the thirteen Loop hotels. Their business had declined steadily since the war. The percentage of hotel rooms occupied was as follows:

1946	92.2
1947	89.8
1948	83.2
1949	76.9
1950	77.1
1951	74.8
1952	72.6
1953	73.1

In 1953 the Chicago Convention Bureau, an organization supported by hotels, retail stores, convention halls, restaurants, taxicab companies, bus companies and airlines, and other businesses that profited from conventions, reported that the bottleneck in the way of increased convention business was lack of suitable exhibition space. The Bureau made up a list of sixteen associations (the American Gas Association, the American Home Economics Association, the American Mining Congress, the American Transit Association, and so on) that avoided Chicago because it lacked adequate exhibition facilities.

The hotels were the businesses most in need of convention trade. But they were also — so the Convention Bureau said — one of the city's chief advantages as a convention center: other cities, even cities with superior exhibition facilities, could not compete with Chicago for large conventions because they lacked sufficient hotel rooms.

It was not surprising, then, that the president of Marshall Field and Company and the manager of the Bismarck Hotel encouraged the *Tribune* to support a convention and exhibition hall instead of a fair or that the Colonel agreed to do so. Such a hall would serve the *Tribune's* purpose as well or better than a fair, and it would attract more powerful and enthusiastic allies in the battles that were sure to come.

Having decided that Chicago must have a hall that would make it the leading convention city of the nation, the directors of the Park Fair employed a firm of architects, Holabird & Root & Burgee, and a firm of engineers, Ralph H. Burke, Inc., to make preliminary studies. In March, 1955, the two firms made a joint report. The hall was to be a single structure, 250 feet wide and 1,200 feet long, with a total exhibition area of 360,000 square feet. There was to be a vast parking space, dining rooms and roof terraces, a helioport on the roof, and an arena with 22,000 seats for special events. The whole was to be air-conditioned and illuminated in the most modern way. Facilities were to be provided for easy handling of the heaviest freight. To get into any other hall in Chicago a rider on an elephant would have to dismount, but to get into the new hall he would not even have to duck his head.

The cost, of course, would be greater than anyone had imagined. A lake front fair, Burke had said when the subject was first broached, could be provided with permanent buildings for $8-$10 million. To build the finest exhibition facility in the country was something else. Such a hall and its equipment, the architects and engineers estimated, would cost $34,286,000.

By the time construction could be started, $9,500,000 would have accumulated in the Race Track Fund. That left another $26,679,000 to be raised in some other way. It was clear that new legislation was needed. A public authority would have to be created and empowered to issue tax-free revenue bonds. There were difficulties in the way of this. If the bonds were to be backed by the full faith and credit of the state, their issue would have to be approved by a majority of the state's voters in a referendum, and it was doubtful, to say the least, if downstate voters would support bonds for a purely Chicago project. The bonds could be backed by the credit of Chicago or Cook County if the voters of one of these political jurisdictions would approve them. But there was a strong possibility that, in a general election, even the Chicago voters would turn them down. If he wanted to, the Mayor might put the bond proposal on the ballot in a primary election, in which his organization would pile up a heavy majority in a light vote. In this event the Democrats would control the Authority. This was repugnant to the *Tribune,* but what was worse — indeed, entirely unacceptable to it — was that such a bond issue would raise the Chicago property tax.

Some other expedient had to be found. This was to permit the state to purchase the Authority's bonds.

Accordingly, Tagge was given another assignment. This time there were two *Tribune* bills. One would create the Metropolitan Fair and Exhibition Authority as a municipal corporation, authorize it to issue revenue bonds, and enable the state and other political bodies to invest in its bonds. The other would authorize the Chicago Park District to lease up to 180 acres of Burnham Park, the 23rd Street Lake Fair site, to the Authority for forty years. Having the support of the Governor, who made special mention of the Authority in his message to the legislature, and of Mayor Daley, the leader of the big Cook County Democratic contingent, Tagge expected a relatively easy time of it. As it turned out, the fair bills caused by far the biggest hullabaloo of the session. Prince, the manager of the Amphitheatre, appeared in Springfield to work against the bills. Certain Chicago civic associations — notably the Chicago Real Estate Board and the Chicago Association of Commerce and Industry — opposed the bill authorizing the lease of the 23rd Street site. A Republican ward politician was employed to co-ordinate opposition. He got $30,000, it was said, to use as he saw fit. But the bills passed in spite of all opposition. "Tagge's Temple," the Exposition Hall was now called by the wags in the Springfield bars.

If the growth of the idea had not been so gradual, the Colonel might perhaps have felt that his position was somewhat anomalous. He inveighed, day in and day out, not only against the Red menace of the New Deal but against the palest pink of "liberalism." Yet here he was, the principal advocate of a socialist enterprise — a publicly owned and subsidized exhibition hall — in a field where there was nothing to prevent private enterprise from operating successfully. It was not easy to see why, if an exhibition hall should be socialized, banks and department stores — yes, even newspapers — should not be so also. That banks, department stores, and newspapers would gain from the subsidization of an exhibition hall was not, of course, a satisfactory answer to the problem, for in principle other businesses might gain from *their* socialization. And even if many businesses gained from public provision of an exhibition hall, why should the taxpayer be forced against his will to support it? That forcing him to do so might in the long run make his city bigger and more prosperous was no justification: it might be that he was satisfied with Chicago as it was.

Such questions did not trouble the Colonel or the other sponsors. They were never raised except by Prince, the manager of the Amphitheatre, whose bias was taken for granted. Maxwell regarded the project as a kind of economic perpetual-motion machine: it would bring in a great deal of income which would be widely diffused throughout the community, and it would do so without adding a dime to anyone's taxes. That it would be given a site which could be sold to a private enterprise for an enormous sum; that race-track betters, many of whom were lower income people, would pay nearly $2 million a year in taxes, and that the value — and therefore the taxability — of the existing, privately-owned convention facilities would be depreciated by construction of the new hall — these considerations Maxwell and the other sponsors, all staunch defenders of free enterprise, disregarded. No one, Maxwell once said, would oppose the Exhibition Hall unless actuated by a selfish motive.

Colonel McCormick died at the end of March, 1955. Maxwell, one of three trustees into whose hands control of the *Tribune* passed, became its editor. He took up the struggle for an exhibition hall with renewed determination: it would be, he felt, a fitting monument to the Colonel.

Maxwell did not take a place as director of the Park Fair or of the Authority which replaced it. He preferred to work from behind the scenes. Sometimes he and Tagge attended meetings of the Board (once Tagge made a report to the Board on a discussion he had at its request with the Governor concerning pending legislation), and he was always consulted when special problems arose. The *Tribune's* law firm, in which the Colonel himself had once been a partner, represented the Park Fair and, later, the Authority. One of its members was always present at meetings of the Board.

Maxwell had a great deal to say in the choice of directors. Appointments to the Board of the Authority were made by the Governor and the Mayor, both of whom took suggestions from Maxwell. When the Authority replaced the Park Fair, the same men were appointed to the new Board.

The composition of the Board nicely reflected the balance of forces that had been brought together in support of the project. There was, for one thing, a balance between the political parties. The Governor and the Mayor were directors ex officio, and each appointed six members to the Board. Parity between them was essential: if one had had a majority, the other could have been counted upon to make trouble. This had become abundantly clear while the bill was before the legislature. The first version of it gave the Governor the appointment of six directors and the Mayor the appointment of five. As the session advanced, Tagge noted a surprising lack of enthusiasm for the bill on the part of the Cook County Democrats. He asked one of them if something was wrong.

"If I were you, George," the Democrat told him, "I would give some thought to that 6-5 provision. Some people would like the bill better if it were 6-6."

"You didn't just dream that up," Tagge said. "Did Daley say that?"

"I think it would help if you changed it," the legislator told him.

Tagge told the Governor what had happened. The Governor was irked. The state was putting up the money, he said, and therefore should have greater weight on the board. But since this was primarily a *Tribune* project, not a project of his own, he would swallow the pill.

In the appointments that were made to the board, some business interests were represented directly. The Illinois Central Railroad, whose tracks ran adjacent to the 23rd Street site, was represented by its president, Wayne A. Johnston. The president of the Marshall Field and Company department store, Palmer, had been one of the early proponents; he soon ceased his active connection with the project, presumably because his presence on the Board would antagonize the other department stores, and his place was taken by David Mayer, Jr., a former president of the State Street Council, a merchants' association. Arthur M. Wirtz, whose family had a half-interest in the Chicago Stadium, a sports arena, represented that interest. Otto K. Eitel, the manager of the Bismarck Hotel, represented the Loop hotel owners. (Wirtz had an interest in the Bismarck and could therefore be considered a representative of it as well as of the Stadium.)

Henry Crown, one of the richest men in the United States, represented two hotels (he was an owner of the Conrad Hilton and of the Palmer House) and the Material Service Corporation, which sold $100 million worth of building materials a year. The Conrad Hilton was closer than any other hotel to the 23rd Street site; Crown, therefore, would have an advantage, and the owners of the Loop hotels a disadvantage, if that site were chosen.

Patrick F. Sullivan, president of the Chicago Building Trades Council, was also a director. It was customary to give labor nominal representation in such undertakings, but there was an additional reason for appointing Sullivan: the building-trades unions could do much to hasten or delay construction.

The other directors represented not particular institutions or organizational interests but points of view, special competences, or opinion groupings within the community. They were C. Wayland Brooks, a former United States senator, and Fred M. Gillies, president of Acme Steel Company, both prominent Republicans; James B. McCahey, a coal merchant who was a prominent Catholic and a Democrat; William A. Sizer, head of a cold-storage company, who understood the bond market and was a Democrat; George A. Williamson, a candy manufacturer and former president of the Illinois Manufacturers Association, and Lenox R. Lohr, president of the Museum of Science and Industry and the successful manager of the Century of Progress Exposition and the Railroad Fair.

Lohr was the first chairman of the Authority. He declined to serve after 1956 and was succeeded by Mayer, the State Street merchant, who was a logical choice for several reasons. He represented a major interest, the retailers, and he was in a position to mediate between the South Side hotel owner, Crown, and the Loop hotel owners represented by Eitel and Wirtz. Moreover, his clothing firm had the distinction of having advertised more than 15,000 consecutive days in the *Tribune* — a record equaled by no other advertiser.

Maxwell had something to say about most of the appointments. Certainly, no member of the Board was obnoxious to the *Tribune*. He and Crown were particular friends. Sometimes they beat drums together in Maxwell's basement rumpus room. Mayor Daley appointed Crown to the Board at Maxwell's suggestion.

The question of a proper site soon arose. So long as the intention was merely to continue the Lake Fair, there was no problem: the fair would be where it was already. Later, when it was decided to build a hall to attract conventions, the site of the existing fair came naturally to mind. It was easy to find reasons in favor of it. The public had come to think of it as *the* place for fairs: the repeated successes of fairs there proved that it was a good site.

Since the whole purpose of the project was to attract visitors to Chicago, the hall ought to be a spectacle. Nothing could be more spectacular than an impressive building on the edge of the lake — one of a group of impressive buildings: the Natural History Museum, the Aquarium, the Planetarium, and Soldier's Field.

There were some who had other ideas. When the Convention Bureau called a meeting of business people in 1952 to present the proposal, some owners of Loop properties raised objections. Twenty-third Street, they said, was too far from the Loop. The sponsors were not sympathetic. "They headed the question of location off," Graham Aldis, a former president of the Building Managers Association, recalled later. "They said, 'Let's not fall to quarrelling among ourselves. Let's get the legislation first.'"

The legislation, as it turned out, authorized the Park Fair to build at 23rd Street and nowhere else. The Colonel, people said, had made up his mind. Nothing would change him.

There were some who opposed him, however. While the *Tribune*'s bill was being fought over in Springfield, the Chicago Plan Commission, at that time an independent agency under an unpaid board, passed a resolution opposing the 23rd Street site. The resolution offered four main principles of site selection: (1) Since its basic character was to be commercial, the hall should not be placed on the lake front. (2) The site should be readily accessible, but not in conflict with traffic from the central business district. (3) It should be on the periphery of the central business district. (4) Strong consideration should be given to the redevelopment needs of the central business district.

The Plan Commission did not explain why these principles should be given paramount importance. There was certainly no reason for regarding them as self-evident. Questions could be raised about all of them. (Why, for example, should the project be excluded from the lake front because of its "commercial" character? Was an unpopular "educational" project more deserving of a site there than a popular "commercial" one?) And there were other principles, not mentioned by the Plan Commission, which had as much to be said for them. (Was it not relevant, for example, that the public had shown that it liked having trade fairs at 23rd Street?)

The directors of the Park Fair had no money to buy land and no authority to build anywhere except at 23rd Street. Unless the Governor was willing to squeeze an appropriation from the legislature, from a practical standpoint the choice was 23rd Street or nothing.

The directors knew, however, that there was bound to be a long public argument over the site. The location of public buildings was always a matter of controversy. When the lake front was involved, the controversy was especially heated.

Anticipating trouble, the directors provided for it. They had the engineer, Burke, evaluate every site, whether public or private, that anyone considered plausible. He rated all sites according to several criteria: adequacy of size, accessibility, availability of transport service, and development cost. The 23rd Street site and others nearby on the lake front were the only ones that passed muster. It had already been accepted by the public as an exhibition area. Highways provided splendid access to it, and there was room for possible future expansion. "Its location on the shores of Lake Michigan," Burke's report said, "capitalizes on one of the major attractions of Chicago. . . ."

Early in 1956 the Authority applied to the Park District for the lease of Burnham Park. The District was run by a professional superintendent, George T. Donaghue, under the direction of five unpaid commissioners appointed by the Mayor. The most important of the commissioners was Jacob M. Arvey, a lawyer, who had long been a leading figure in the Democratic machine and was still a National Committeeman. Arvey was very much interested in the large amount of patronage the District afforded him. So long as this remained undisturbed, he was willing to let Donaghue run things pretty much as he saw fit.

Donaghue's impulse was to resist the request for Burnham Park. As a professional park administrator, he did not want any buildings in his parks that were not essential for park maintenance. But he knew that in this case resistance was hopeless. "This was something important to the businessmen of the city — to the people who pay the taxes," he explained to an interviewer later. "I have to work with my board. Besides, that site had never been developed as a park and it was cut off by the Outer Drive from any normal group of users."

Long before the Authority applied for the lease, Donaghue and his staff had entirely reconciled themselves to the inevitable. It was a Park District lawyer who, in 1954, proposed that the hall be financed with bonds to be purchased by the state.

As a matter of course, however, the District held public hearings on the Authority's application. At the first hearing, Major Lohr made a statement for the Authority, and the engineers and architects outlined their proposals in general terms. Ferd Kramer, president of the Metropolitan Housing and Planning Council, spoke in opposition to the site. It would, he said, encroach upon Chicago's most envied civic possession, an open recreational and cultural belt along the lake. It was on the flank of a crowded section of the city that was greatly in need of park and recreational facilities. While a few interests might benefit from the hall, the people who lived in the city would be deprived of a resource that should be available to them free. "We do not believe," he concluded, his tongue doubtless in his cheek, "the Park District would intentionally subordinate the recreational needs of all the people to the interests of certain groups, important as they may be."

William Spencer, the businessman who was chairman of the Plan Commission, said that he did not think anyone in his right mind would deny that the city needed a convention hall. The 23rd Street site, however, violated some cardinal principles that the Commission had long ago laid down. One of these was that the lake front must be used only for educational and recreational purposes. The legislature should be asked to provide funds to buy a convention hall site from private ownership. That would involve two year's delay, to be sure, but delay was justified in order to preserve the lake front.

To this, Arvey responded that the Park District could only decide whether or not to give a lease. If it decided against leasing, it might kill the convention hall altogether.

In his opinion, he said, the hall was a "quasi-public" and not a "commercial" purpose. "It doesn't penetrate any particular group," Arvey said. "It benefits all of our population."

Joel Goldblatt, a State Street merchant who was a member of the Plan Commission, took issue with Spencer. He had made a dozen trips to the proposed site, he said, and had seen there "nothing but the breeding of juvenile delinquency." Commercial exhibits such as would be shown in the hall were, he thought, very educational.

After another hearing two weeks later, the Park commissioners voted unanimously to give the lease. The legislature, Arvey observed, had held hearings on the subject and had decided to authorize the Authority to enter into a lease. This, he thought, constituted a mandate to the District.

It was his opinion, Arvey went on, that the 23rd Street site was not the most suitable one. It would be better to have enabling legislation and an appropriation that would make possible the selection of a site having some slum-clearance value. But the matter had been under discussion for three years and no definite plan of this kind had been offered. In view of the legislature's position and in view of statements by the Mayor and the Governor that a hall was essential, he would vote aye.

He was saying, in effect, that if the *Tribune* and the Governor would not exert themselves to get an appropriation for another site, nothing could be done. The choice was 23rd Street or nothing.

Within the Authority itself there was a last-minute flurry of disagreement over the lease. Wirtz, one of the owners of the Bismarck Hotel, said that he had been under the impression that the Authority was not authorized to buy land. (The Park Fair had not been authorized to buy it; the Authority was authorized but had no money for the purpose.) When he discovered, a few days before the lease was to be signed, that there existed no legal obstacle to the choice of another site, he told the Board that no unbiased economic survey would support 23rd Street. The hall should be close to the Loop, he said. He proposed buying a site and building a multiple-story structure.

Despite his objection, the Board approved the lease. The 23rd Street site, the directors believed, was the best available. In any case, the lease would not bind the Authority: it was essentially an option.

Mayor Daley, one of the directors of the Authority who voted to enter the lease, remarked that it would be well for the Authority to hold hearings at which members of the public could express their views on the site. The public would feel that the Authority had acted high-handedly if it failed to hold hearings. As a municipal corporation, it was under an obligation to listen to the public.

Accordingly, three months later, the Authority held a day-long hearing. A lawyer, an architect, and a real estate man appeared jointly to propose building the hall on the air rights over the Union Station. These could be had, they said, for $6 million. Their proposal was backed by a committee of prominent men who managed Loop properties. Except for this proposal, which the Authority did not take seriously, the hearing developed nothing new. At the end of the day, the situation was unchanged except that the Authority had now satisfied convention by listening to the voice of the people.

A few days after the signing of the lease, Eitel, the manager of the Bismarck, told the Board that the directors of two Loop hotels, the Sherman and the Bismarck, opposed the 23rd Street site and wanted a centrally located one. He asked the Board to have additional site studies made. To satisfy him and other objectors, the Board instructed Burke to evaluate more sites. The endless process of site evaluation, a planner employed by Burke later told a court, was mainly a matter of public relations. The planner said:

> There was a great deal of adverse comment in the newspapers. Every amateur traffic expert and everyone who had an axe to grind, or a piece of property to sell, decided that their particular scheme should be brought to public attention. There were many hearings. . . . I did not attend them, but at all these hearings there were, you might say, constituent complaints that were being registered, and we realized in advance that those complaints would be made, and that is why we had originally put in private sites in the report, and the Fair Authority said, "Well, let's take some more," because someone would start boiling the pot in the newspapers, to the effect that future generations were getting their lake front taken away from them, or something like that.

Site selection was not the Authority's most serious worry. For a time it appeared that the project might not be feasible on any site at all.

First reports had been encouraging. Burke estimated that the normal income of the hall would be $4,358,425. More than half of this ($3,630,000) would come from the rent of space; the rest would come from concessions, parking, and charges for equipment and freight handling. Expense would be $1,741,750 leaving $2,616,675 for debt service. This was almost a million dollars more than required.

These were, of course, estimates. Burke employed experienced market analysts who assembled a great deal of information about the convention business and interviewed many prospective users of the hall. It was reasonable to assume that the estimates would not be far off. Yet, there was a possibility that they might. Critics might even claim that his report was concocted to justify a course of action to which the Authority was committed. Wirtz, in fact, had intimated something of the sort when he said that no unbiased survey would support the 23rd Street site.

To guard against error and against criticism, the Board employed a nationally known firm of management consultants, Booz-Allen-Hamilton Inc., to make another study of economic feasibility.

Late in the summer of 1956, Booz-Allen-Hamilton submitted a report which put the whole enterprise in doubt. No matter how elaborate and well located it might be, the report said, the new hall would not significantly increase the number of conventions coming to Chicago. Of the 18,000 conventions held in the United States, only 48 required more than 25,000 square feet of floor space. Whether or not these 48 came to Chicago depended upon other things than the hall.

This was a disturbing conclusion. The whole purpose of the project was to attract conventions that would not otherwise come.

There was another irony: "Lack of present hotel facilities," the report said, is a very serious barrier to attracting more major conventions." Previously, it had been alleged that conventions were needed to bring business to the hotels. Now the opposite was asserted: more hotel rooms were needed to bring conventions.

With the possible exception of the New York Coliseum, the report said, all major convention halls operated in the red. Chicago was not likely to be an exception. Total operating income, Booz-Allen-Hamilton estimated, would be $1,915,000. Total operating expenses would be $1,550,000, leaving a net of $365,000. Interest and amortization of bonds would require $2,171,000. The subsidy from the Race Track Fund was $1,777,580 in 1956. Assuming it was that much in the future, the subsidy and the net operating income would, together, almost — but not quite — cover the interest and amortization charges. There was a danger, of course, that in some years the subsidy might fall off: no one could be sure how much would be bet and, therefore, how much would be collected in taxes. In bad years the Authority might incur a big deficit. At best, the outlook was uncertain.

Lohr, the chairman of the Authority, gave the press a full and frank statement of these difficulties. "While many of those who have criticized the project have based their arguments on location." he said, "the primary question before the Authority is whether funds will be available to construct it and continue its successful operation."

Observing that the Plan Commission, the Metropolitan Housing and Planning Council, and the Real Estate Board had made "most helpful and welcome" suggestions, he rebuked them gently for opposing the 23rd Street site without realistically considering the alternatives: "All studies must give full consideration to the economics of the problem. It is immaterial how desirable a plan may be if it is beyond the economic feasibility of the Authority to pay for it."

To meet the challenge posed by Booz-Allen-Hamilton, the directors of the Authority changed somewhat the design of the hall. By eliminating underground parking and a sports arena (a change especially welcome to Wirtz, whose family owned a half-interest in the Chicago Stadium), they reduced the estimated cost from $35 to $28 million while increasing somewhat the space that could be rented.

Even with these changes, the feasibility of the project depended upon the willingness of the state to buy the Authority's bonds. Now that interest and amortization charges had been reduced, the revenue from the Race Track Fund would almost certainly be sufficient to prevent a deficit. But since one legislature could not bind the acts of another, there was always some possibility, however remote, that a future legislature would take away the subsidy.

So long as this possibility remained, the Authority would have trouble finding buyers for its bonds. If, however, the state bought some of the bonds, private investors would be encouraged to buy the rest. As Lohr explained frankly in the press, ". . . the purchase of some of the bonds by the state would be an added incentive, if one were needed, to assure continuation of the subsidy, and thus make the remainder of the issue more attractive to the general purchaser."

The law empowered the state treasurer, acting with the approval of the governor, to buy the bonds with any surplus funds that might be in the treasury. No one doubted that the state treasurer then in office, Elmer J. Hoffman, would buy the bonds. He intended to run for governor some day, and therefore he was not likely to offend the *Tribune*.

The race-track and the Amphitheatre owners had been the first opponents of the exposition hall. In 1956, other opponents moved from the background to the center of the stage.

These new opponents represented three principal forces. One force consisted of planning-minded people. These were businessmen, architects, engineers, professors, and others who identified with the city-planning movement. Without exception, they were opposed to the 23rd Street site, which they said violated every canon of planning. The same people were conservationists. Building anything on the lake front — especially anything "commercial" —struck them as a desecration of nature.

A second force consisted of property owners who wanted the hall closer to the Loop. The Chicago Real Estate Board was one of these. The Association of Commerce and Industry was another. Certain hotels and retail stores were others.

A third force consisted of one man — James A. Cunningham, the investment banker who sometimes handled special matters for the Mayor and the President of the County Board. Cunningham was negotiating for the consolidation of several South Side railroad terminals. He wanted the exhibition hall and the Chicago branch of the University of Illinois both located on a site that would be freed by the consolidation of terminals.

These forces were brought together into a coalition by the

Metropolitan Housing and Planning Council, whose president, Ferd Kramer, a leading realtor and manager of residential property, was an ardent advocate of planning. He had opposed building at 23rd Street from the first.

The one most directly responsible for creating the coalition of opponents was the Council's salaried director, Mrs. Dorothy L. Rubel. She was an energetic woman with a talent for managing and manipulating. Running a civic association was not a way of making a living (her husband was an investment banker) but of exercising her talents for behind-the-scenes management. Mrs. Rubel was very careful to work within the policies laid down by her board of directors. But these were all busy men of large affairs, and they expected her — as they did the executives who worked for them in their businesses — to assume responsibility and initiative within the sphere marked out, sometimes vaguely and sometimes definitely, as "overall policy."

Having an office with telephones, files, and stenographers, and having her full time to devote to such things, Mrs. Rubel was in a position to take charge of the opponent forces. Most of the opponents lacked time or facilities to do very much. Mrs. Rubel could act for them. It was essential that they all be kept informed and that their activities be co-ordinated. She could serve as a center of communication and control.

Accordingly, she organized a citizens committee to speak in the name of the coalition. The committee consisted principally of leading figures in the Housing and Planning Council. Its letters and press releases went out from the Council's office on the Council's letterhead. However, the committee included a number of important people and organizations, among them Cunningham and the Chicago Real Estate Board, not usually associated with the Council. This justified its existence.

Early in 1956, Kramer was succeeded as head of the Council by Joseph Pois, who thereupon became, with Mrs. Rubel, one of the leading spirits of the committee.

Pois was a business executive who loved to master large bodies of knowledge and to solve complicated technical problems. After undergraduate work at the University of Wisconsin (where he was Phi Beta Kappa) he took an M.A. in international relations and a Ph.D. in political science at the University of Chicago. Later, while employed, he earned a law degree and was admitted to the bar. He worked as a field supervisor for the Public Administration Service, as a section chief in the United States Bureau of the Budget, and as chief of the administrative management division of the Coast Guard during the war. After the war, he joined the Signode Steel Strapping Company and soon became its vice-president and treasurer and a member of its board of directors.

Business success did not give Pois the intellectual stimulation he needed. He soon became involved in a variety of public affairs. For a time he took leave from his firm to serve as Governor Stevenson's director of finance; later, he became a member of the Chicago Board of Education. A day seldom passed without his attending at least one luncheon devoted to civic affairs (sometimes he went to one from 11:30 to 12:30, and then to another from 12:30 to 1:30) and meeting in the afternoon or evening with some civic committee or board.

Pois was appalled at the lack of study given to civic affairs. He was not satisfied with any decision that was not based on an extensive and exhaustive examination of all relevant considerations. The right way to solve policy problems, he thought, was by conscientious fact-gathering and analysis followed by intelligent discussion.

Although he was by no means contemptuous of politicians and even had a high regard for Mayor Daley, Pois did not enjoy dealing with them or entering into any situation where unrehearsed give-and-take occurred publicly. This was part of a larger aspect of his personality. He did not relate easily to people. He could not make small talk and did not enjoy those who did make it. At affairs where cocktails were served he would often find a quiet spot where he could be by himself to study a report until the time came for the serious business to begin.

Kramer as president had devoted an enormous amount of time to the Council's affairs, but he had been willing to let Mrs. Rubel work without interference or detailed supervision. She had, for example, written speeches and press releases, following the general lines laid down by him and by the Board, and these had been used without further checking. Pois' style was different. He insisted upon writing his own speeches and upon approving press releases before they went out. He wanted to know the details of Council affairs, and he seldom allowed Mrs. Rubel to act in his name. He would not himself talk to politicians if he could help it, however, and therefore Mrs. Rubel's efforts at indirect management were to some extent hampered.

Within these limitations, however, Pois and Mrs. Rubel led and co-ordinated the opposition to the hall in 1956.

Kramer, Pois, and the other leaders of the Metropolitan Housing and Planning Council were against the 23rd Street site primarily because they wanted to preserve the lakefront, which they regarded as the city's greatest asset. In itself, an exhibition hall might not make a crucial difference. But there was constant pressure to build along the lake, and every encroachment would make the next one easier. Unless a halt was called at once, the lakefront would be destroyed. Public improvements, the Council leaders also thought, ought to be used to facilitate urban renewal. They should replace slums and eye sores, not green spaces, and thus do double duty.

These were the controlling considerations. There is reason to believe, however, that none of the Council leaders was enthusiastic about an exhibition hall at *any* location. If it had been proposed to locate one at the right place (on the south edge of the Loop close to mass transportation and within walking distance of some of the hotels), the Council leaders would have supported it. But no matter where it was put, an exhibition hall was not really their kind of a project. It did not solve social problems, and it was not culturally improving. Bringing people to Chicago to see housewares, paint, and roadbuilding equipment did not (it seems safe to conjecture) strike them as particularly important, even though it might bring profit to merchants and hotelkeepers.

This indifference — in some it was a positive antipathy — to the ideal of boosterism was not shared by the newspapers, the civic associations, and the politicians. These took it for granted that publicity and dollars made cities great. The directors of the Authority, when they sought to justify the project to the public, did so in these terms: "It would bring prestige to Chicago, creating favorable nationwide publicity, such as the new Coliseum in New York has done for that city. It would bring new conventions to

Chicago which would not otherwise come. Through their expenditures while in Chicago, the additional visitors would mean much to our local economic welfare. Similarly, the expenditure of the many millions involved in the construction of an Exposition Center would be an asset to the local industry and local labor."

Not understanding or sharing the planning-minded people's contempt for mere boosterism, the rest of the city would have little patience with them if they based their opposition to the hall on it alone. Mayor Daley, for example, being a booster himself, would probably regard such opposition as frivolous or downright perverse. In order to make their opposition at all effective, the planning-minded people saw, they would have to base it on grounds that were intelligible to the boosters who comprised the vast majority. As a member of the Metropolitan Housing and Planning Council's board later explained: "Personally I would rather have seen the money used for something else altogether. But it would have been unrealistic to take that position. You had to agree that we needed a hall. Otherwise people would say, 'What are you anyway? A professional objector?' They'd think you were being too negative."

Under the circumstances, the sensible strategy was to support the principle of the hall very vigorously while opposing the only site at which it was immediately practicable to locate it. This strategy was all the more appealing because the site in question was, from a planning standpoint, about the most objectionable that could be found. Even if the project had been considered a culturally improving one, most planning-minded people would probably have been unwilling to have it at 23rd Street.

Since they were opposing — so they said — not the hall per se but only the hall at that particular site, the planning-minded people could enter into a mutually beneficial alliance with the second force of opponents — those boosters who, although favoring a hall, wanted it closer to their Loop properties.

These exigencies of rhetoric and of strategy accounted for the name which the coalition of opponents gave itself: The Citizens' Committee for a Chicago Exposition Hall.

The Governor was obviously working closely with the *Tribune*.

The best hope of the opponents, therefore, was with Mayor Daley. To be sure, from a formal standpoint there was little he could do. He was only one of fourteen members of the Authority's board. Its negotiations would not be with the city of Chicago but with the Park District, an entity legally as distinct as Milwaukee.

Informally, however, there was a great deal he could do. He was the Democratic boss of Cook County. There was no doubt that the Park District board would accept any suggestion he might make. Besides, he controlled the largest single bloc of votes in the legislature; without his co-operation the exposition hall was not likely to get very far.

There was, however, little reason to suppose that he could be induced to oppose it. He had been on record in favor of a hall for many years. He was, as everyone knew, an ardent builder and booster. There was, in fact, no hope at all of persuading him to oppose an exhibition hall as such. No mayor in his senses would publicly oppose a project of this kind. To do so would make him seem lacking in enterprise and civic spirit.

This would have been true with any such project. It was especially true with this one. For this one was a *Tribune* "must." "The Mayor," a big businessman told an interviewer, "isn't going to oppose it and have the *Tribune* kick the ——— out of him. Why should he? He's got nothing to lose by going along."

No one expected the Mayor to provoke the *Tribune* gratuitously. There were many who suspected, however, that he might secretly be pleased if it stubbed its toe and fell on its face. He might even be sly enough to contrive the situation so that this would happen without his seeming to be in any way responsible for its happening.

When the heads of the Metropolitan Housing and Planning Council waited on him to explain their objections to the 23rd Street site, the Mayor told them to "go ahead and push a site of their own." He probably meant that they should be constructive rather than destructive in their criticism. But this was not the interpretation that the Council leaders placed upon his words. He meant, they thought, that he would like to see such pressure brought that the *Tribune* would withdraw from the field in defeat.

The most active of the opponents decided to direct a steady stream of pressure on the Mayor through the press, by resolutions from civic organizations, and by personal interviews. Whether any amount of such pressure would change his mind or influence his behavior, they had no notion. Possibly, the pressure would make no difference. Even so, they felt, it was their duty to create it. When things were being done wrong, thoughtful and public-spirited people had an obligation to say so, even though they might not get them done right. Even if the Mayor were not influenced by the pressure, there might be some gain in educating public opinion so that on another such occasion opposition might succeed. At any rate, the Housing and Planning Council had to speak up publicly or else lose the confidence and respect of its members. Speaking upon such occasions was what it was for.

The Mayor's suggestion that they push a site of their own did not appeal to the opponents. Pois later explained why not: "We shied away from a specific site. If we had come out for one, they [the proponents] would have labelled us. We tried to encourage people to propose alternative sites, but we would have lost some [supporters] on any specific plan. At the end, we came up with the South Side and I was afraid of the charge that 'you are tied up with the south-end group.' So I felt that it was better strategy to stimulate the others [to propose specific sites]. . . ."

In their attempt to apply pressure, the opponents made use of the Plan Commission. Recalling that it had once opposed the 23rd Street site, Pois publicly suggested that the Authority call on it for advice. The Authority did so, and in December, 1956, the Commission reaffirmed its earlier position. It presented the Authority with a map on which several possible sites on the periphery of the downtown business district were designated. The 23rd Street site was not among them.

Spencer, the chairman of the Plan Commission, believed that the hall should be close to the Loop. He favored putting the project where it would contribute to the renewal of a blighted area. To do this in the area he had in mind, it would be necessary to tear down the large and valuable Transportation Building. Major Lohr, the chairman of the Authority, and Maxwell, the editor of the *Tribune,* went with him one day to see the site.

"You don't know what you're talking about," Lohr told him. "It would cost a terrific amount to tear this building down and a lot more to rehabilitate the neighborhood around it."

As it seemed to Lohr and Maxwell, the Plan Commission had taken a position without first getting the facts. Unless they knew what the site they recommended would cost and unless they had some reason to think that the Governor would agree to an appropriation of that amount, it was irresponsible of them to enter the controversy at all.

The *Daily News* and the *American* played up the story of the Plan Commission's opposition to the 23rd Street site, and Pois and the opponents were delighted with the effect they had created. The Mayor, they thought, was on the spot. If he endorsed the site now, he would be repudiating his Plan Commission. The businessmen on the board of the Authority were somewhat shaken, Pois believed, at finding themselves out of step with what the experts said were sound principles of planning. "There is something about a plan," he told an interviewer. "Maybe it is becoming a fetish, but it is for a good purpose. . . ."

The Mayor seemed unperturbed, however. Early in 1957 he created a city-planning department under a professional head, Ira Bach, who was directly responsible to him. The old commission was retained, but in a purely advisory capacity. Spencer, who was criticized in a *Tribune* editorial and who believed that a planning body ought to be independent of executive control, resigned.

The new Department of Planning was only a few months old when its commissioner was asked to explain his department's position to a meeting of opponents of the 23rd Street site. Paul Hedden, his deputy, reiterated the stand of the former commission.

When he heard what Hedden had done, the Mayor was irked. "Hedden is not protesting in behalf of the present mayor of Chicago," he told reporters. "He has never discussed this with me," he went on. "We need an exposition hall. The city has waited too long for this. We need it if we are to keep up with modern ideas, and the campaign to make Chicago greater. The plan has been thoroughly studied by all agencies and phases of government. We've had adequate time to consider all sites."

When a reporter asked him specifically about the 23rd Street site, he said, "I've said repeatedly we should not delay building a new hall. Those who have selected the site hired engineers to make studies and the engineers approved the site. We should proceed."

A few days after this, the Mayor appeared before the executive session of the Plan Commission to urge approval of the 23rd Street site. The Commission agreed to go on record in favor of the site at its next regular meeting. However, when the meeting was held and a motion made endorsing the site, a real estate man who was a member remarked that some people felt that not enough consideration had been given to other possible sites and that there should be more public hearings. "We're working in reverse order," another member remarked. "We should make a recommendation first on a site and then they can follow it or not follow it." To avoid dissension, the motion was tabled.

As the Mayor's subordinate, Bach, the head of the Planning Department, had no doubt that, no matter what the advisory Commission might do, the proper thing for him was to follow the Mayor's orders. To the planning-minded opponents of the 23rd Street site, this looked like weakness. "If Bach had any guts," one of them said, "he wouldn't take that. He's too much of a Milquetoast guy."

Meanwhile the opponents were trying to stir up opposition in other quarters. Taking it for granted that Negro leaders would object to having the Black Belt cut off from the lake, an opponent of the site pointed out to several of them that the Authority was proposing to turn Burnham Park into a trade fair. They said, "Fine." Apparently, they preferred commercial exhibitions to grass and trees. In any case, they were not going to get excited about an issue which was not "racial."

Mrs. Rubel had a similar experience with organized labor. The Cook County Industrial Union Council gave the opposition to the hall some slight support for a time. The AFL, however, did not. Patrick Sullivan, who was on the board of the Authority as the representative of the building trades unions, saw to that. When Mrs. Rubel sent protests to the Mayor and the Park District in the name of a group of prominent citizens, she could not put any labor leaders on the list. What was true of Negroes was true also of labor: the issue concerned labor but it was not a *labor issue.* Where the central concerns of their unions were at stake — as they were, for example, in the case of the building trades — union leaders were very much on the job. Where the central concerns of the unions were not at stake, the leaders were not interested.

With one press release, Mrs. Rubel suffered embarrassment. Following her usual practice, she issued the release in the names of several persons of whose support she had been assured. She did not, however, check with each of them as carefully as she might before the release went out. Tagge of the *Tribune* called them and found that about half did not know exactly what had been said in their names and had not specifically authorized it. This, of course, was front-page news.

To Maxwell and Tagge it was incredible that anyone would oppose such an obviously good thing as the exhibition hall except for selfish reasons. The interest of the Loop property owners who wanted the hall closer to them was plain enough. The other opponents, Maxwell and Tagge reasoned, must have similar interests. Tagge actually called Pois on the telephone to ask what real estate he owned. Kramer, who had very extensive real estate interests, was hurt by intimations that his motives in opposing the hall were selfish. The fact was that Michael Reese Hospital, of which he was a director, and the Prairie Shores redevelopment project, which was being promoted by his firm (but in which he personally had no financial interest), stood to gain from the building of a hall at 23rd Street: both were in the vicinity, and improvements there might enhance the value of nearby land. Kramer, however, did not explain this to the *Tribune.*

While it was firing salvos at the Mayor and the Park District the Citizens Committee for a Chicago Exposition Hall was also studying the legal situation. If the Governor and the Mayor could not be persuaded or cajoled with press releases, perhaps they could be checked by court action. Two lawyers who were active in the Metropolitan Housing and Planning Council volunteered to look into this possibility.

These were by no means the first efforts to stop the project by legal action. The Metropolitan Fair and Exposition Authority Act was only a few days old when its constitutionality was challenged in the courts by several downstate county fairs and the state's attorney of Sangamon County. These suits were not necessarily hostile to the Authority: it was essential that its legal position be established quickly; suits of this kind were routine. Despite the promptitude with which the legal testing began, it was sixteen months before the constitutionality of the Act was finally established by two decisions of the Illinois Supreme Court.

These decisions did not mean that the Authority could not be stopped on other than constitutional grounds. The lawyers who looked into the matter for the Citizen's Committee reported that the Park District held the 23rd Street site for park and boulevard purposes only. If a court could be shown that the exhibition hall was for "commercial" purposes, it might decide that the Park District had no right to lease land to it. "However," the lawyers told the Committee, "it would be necessary to commence a law suit to get the question determined. There are all sorts of practical difficulties in the way of commencing such a proceeding, including public relations and financial." By this last they meant that public opinion might be alienated by an attempt to stop the project in this way and that in any case the Committee had no money to prosecute a suit.

There was also, they went on to say, a legal obstacle. The courts had held that a plaintiff had no standing to sue as a taxpayer unless he could show that taxes assessed against him were involved. It was doubtful if any one could be found who would be specially injured by the building of the hall. The advice ended on a note of futility: "As Mrs. Rubel has suggested," the lawyers' memorandum said, "perhaps this argument could be used to needle the Park District in negotiation. Perhaps also it could be used effectively as propaganda if the right materials were placed in the hands of our newspaper friends."

As it turned out, it was not until the end of 1957 that the opponents found a way to make an effective legal attack. By then it was clear that the Authority would have to sell its bonds to the state. If the courts could be persuaded to restrain the State Treasurer from buying them, the Authority would be dealt a damaging and perhaps even a fatal blow.

This was a likely enough possibility to arouse the interest of Calvin Sawyier, a member of the law firm that had represented Prince, the manager of the Amphitheatre, in his earlier attempts to block the project. Sawyier had long been active in the Metropolitan Housing and Planning Council — he was a member of its board of directors — and he was personally very much opposed to building on the lake front site. He had not taken an active part in the Council's opposition to the hall, however, because, since he was known as one of Prince's lawyers, his participation might embarrass the Council.

Sawyier eventually offered to institute a taxpayer's suit. "You get me a plaintiff and I'll give my time if the plaintiff is one who cannot afford to pay for it."

Sawyier knew that Prince would not appear as plaintiff in such a suit himself. He might, however, finance the suit if an acceptable plaintiff could be found. In that case Sawyier would be able to devote more of his time to it than otherwise.

However, it was not easy to find a plaintiff. As someone later explained, "No one wants to buck the *Tribune*." Kellogg Fairbank, a well-to-do real estate man, finally agreed to lend his name for the purpose from motives of public service. The lake front, he believed, should be kept free of buildings. He was not against a hall provided it was built elsewhere. When he learned that Prince would finance the suit, Fairbank insisted that Prince agree that the suit was to prevent building on the lake front, not to prevent building elsewhere. As a practical matter this was not a very serious limitation from Prince's point of view. If the Authority was prevented from building at 23rd Street, the threat to the Amphitheatre would be lifted for a long time to come.

The chance that the courts would find for the plaintiff was negligible. Of necessity, the finding would turn on judgment — was this a "reasonable" and "prudent" investment for the State Treasurer to make? The practice of the courts was to give elected officials the benefit of the doubt in such matters; since the State Treasurer and the Governor believed that the investment was proper, there would be a presumption in its favor. But apart from this, there was reason to suppose that the plaintiff would lose. By its very nature the case afforded wide latitude for the exercise of judicial discretion. It would therefore be easy for political bias to creep in. All of the judges were politicians who depended upon the party bosses, especially upon Governor Stratton (of the seven Supreme Court justices, five were Republicans), to "slate" and to elect them. Perhaps no judge would do what his conscience told him was wrong merely to curry favor with a boss. But it was likely that in this case, where there was a presumption in favor of the judgment of the elected officials, the judges would find themselves inclined to do what they knew their parties leaders wanted.

The advantage of the suit was not in the small prospect of winning but in the large prospect of delaying. Until the suit was decided, the Authority could not sell its bonds. And if the normal procedures were followed, it would be at least two years before it was decided.

The case would come first before a circuit court. Allowing the usual preliminary period for preparing the case for trial and allowing about six weeks for the trial itself, it would be three or four months before the judge would hand down an opinion. Then there would be an appeal to the Appellate Court. If the usual practice were followed, the court would allow the lawyers forty-five days to make an abstract of the record and another thirty days for the preparation of their briefs. Two or three extensions of this might be expected. Taking everything into account, a decision could not be expected in less than five or six months from the time appeal was taken. Then, of course, there would be a further appeal, this time to the Illinois Supreme Court. This would take several weeks more. If by good luck the judges' long summer vacation intervened, it might take several months.

And this was not all. If the case offered some toehold on federal jurisdiction, it might be appealed to the United States Supreme Court. The justices of that court would care nothing whatever about Illinois politics, and so there was even some chance that they might favor the plaintiff. At the worst — if the court refused to hear the case — something would have been achieved; if advantage were taken of every possibility for delay, it might be six or eight months before the court ruled.

Even then there would be opportunities for more delay. The

initial suit need not raise every possible objection. Thus, when the objections it did raise were finally decided, there would be others waiting to step into their places. On the basis of these, a new suit could be started on its long road.

Rather than suffer two or three years' delay when building costs were rising rapidly, the directors of the Authority might come to terms, agreeing to ask the legislature for an appropriation with which to build somewhere else.

There was another possibility. In November, 1958, a new state treasurer would be elected. It was likely that the winner would be Joseph D. Lohman and that he would refuse to buy the bonds. Lohman, everyone knew, considered that he had been unfairly treated by the *Tribune*. Although a Democrat, his appeal was largely to "reform" and "good government" elements and therefore, far from being amenable to suggestions from Mayor Daley, he might welcome an opportunity to demonstrate publicly his independence of the Mayor by opposing a project with which the Mayor was identified.

Lohman did not commit himself, but when Sawyier talked to a lawyer who represented him he got the impression that all might be well if the sale of the bonds could be postponed until after he took office as state treasurer. Later, during his election campaign, Lohman told a television interviewer that he did not look on the bonds with favor.

Sawyier filed suit at the end of January, 1958, a few days before the Authority was to receive bids on $25 million of bonds. The judge assigned to the case was one he thought likely to be fair and reasonable. It soon developed, however, that the judge was about to go on a vacation. When he found that the case was likely to run for some time, he turned it back to the executive committee of the court for reassignment.

Judge Julius Miner, a friend of both Maxwell and Crown (he and Crown sometimes listened to Maxwell play the drums in his basement), was a member of the executive committee. When the Fairbank case was first assigned, Miner was in Washington, but he had returned by the time it came up for reassignment, and, whether for this reason or not, the judge assigned, Thomas E. Kluczynski, was one whom Sawyier was to find unsympathetic.

Sawyier asked that the trial be scheduled for May 1. That would allow three months for preparation. The defense lawyer, a member of the firm in which Colonel McCormick had been a partner, protested at so much delay; Judge Kluczynski said that the matters involved were of urgent concern and that May was too far away.

"Let's get this case moving," he said. "I'll set it for trial March 17."

Sawyier soon got another shock. A lawyer named Ferre C. Watkins asked the court, as a taxpayer, for permission to intervene as a plaintiff. He said he wanted "to get a complete review of every issue in this case by the Supreme Court as fast as possible." The Fairbank suit, he said, failed to raise a number of issues which should be explored. Judge Kluczynski agreed and allowed him to intervene.

Watkins did not reveal who his client was, and there were some who suspected that it might be the *Tribune.* Maxwell admitted later it was fortunate that Watkins had entered the suit. "We didn't have to wait on the whims of the Prince lawyers," he said. "They could have delayed two years by taking the thing to the Supreme Court. We prevented that." He denied, however, that the *Tribune* employed Watkins. "We had a pretty good law firm," he remarked.

Sawyier's case rested upon two main contentions. One was that the bonds were not a reasonable or prudent investment for the state treasurer to make. The other was that the Park District had no right to reclaim and dispose of submerged land, some of which was part of the 23rd Street site. In six weeks of daily sessions he sought to establish these points by the testimony of Authority officials, planners employed by Burke, the State Treasurer, and various financial experts.

Getting financial experts to testify proved difficult. Sawyier talked to the trust officers of all the major banks and to at least five investment bankers. All agreed that the Authority's bonds could not be recommended for purchase by trust accounts. But when Sawyier asked if they would testify to this in court, all answered no. The reason was, a banker explained later, that all of them had nothing to gain and, possibly, something to lose by testifying. A banker who went out of his way to hurt the Authority could expect no favors from it or from its backers when at some future time there was business to be done. As one of them explained later:

Investment bankers use their own capital and capital borrowed from banks to buy bonds for resale to investors. The big houses head syndicates. Halsey-Stuart, one of the big houses, was rumored to be forming a syndicate for the convention hall bonds. If you have been "contrary," they might say "the hell with you" when the time comes to join their syndicate, if not their syndicate in this matter then in some other. Naturally, those who are members of the syndicate won't testify against it. Four or five years before, when the convention hall was first talked about, they may have given Halsey-Stuart informal assurance that they would join the project. Naturally, they can't turn around now and try to kill it.

And you never know who is in the syndicate. They keep it to themselves. So Sawyier wouldn't have had any way of knowing whom to go to.

"What do I get out of it?" That's the attitude of anyone who might be asked to testify. For example, of the trust department of a bank. I talked to someone in the trust department of the American National. He said, "Of course I'm against it. But why should I testify?"

One financial expert who did testify was Rex J. Bates, a junior partner in the investment counseling firm of Stein, Roe and Farnham. Bates was a member of the board of the Metropolitan Housing and Planning Council and had been an active opponent of the 23rd Street site from the first. One of the senior partners in his firm, Sidney Stein, was a brother-in-law of Ferd Kramer and had himself been active in the Metropolitan Housing and Planning Council. Sawyier "cleared" through Stein before asking Bates to testify.

When Bates's testimony was reported in the press, one of the senior partners in his firm, Wells Farnham, was very much annoyed. Farnham thought the lakefront site was a good one and he was a friend of one of the architects who had designed the hall. Apart from this, he thought it inappropriate for a member of the firm to take a position in a controversial public question. When Bates pointed out that he had testified in a personal capacity rather than as a representative of the firm, Farnham was unimpressed.

"You were there only because you were connected with the

firm," he was later said to have replied. "We are in the business of selling advice to investors. Why should we get involved in a nasty political row?"

On the first day of May the judge decided against the plaintiffs. This was no surprise, and Sawyier made ready for an appeal at the latest possible date to the Illinois Supreme Court. At this point, however, the intervening plaintiff, Watkins, took the initiative by appealing at once; he made the appeal the day after the decision was handed down.

That court at once agreed to a defense motion to advance the case so that it could be heard before the summer recess.

Sawyier was very much put out. From first to last the judges had shown an extraordinary desire to hurry things along. It might be, of course, that they were motivated by nothing more than concern to get an urgent public question settled. On the other hand, it might be that they were playing the *Tribune's* game for their own ends. However this might be, their haste, Sawyier maintained, had denied his clients some of their rights.

In his brief to the Illinois Supreme Court, he made this part of his theory of the case. To his two previous contentions(that the bonds were not a proper investment and that the Park District had no right to reclaim and dispose of submerged lands), he added a third: that the plaintiff had been denied his right to due process of law and to a fair and impartial hearing. He had not, he said, had time to discover all of the relevant facts before the suit was called to trial, and Watkins had entered it to "sabotage" it by an extraordinarily prompt appeal. Had he been allowed the normal delay, he told the court, the case might not have been decided until the incumbent state treasurer had left office.

With his argument about due process Sawyier was establishing a basis for an appeal to the Supreme Court of the United States and, in effect, serving notice that an appeal was to be expected.

The Illinois Supreme Court on August 1 handed down a unanimous decision supporting the Authority on all points. It flatly denied the allegation that Fairbank had been denied due process by an unduly speedy trial. "Actually," it said, "the case was thoroughly prepared, well tried, and argued on behalf of all parties.

Permission was given, and accepted, to exceed the length of briefs authorized by our rules."

The decision was handed down during the court's vacation period. This was evidence of unusual haste. Opponents of the hall suspected that the justices had hurried in response to signals from the Tribune Tower. Proponents, however, thought they gave the decision quickly simply because they felt that the public interest required it.

Sawyier ordered a copy of the record. This was the first step toward taking an appeal to the United States Supreme Court. He had until December 15, 1958, in which to file the appeal. If Hoffman, the state treasurer, waited for this deadline to pass before buying the bonds, he would not be able to buy them at all, for his term of office expired on January 12, 1959.

Hoffman did not wait, however. After studying the Illinois Supreme Court opinions, he and his advisers decided that if there was further litigation, the Authority would surely win it. Accordingly, he bought $20 million dollars of bonds on November 17th.

After Hoffman bought the bonds, there was talk that the opponents would appeal to the United States Supreme Court. Early in 1959, however, Prince, who was then in Paris, sent word that he was keenly interested in getting the 1960 Republican national convention for his Amphitheatre. He wondered whether Maxwell would stand in his way because of the long battle over the exposition hall. Maxwell at once set word that, on the contrary, the *Tribune* would do everything it could to bring the convention to Chicago. The new hall on the lakefront could not be ready in time for the convention, but this made no difference. It was, Maxwell said, a matter of helping Chicago.

Prince did not say that in consideration for the *Tribune's* help in getting the Republican convention he would not take his case to the United States Supreme Court. Maxwell did not ask him for such a pledge. But after their exchange of courtesies, common politeness required that Prince drop any notion of fighting a bitter-end delaying action. As it turned out, Chicago — and Prince's Amphitheatre — got the 1960 G.O.P. convention, and the case against the exhibition hall never reached the nation's highest court.

The exhibition hall's legal troubles were not over, however. Two weeks after the Supreme Court decided the Fairbank case, a suit was brought to enjoin the Park District from leasing land to the Authority. Several residents of the University of Chicago neighborhood were the plaintiffs. They had been active in planning for a local urban renewal project, and this had brought them into other matters affecting the South Side.

Fred Zimring, a research associate in psychology at the University, was one of those in whose name the suit was brought. He and his wife (she felt more strongly on the subject than he) believed that it was much too easy for the authorities to give away park land. They had no objection to the exhibition hall as such — in fact they rather favored it — but they thought it was essential to establish the principle that parks should remain parks. Zimring knew Sawyier slightly and had followed the Fairbank suit with interest. When it failed, he and others decided to try.

The expense of the suit was borne by the owner of the *Hyde Park Herald,* a community newspaper. Fighting to save the parks was something to make a community newspaper known and respected. Legally, however, the case was hopeless, and it was soon dismissed.

Meanwhile, still another suit had been filed in Springfield by the Sangamon County Fair Association through its attorney, James C. Craven. The Association contended that the Authority had failed to comply with various provisions of the law, and it asked that the money turned over to it from the Racing Fund be returned.

The chance of the suit's succeeding was remote. Nevertheless, it was a nuisance. Although Hoffman had been willing to run a slight risk in buying the bonds for the state while some legal questions remained unsettled, the investment houses which would offer the remainder of the bonds to general investors could not be expected to act until the legal position was unassailable. Thus there was some possibility that the Authority would find itself in the embarrassing position of having the hall two-thirds built and being unable to finish it.

When Tagge looked into the matter, he found that Craven had begun the suit without a retainer in the hope of influencing the

State Department of Agriculture to cease what he considered to be discriminatory regulation of the Sangamon County Fair. Craven would drop the suit, he told Tagge, when the Department of Agriculture agreed to give the local fair the same treatment it gave the Chicago one. Tagge called the director of the Department of Agriculture. His office had not made any special difficulties for the Sangamon fair, the Department of Agriculture man said. In fact, believing Craven to be a very touchy fellow, it had leaned over backward to avoid antagonizing him. The Department would, however, assure Craven once again of equal treatment. Matters were soon arranged on this basis, and early in 1959 the suit was dismissed by agreement.

Whatever may have been its value to the county fairs, Craven's zealous efforts probably enhanced his standing with the local folks. For a young man who looked forward to a political career (he had graduated from law school in 1949 and had run unsuccessfully for state senator and for county judge), this was in itself a considerable advantage. People in Sangamon County would remember that Craven had not hesitated to challenge the city colossus on their behalf.

Craven, at any rate, was pleased with the outcome of the suit. "We were able to be a considerable nuisance to the *Tribune*," he later told an interviewer with satisfaction.

While the hall was under construction there was talk of naming it for Colonel McCormick. The editors of the *Daily News* and of the *Sun-Times* intimated to Maxwell that they would have no objection. The hall had been the Colonel's idea, and the *Tribune* pushed it through.

Maxwell believed the directors of the Authority would gladly name it for the Colonel. However, he decided against it.

"I'm not going to do that," he told an interviewer in the spring of 1959. "I'm going to name it 'The Chicago Lake Front Exhibition Hall.' I think it would be a mistake to name it for the Colonel. In the long run naming it for him might harm the *Tribune* and harm his memory. The public might not like it. It might not sit well. I believe we'll put a plaque on the wall near the entrance saying, 'This exhibition hall was conceived by Robert R. McCormick, editor and publisher of the *Chicago Tribune,* soldier, statesman, etc.' That would be only proper, I think."

Although there might be some disagreement about what ought to be said on the plaque, those on the inside of civic affairs agreed that the *Tribune* was chiefly responsible both for the hall itself and for the site. In the end the hall was officially named "McCormick Place."

The story of the hall demonstrated, some said, the ruthlessness and the power of the *Tribune.* The hall was at 23rd Street, they said, because all who might effectively have opposed it — the Governor, the Mayor, the Park District, the judges, and most of the civic association leaders — were afraid of the *Tribune.*

"I told Spencer to go along [with the *Tribune*] on 23rd Street," a member of the Plan Commission told an interviewer while the struggle was still at its height. "I said, 'if you don't, you'll get slaughtered . . . dirtied up by the press.' I've got a simple philosophy. I'll fight the sons-of-bitches if I have something to gain. This is just what happened with Spencer. [He was slaughtered.] They got all of his friends, and the *Tribune* smeared him editorially. There was no retraction. What does a retraction mean? What did Bill gain? What is Bill now? Forgotten. A nobody. And they talk of, 'Make small plans. . . .' "

This was a somewhat exaggerated version of the general view. When they proposed a resolution in a civic association or addressed an open letter to the mayor, people liked to feel, apparently, that they were playing dangerous parts in a real-life drama such as might be seen almost any night on television. The *Tribune* was the barroom bully — the gunslinger who forced timid citizens to stay at home and keep the blinds down. It took guts to walk up to the bar and order a glass of whiskey when the gunslinger was on a rampage.

This picture of the *Tribune's* power and ruthlessness was ridiculous, of course. The *Tribune* had persuaded the Governor to help, and it and he together had brought enough downstate legislators into coalition with the Chicago bloc to pass the crucial legislation. But this had not involved either coercion or threats of coercion. Tagge was effective because he was liked and trusted, not because he was feared. The Governor valued the *Tribune's* support and was glad to do it favors, but he would have favored the exhibtion hall anyway. And, in fact, he did not exert himself fully on behalf of the hall; there were times when, if it had not been for Tagge, the legislation would probably have failed.

Mayor Daley, it was reasonable to suppose, liked to be spoken well of in the *Tribune*. If he ever ran for governor, the *Tribune*, with its big downstate circulation, could help him a good deal merely by not going "all out" in opposition. But this did not mean that the Mayor would make a deal with the *Tribune* or that he had been compelled to do something he did not want to do. "We didn't try to persuade the Mayor," Maxwell said later. "Why should we? Any mayor would be soft in the head not to want an improvement like that for his city."

The Mayor probably would have preferred a different site than 23rd Street. He had to take 23rd Street or nothing because the Governor and the downstate Republicans, under the influence of the *Tribune,* would agree to no other. To this — but only this — extent had he been influenced.

With the judges, too, the *Tribune* had exercised less influence than many supposed. It had played the legal game cleverly, and it had held a good hand. In the main, these were the sources of its influence on the courts.

As for the civic associations, some of them had opposed the 23rd Street site vigorously in spite of the *Tribune*.

Even the Plan Commission had entered the fray, although it had been armed with not much more than its good name and good intentions. Spencer, its chairman, had not been "dirtied." He had merely been called feeble. Far from being a friendless and broken man afterwards, he was, so far as one could tell, a healthy, happy, and prosperous one. When he heard that Maxwell's wife played the piano, he invited the Maxwells to his home so that Mrs. Maxwell and he might play duets in his drawing room. Later, as chairman of the membership committee of the Commercial Club, he arranged for Maxwell to join.

Nevertheless, the general impression was that the *Tribune* got its way by "slaughtering," or by threatening to "slaughter," its opponents.

Why, people asked, did it go to such great lengths in such a matters? Why did a newspaper undertake to build an exhibition hall anyway?

Some said it was because the *Tribune,* as one of the sponsors of the Lake Front Fair, shared an obligation to restore the 23rd Street site to its original condition. It would cost a large amount — some said $50,000 and others $150,000 — to meet the obligation. If an exhibition hall were built at 23rd Street, the obligation would not have to be met. The *Tribune* was simply trying to save money.

This was not plausible, since $150,000 was not much money to the *Tribune.* It was also false. The sponsors of the Lake Front Fair had been bonded and had no further obligation to restore the site themselves.

Others said it had been the Colonel's dying wish to have an exhibition hall built there. There was a grain of truth in this: the Colonel had been very much in favor of the hall, and Maxwell and the other trustees of his estate were mindful of his wishes. But the exhibition hall was probably not quite so important to the Colonel as the story implied. He was an old man and he had other things to think about. When a board member of the Metropolitan Housing and Planning Council asked his widow if he had had his heart set on having the hall at 23rd Street, she said no, he did not care.

The truth seems to be that the *Tribune,* like some of its critics, thought that it was playing a part in a real-life drama. But it saw itself not as the gunslinger who kept the town at bay but as the clean-cut champion of law and order — fast on the draw, to be sure, but always in the cause of right. As Maxwell explained later to an interviewer:

> You want to see your city continue to grow rather than to die. We have nowadays — what do they call it? — "urban movement" or something like that. The core of the city is being gutted. There are great investments at stake. You can't stand by and let it die. We thought we could prevent it from dying by bringing conventions here, on the front porch of the city.

> We fought the NRA [National Recovery Act] for the people. We fight crime and vice. I don't know any paper that is strong and dominant that doesn't crusade for something.

Both images of the *Tribune,* its image of itself and its opponents' image of it — the image of the champion of law and order and the image of the gun-toting bully — had one thing in common: power — the gun. The *Tribune* wanted to appear "strong and dominant." That was the way it did appear.

Appearing so was good for business. It was hard to say what part of the mixture was public service and what part was organizational enhancement. Maxwell said:

Why did we put so much time into this? Because it's good for the city. But partly from selfish motives too. We want to build a bigger Chicago and a bigger *Tribune.* We want more circulation and more advertising. We want to keep growing, and we want the city to keep growing so that we can keep growing.

We think the community respects a newspaper that can do things like that. People will go by that hall and say, "See that? The *Tribune* did that singlehanded." That's good for us to have them say that.

If it hadn't come off — if those law-suits had turned out wrong — it would not have been good. It's good that people should think that their newspaper is powerful. It's good that it be powerful.

PART II

8

The Structure of Influence

THE Chicago area from *a purely formal standpoint,* can hardly be said to have a government at all. There are hundreds, perhaps thousands, of bodies each of which has a measure of legal authority and none of which has enough of it to carry out a course of action which other bodies oppose. Altogether, these many bodies are like a great governing committee each member of which has, in matters affecting it, an absolute veto. Moreover, the "committee" is (from a formal standpoint) one in which the members can have no communication with each other. Each legally separate body acts (from a formal standpoint) independently and without knowledge of the others. This being the case, it is of course extremely easy (from a formal standpoint) for any opponent to forestall any action. An opponent has only to find, among the countless independent bodies whose consent is required, one which can be induced to withhold consent in order to obstruct action. From a formal standpoint, virtually nothing can be done if anyone opposes — and, of course, everything is always opposed by someone — and therefore every opponent's terms must always be met if there is to be action. Every outcome must therefore be an elaborate compromise if not a stalemate.

For example, the government of Chicago proper consists of executive, legislative, and judicial bodies which are formally separate. The City Council may check the executive. The executive may check the Council. The courts may check them both.

The executive, however, is not a single body. It is several. The mayor is one. The city treasurer and the city clerk, both elected and therefore no more responsible to the mayor than he to them, are others. Schools are run by a board appointed by the mayor but not removable by him. Public housing is run by another such board, the transit authority by another, and parks by still another.

The City Council consists of the mayor and fifty aldermen, each of whom represents a ward. From a formal standpoint, the mayor can only preside, offer recommendations, and exercise a veto. Each of the aldermen has (from a formal standpoint) equal power. A majority of the Council can check the mayor (and of course all of the other executives) in almost anything.

Cook County (from a formal standpoint) is not a government but a congeries of unrelated governing bodies. It has several executives, all of whom are elected and therefore independent of each other. (These include the president of the County Board, the sheriff, the coroner, the county clerk, the state's attorney, and the county treasurer.) It has a legislative body whose fifteen members have equal authority, and it has courts of co-ordinate standing. There are, in addition, various other county governing bodies: the Zoning Board of Appeals, the Forest Preserve District, the Sanitary District, and so on. From a purely formal standpoint, all are independent, or nearly so, and thus able to check each other.

Even if all of these bodies were to agree upon a course of action (and if only the formal elements of the situation are regarded, it is hard to see how they ever could agree), they might be checked or overruled by the state of Illinois. Legally, the city is a creature of the state, and the county is an arm of the state. The state can reverse any decision that may be made by the city or county; it can even abolish them both. But the state is not a single body either. It consists of several elected executives, one of whom is called governor; of two legislative bodies, a senate and a house of representatives, with ample authority to check each other and the governor at every turn (but subject also to being checked by him), and of independent courts.

This account of the formal fragmentation of authority in the Chicago area could be carried much further. What has been said should suffice, however, to make clear that a single actor — say, the mayor of Chicago — can pursue a course of action only insofar as the formal decentralization is somehow overcome by informal centralization.

By far the most important mechanism through which this is done is the political party or machine. (A "machine" is a party of a particular kind: one which relies characteristically upon the attraction of material rewards rather than enthusiasm for political principles.) The Mayor of Chicago is chairman of the Cook County Democratic Committee.[1] (Although it is not necessary that the same person occupy both offices, a mayor has good opportunities to take control of the party machinery, and the head of the party has much to say about who will be nominated for mayor.)[2] As party "boss," the mayor plays the principal part in making up the "ticket." One who defies his control may be "dumped" at the next primary, and one who is loyal to him may be chosen for rapid advancement. In addition, he has a vast amount of patronage at his disposal; he can give or withhold the hundreds of jobs without which most ward committeemen could not maintain their positions. Without being dishonest himself, he can regulate the "take" of those who profit financially from their connection with politics. Having control of the police force, he can decide how rigorously laws are to be enforced.

Normally, the Cook County Board is controlled by a Democratic president much as the City Council is controlled by the mayor. Between the two Democratic political heads — the mayor and the county president — there is a good understanding of relative power and mutual interest. Each runs his own bailiwick, but when the need for joint action arises, the mayor, who is the more powerful, is the senior partner.

The governor is normally a Republican. He is the boss of a machine whose greatest strength lies in the suburbs of Chicago and in the towns and villages downstate. His supply of patronage and other favors, although large, is not sufficient to assure him control as complete or dependable as that of the Democratic political heads. Nevertheless, he can usually — if he wishes to pay the price — control the action of the Republicans in the legislature on the few measures he deems crucial.

Although the machines go far toward overcoming the constitutional decentralization of authority, they do not overcome it entirely. There remain some obstacles which a political head may circumvent only with difficulty, and others which he may not get around at all. The latter are of three general kinds:

1. He may be checked by elected official whose co-operation is essential. In general, elected officials are subject to the discipline of the party machines and thus of the political heads; to this extent their "independence" is nominal rather than real. The machine and its head are not all-powerful, however, and there are usually "irregulars" within the party who can afford to defy its discipline. Thus, it happens sometimes that a political head is checked absolutely by an elected official of his own party. In the Exhibition Hall case, many people hoped that would happen: the state treasurer-elect, an "independent" Democrat, was expected to refuse to buy certain bonds, thus frustrating a plan which the Mayor and the Governor strongly supported.

Usually, of course, the checking is done by an elected official of the opposite party. In the most common and important case, the governor checks the mayor. Although Chicago has what is called "home rule," it is nevertheless the creature of the General Assembly.[3] The governor usually dominates the legislature, and he is always in a position to give or withhold co-operation essential to the success of many of the mayor's undertakings. Those who wish to check the mayor are therefore likely to turn to the governor for help, as was done in the Welfare Merger case.

The mayor is not entirely at the governor's mercy, however. Occasions arise when the governor needs some of the votes the mayor controls in the legislature and then the mayor can demand a *quid pro quo*. The mayor's main defense, however, is public opinion. He can arrange matters so that the governor, if he withholds co-operation, will bear the onus of "playing politics" or of obstructing a program which the voters approve. In the Chicago Transit Authority case, for example, the Governor, whatever his personal inclinations, could not afford openly to refuse collaboration with the Mayor in an effort to solve the city's transit problems. This circumstance gave the Mayor some bargaining power.

2. Courts are often impervious to the influence of the political

head. The principle of the separation of powers, which assures the courts their independence, is generally respected by politicians, most of whom are lawyers. In civil cases especially, political heads rarely attempt to exercise influence. When the issue is public and essentially political (e.g., the Exhibition Hall), judges frequently take cues from the appropriate political heads. They may do so because the political head can give or withhold some advantage (like all who run for office, judges must be "slated"; but because they have long terms and the party is not likely to "dump" a judge who is endorsed by the Bar Association, they are relatively independent); more often, however, a judge accepts cues from the political head out of friendship or respect (the judge and the political head are likely to have gone to school and to have risen in politics together) or because he feels that it is right and proper to give the views of the chief executive special weight. As a rule, the political head and the judge are not in direct communication, although there is nothing to stop the political head from picking up the telephone and calling the judge if he wants to. The judge gets his cues by reading the newspapers and by discussing public affairs as other people do with friends and associates. In the Exhibition Hall case, for example, it may be taken for granted that the judges knew, without being told, where the Governor and the Mayor stood and why the proponents wanted the decision expedited.

The one sure way to remove an issue entirely from the influence of the political heads is to take it to the United States Supreme Court.

3. The political head may be checked by the voters at the polls. It goes without saying that he is checked when he is voted out of office. But there are other checks which the voters may apply. Bond issues, usually, and constitutional amendments, always, require the approval of the voters. So long as they turn down a proposal that has been placed upon the ballot, nothing can be done about it.

This element of decentralization has also been partially overcome in practice. A proposal may be put on the ballot in an off-year or a primary election when the total vote is sure to be light. The machine can then turn out enough disciplined voters to carry the day. But even so, the referendum is an important check. Some proposals would certainly be voted down even in a primary election, even in Chicago, where the machine is strongest. There are many more which could never pass a state-wide referendum.

These three obstacles — i.e., elements of decentralization which remain effective despite the enormous amount of informal centralization brought about by the machines — tend to generate civic controversies of the kind described here and, in general, to make political issues out of what otherwise would be administrative decisions. That a real possibility exists of checking the political head encourages people to try to do so. Interests that are adversely affected by the course of action he proposes endeavor to maneuver the situation so that one or another of these obstacles can be placed in his way. If they are fortunate, they may check him absolutely. But even if they do not succeed in this, they may compel him to make compromises.

When it is the mayor who is to be checked, the most readily available obstacle to place in his way is, normally, the opposition of the governor. Thus, in the Welfare Merger case, when IPAC found itself unable to get along with the city welfare commissioner, it asked the Governor to transfer the city department to the county. If the governor has decided to follow the same course of action as the mayor, some other obstacle must be found. In the Exhibition Hall case, proponents of the hall eluded one obstacle, to begin with, by securing the agreement of the Mayor and the Governor. This enabled them to secure legislation providing for the financing of the hall without the necessity of a referendum, thus eluding another obstacle. Not being able to use the Governor against the Mayor or the voters against them both, the opponents of the hall relied upon the only obstacles left to them: the courts (six suits were filed against the hall) and the independent powers of an elected official, the State Treasurer, who might defy the Mayor and the Governor.

The importance to the structure of influence of this formal decentralization of authority does not, however, rest solely upon the possibility of bringing one or more of these three obstacles into play so as to check the political head absolutely. Even where formal decentralization is entirely overcome by informal arrangements, decentralization of formal structure is of great importance. For the overcoming of it almost always represents a cost to the political head (i.e., he has to give up something, if only time and effort, to secure it), and this cost is often so great as to deter him altogether from the course of action he would otherwise pursue or to incline him to make compromises and concessions.

There are, indeed, a few circumstances in which formal decentralization can be overcome at trivial cost. Use and wont give the political head the right to issue instructions to some "independent" bodies almost as if they were a part of his office. (Even here, however, a certain amount of protocol must usually be observed by him, and this may be regarded as a cost.) But such cases are the exception. As a rule, the political head must give up something or incur some disadvantage of consequence — he must "pay" — in order to acquire for his own use the authority which the law places in other hands. For example, had he wanted to do so, it is likely that Mayor Daley could have acquired control over Ryan and the County Board in the Branch Hospital case. But to have acquired it would have been costly in one way or another. He would have had to give Ryan some juicy plum, or else he would have had to incur his enmity and run the risk of splitting the party. Even if the branch hospital matter had been very important to him, he might well have decided that the cost of acquiring control (giving up a plum or creating a split) was more than he wanted to pay. It is often the case that the "price" of acquiring control is so high that the political head decides that the transaction is out of the question. Thus, formal decentralization, even when it does not present an insuperable obstacle, may check the political head by imposing costs so high as to render action "unprofitable."

In a system in which the political head must continually "pay" to overcome formal decentralization and to acquire the authority he needs, the stock of influence in his possession cannot all be "spent" as he might wish. Some of it is "working capital." He gets his stock of influence by "buying" a bit here and a bit there from the many small "owners" who were endowed with it by the constitution-makers. Those who "sell" him their bits of influence demand something in return: jobs, favors, party preferment, *or other bits of influence.* Thus, some of the influence he has centralized he must again decentralize by trading it for other bits that he particularly needs. He may have a sizable "inventory" and many "accounts receivable," but if his "accounts payable" are large, his net position is not good. If, for example, he has control over a state senator in a certain matter, it may be because he has given the senator control over him in another matter. With regard to this other matter he may still *seem* to have control, but he does not really have it, for he has traded it.

It goes without saying that if he is to stay in business very long, the political head must, like any trader, maintain his capital and support himself while doing so. He must, in other words, employ the incentives at his disposal so as to: (a) secure the co-operation he needs to accomplish his immediate purposes (e.g., get certain bills passed and ordinances adopted), and (b) replenish the supply of incentives (and if possible increase it) so that he can accomplish other purposes on future occasions. In the CTA subsidy case, for example, it may possibly have been within the Mayor's ability to offer the Governor such incentives as to induce him to exert himself to the limit to get the subsidy bill through the legislature. But the Mayor had to consider whether this would be a wise investment of his limited stock of influence. He had to consider whether passage of the subsidy bill would so much increase his standing with an important bloc of voters or would bring him such patronage or other benefits as in the long run to make the transaction "profitable," i.e., as to yield a net gain in his influence. To be sure, on any particular occasion the Mayor might indulge himself in the luxury of "consuming" rather than "investing" influence, i.e., of using it for present purposes without regard to its replenishment. But if he consumed it for very long, he would be out of business.

It need hardly be remarked that if the political head had formal authority commensurate with requirements of the tasks he undertakes, he would not have to engage in this kind of trading. He would not have to offer jobs, favors, party preferment, and bits of influence in order to induce others to act as if they were his subordinates; they would have to act so because he could replace them if they did not.[4]

In some instances, it must be acknowledged, control acquired and used informally is more reliable in its operation than control provided by law. But this is not the general case, and it must be counted a disadvantage of informal control that its operation is, generally, highly uncertain. Here again the question is often one of "profitability." If the political head pays a high enough price, he may be able to buy the certainty of being obeyed. But there seems to be a principle of increasing costs at work: beyond a point, each increase in the probability of being obeyed costs more than the one before it, and the total cost becomes prohibitively high long before certainty is reached.

In part, the reason for this is that "debts" of influence owed to the political head, like gamblers' debts, cannot be collected in courts of law. If business is to be done in these circumstances, it must be under a set of extra-legal rules which will secure enforcement of contracts. Such rules exist. In some instances they are effective because politicians feel a moral obligation to abide by them, just as traders in the grain pit respect commitments the evidence of which is no more substantial than a raised eyebrow. In some instances they are effective because the one who "owes" influence fears his "creditor's" ability to make reprisals. When this motivation is paramount, the debtor is likely to test the influence of the creditor by acts of insubordination. This process of testing, which is a means that politicians use to get and to give information about their relative influence, has the incidental effect of introducing an element of uncertainty into the operation of the whole system of influence. Thus, for example, the governor may find that one of his leaders in the General Assembly unexpectedly refuses to carry out his wishes; the leader, it may be, has nothing more in mind than to establish the fact that he is strong enough to "buck" the governor and that, accordingly, his "price" must be raised.

Since he takes and uses authority which the constitution-makers intended to put beyond his reach, the political head is frequently excoriated in the press and elsewhere as an enemy of democracy. He is told that he ought to be ashamed of himself for being a boss, although the system of government could not possibly do the things the critics want done unless the decentralization of authority were somehow overcome. He must, therefore, boss while pretending not to. Although he is well aware that the system could not function satisfactorily if he did not assume powers that do not legally belong to him, he is likely to share somewhat in the general misgivings, and he must therefore either convince himself that he is not bossing or else feel guilty for doing so.[5]

To understand how the political heads evaluate their opportunities, i.e., how they decide the terms on which they will use influence or allow it to be used upon them, it is necessary to look at some salient facts of political geography.

"Downstate" (all of Illinois outside of Cook County) is white, Protestant, Anglo-Saxon, rural, and normally Republican. It elects the governor (a Democrat has held the office in only 16 of the last 58 years), and it controls the General Assembly. Under a recent reapportionment, the Senate is safely downstate and Republican; a narrow majority of the House may be from Cook County, but some of the Cook County representatives are sure to be Republicans, and some downstate Democrats are almost sure to vote with the Republicans. Downstate hates and fears Chicago, which it regards as an alien land.

Chicago is heavily Democratic. The Democratic heartland is the slums and semi-slums of the inner city; here, in wards which are predominantly Negro, Italian, Polish, Lithuanian, or Irish, and (except for the Negroes) almost entirely Catholic, the machine gets the hard core of its support. The lower the average income and the less average education, the more reliably Democratic is the ward.

The vote is less Democratic as one moves outward from the center of the city. Some of the outlying wards are usually Republican. So are most of the "country towns" (that part of Cook County which lies outside Chicago); for the most part, the suburbanites of the "country towns" are white, Protestant, and middle-class. Their affinity is with downstate rather than the inner city.

The inner city wards are so populous and so heavily Democratic that they can usually offset the Republican vote of the outlying wards. In the future, the ascendancy of the inner city wards is likely to be even more complete. White, middle-class families are moving to the suburbs, and their places are being taken by Negroes and poor whites from the South. Since the newcomers are almost all Democrats, and since many of those who leave are either Republicans or upward mobile types likely to become Republican, the proportion of Democrats in the inner city is increasing.

One might expect, then, that a mayor of Chicago would make the maintenance of the Democratic machine his most important business. So long as he controls the machine and it controls primary elections in the inner wards, he is invincible. And, of course, the way to maintain the machine is to pass out "gravy" with a generous hand — to give jobs, favors, and opportunities for graft and bribery to those who can deliver votes in the primaries.

This is, in fact, the strategy followed by the bosses of the most powerful machine wards.

It is not, however, the strategy of the mayor. He is normally the chairman of the county Democratic committee and therefore the leading figure in the party in Illinois and one of its leading figures nationally. Consequently, it is not enough for him merely to maintain himself in office in Chicago. He must take a wider view. He must carry the county and, if possible, the state, and he must contribute all that he can to the success and prestige of the party nationally. When the interests of the party on the larger scene conflict with its interests in the inner city of Chicago, the interests of the party in the inner city must usually be sacrificed.

As the table shows, to win a county-wide election a heavy vote in the inner city wards is not enough. There must also be a fairly strong Democratic vote in the outlying wards and in the suburban "country towns." The voters in these places are not in the habit of doing what the precinct captains tell them to do; their incomes are generally high enough, and their positions in society secure enough, to make them indifferent to the petty favors and advantages the machine has to offer. Many of them even seem to have absorbed the idea that "independence," i.e., splitting the ticket, is a mark of middle-class sophistication. To get the vote it needs from these outlying areas, the Democratic party must appear not as a "machine" but as a "force for clean and progressive government." To do this it must offer "blue-ribbon" candidates, and it must give the city and county the kind of administration that will win the approval of the press and of "good government" forces generally. ("Good government" is some kind of a mixture — the proportions vary greatly from context to context — of the following principal ingredients: (a) "reform" of the old-fashioned kind, i.e., the suppression of vice, crime, and political corruption; (b) "efficiency" in the sense of doing what public administration "experts" recommend with respect to organization structure and "housekeeping" functions like budgeting and personnel management; (c) following "progressive" policies in the fields of housing, planning, race relations, and welfare; and (d) executing big projects — airports and exhibition halls, for example — to boost the size, business, and repute of the city.)

Relative Importance in the Cook County Electorate of Inner City Wards of Chicago, Outlying Wards of Chicago, and "Country Towns"

	Population (in thousands)		Per Cent Change	Per Cent Contributed to County Democratic Vote	
	1950	1960*		1948	1956
18 Inner City Wards	1,257	1,291	3	37	31
Outlying Wards (Rest of Chicago)	2,364	2,616	11	50	51
"Country Towns" (Suburbs)	888	1,532	73	13	18
Total Cook County	4,509	5,439	20	100	100

* Estimate

The preference of the outlying wards and "country towns" for good government has for a good many years been a force which the inner city machine has had to take into account. Its importance, moreover, is growing every year. In part, this is because the whole population — and especially that of the outlying wards and "country towns" — is becoming more discriminating in its voting behavior. In part, also, it is because the numerical strength of the outlying areas is growing while that of the inner city remains approximately the same.

In this situation, a rational county Democratic leader will be less attentive to the inner city wards, whose vote he can count on, than to the outlying areas, whose independence is a danger. His strategy in dealing with these outlying areas is clear: he must help his party live down its reputation as a "corrupt machine" and establish a new one as the honest and energetic servant of the people. The welfare of the suburbs must be his special concern; he must show the suburbanites that they have nothing to fear and much to hope for from the Democratic organization in the central city.

By the same token, a rational Republican leader will endeavor to keep alive the old image of the "boss-riden" and "crooked" machine. He will do his best to frighten suburbanites and downstaters with stories of the growth and spread of the machine and of its designs on them.

These strategies are the ones the Democratic and Republican political heads do, in fact, follow. Mayor Daley, whose slogan is "good government is good politics and good politics is good government," has made it clear that he will not tolerate corruption in office and has kept a very tight rein on gambling, prostitution, and other organized crime. At the same time, he has inaugurated many reforms: he established an executive budget, introduced the performance-type budget, passed a performance zoning ordinance and housing code, extended the merit system, established a centralized purchasing system under a respected administrator, took control over contracts from the City Council, and transferred authority to issue zoning variation permits from the City Council to a Zoning Board of Appeals. His policy toward the suburbs has been sympathetic and generous: through James Downs, the highly respected businessman who is his consultant on housing and planning, he has offered them the assistance of the city-planning department and of such other technicians as might help with their transportation, water, drainage, and other problems. In his campaign for re-election in 1958, the Mayor presented himself as an efficient and non-partisan administrator. His principal piece of campaign literature did not so much as mention the Democratic party or the Democratic slate.

The Republicans have also followed a rational strategy. They have tried to paint the Mayor as a "boss" and the Democratic

organization as a corrupt and rapacious "machine." In the 1958
election, for example, Daley was dubbed Dictator Dick, and the
Republican organizations distributed buttons marked "S.O.S." —
"Save Our Suburbs from the Morrison Hotel Gang" (the Morrison Hotel is Democratic headquarters in Chicago). Some buttons showed the Democratic machine as an octopus reaching out
to grasp the unprotected suburbs.

These and other antagonisms put adoption of any plan of
metropolitan area organization out of the question. Because of
their strength in the outlying wards and in the suburbs the Republicans would have a good chance of controlling a metropolitan
area government. But in order to avail themselves of the chance,
they would have to relinquish their present control of most of the
suburbs. For if the whole metropolitan area were, so to speak,
put in the same pot, the Democrats might now and then win the
whole pot, and even when they could not win it they could offer
a troublesome and expensive contest. Therefore, although the
bolder Republicans and the Republicans whose interests are mainly
metropolitan favor proposals for putting one or more functions
on an area-wide basis, the more timid ones and those whose
interests are in particular "safe" suburbs are opposed to it. With
the Democrats the situation is similar. Mayor Daley would
probably be glad to take his chances with the electorate of the
metropolitan area. But the leading ward committeemen of Chicago
much prefer certain success in the central city to occasional
success in the metropolitan area.

The central city-suburban cleavage is the fundamental fact of
party politics in the metropolitan area. But the cleavage is not
simply a party one. As the Welfare Merger, Transit Authority,
and Chicago Campus cases show, party differences reflect differences of interest and outlook that are deep-seated and pervasive.[6]

It will be seen that the influence of the mayor depends largely
upon his being "boss" of the party in the county and that this
in turn depends upon his ability to maintain the inner city machine
while attracting support from the "good government" forces in
the outlying wards and suburbs. In short, the mayor must bring
the machine and the independents into a working alliance.

To become the county boss, one need only have the backing of the principal ward bosses of the inner city. There are 80 members of the county committee, 50 from the central city and 30 from the "country towns," and their votes are weighed according to the number of Democratic votes cast in each district in the previous general election. The inner city wards are therefore in a decided majority. These are grouped into ethnic blocs each of which has its own boss: there is a bloc of Negro wards under the control of Congressman William L. Dawson, a bloc of Italian wards under an Italian leader, a bloc of Polish wards under a Polish leader, and certain mixed wards under Irish leaders. Four or five of the most powerful bloc leaders, together with the president of the County Board, can, by agreeing among themselves, choose the county chairman.

Left to themselves, the bloc bosses would doubtless prefer someone who would not trouble them with reform. They realize, however, that the voters in the outlying areas will not leave them to themselves and that, unless the machine's reputation is improved, it will be swept out of existence altogether. They accept, therefore — although, no doubt, as a necessary evil and probably without fully realizing the extent of the evil — the need of a leader who will make such reforms as will maintain the organization.

In choosing a leader, the bloc bosses look for someone whose identifications are with the inner city wards (he has to be a Catholic, of course, and one whom ward politicians will feel is "their kind"), whose "nationality" will not disturb the balance between the Italians and the Poles (this virtually means that he must be Irish), who knows the workings of the organization from long experience in it and who is felt to have "earned" his promotion, who has backers with money to put up for campaign expenses (for it will be assumed that the county chairman will have himself nominated for office), who is perfectly "clean" and has a creditable record of public service, and who has demonstrated sufficient vigor, force, and shrewdness to maintain the organization and lead it to victory at the polls.

Once he has taken charge of the machine, a new leader need pay very little attention to the ward bosses who selected him.

If he can win elections, he is indispensable to them. Moreover, possession of office — of the county chairmanship and the mayoralty — gives him legal powers (patronage, slate-making, and control of city services, including police) which make the ward bosses dependent upon him. Without them to hold the ladder, he could not climb into his position. But once he is in it, they cannot compel him to throw something down to them.

He is likely, therefore, to prove a disappointment to them and a pleasant surprise to the friends of good government. The bloc bosses need him more than he needs them. They want "gravy" to pass out to their henchmen. But he is a county, state, and national leader, and as such his task is to limit or suppress the abuses upon which they fatten. To win the respect and confidence of the independent voters in the outlying wards and the suburbs, he must do the things that will hurt the bosses most.

The requirements of his role as a leader who must win the support of the independent voters are enough to account for his zeal to show himself honest and public-spirited. But it is likely that another circumstance will be working in the same direction. Ethnic pride may swell strongly in him and make him want to show the skeptics and the snobs that a man from the wrong side of the tracks can be as much a statesman as anyone from an "old family" or an Ivy League college.[7]

The political head is not likely to take a lively interest in the content of policy or to be specially gifted in the development of ideas or in their exposition. If ideas and the content of policy interested him much, or if he were ideologically-minded, he would not have made his career in the machine, for the machine is entirely without interest in such matters. Similarly, he is not likely to be a vivid public personality, to be eloquent, or to have a flair for the direct manipulation of masses. The qualities that make a popular or charismatic leader would tend to prevent a man from rising within the organization. The kind of leader produced by it is likely to be, above all, an executive.

Any mayor of Chicago must "do big things" in order to be counted a success. It is not enough merely to administer honestly and efficiently the routine services of local government — street cleaning, garbage collection, and the like. An administration that did only these would be counted a failure, however well it did them. As a businessman member of the Chicago Plan Commission explained to an interviewer:

The Mayor — no public official — is worth his salt if he isn't ambitious. That's true of you and everyone else. Now, what's a political person's stock in trade? It's government, of course. For a public official to just sit back and see that the police enforce the laws is not dynamic enough. I don't know that he would reason it out this way, but you have to get something with a little sex in it to get votes. In the old days, there were ward-heelers with a fistful of dollar bills. But that, even in Chicago, is passé.

What makes a guy have civic pride? A worker in a factory, a cab driver? He gets a sense of pride in taking part in an active community. The Mayor's smart enough to realize it. Today the tendency all over the country is for the public officials to take the lead more than they did a few years ago. . . .

Wanting to do "big things" and not caring very much which ones, the political head will be open to suggestions. (When Mayor Daley took office, he immediately wrote to three or four of the city's most prominent businessmen asking them to list the things they thought most needed doing.) He will be receptive, particularly, to proposals from people who are in a position to guarantee that successful action will win a "seal of approval" from some of the "good government" groups. He may be impressed by the intrinsic merit of a proposal — the performance budget, for example — but he will be even more impressed at the prospect of being well regarded by the highly respectable people whose proposal it is. Taking suggestions from the right kind of people will help him get the support he needs in order to win the votes of independents in the outlying wards and suburbs.

For this reason, he will not create a strong staff of policy advisers or a strong planning agency. The preparation of policies and plans will be done mainly within those private organizations having some special stake in the matters involved and by the civic associations. Quite possibly, the political head might, if he wished, assemble a technical staff of first-rate ability and, working closely with it, produce a plan far superior to anything that might be done by the private organizations and the civic associations. But a plan made in this way would have one fatal defect: its makers could not supply the "seal of approval" which is, from the political head's standpoint, its chief reason for being. On the other hand, a plan made by the big business organizations, the civic associations and the newspapers, is sure to be acclaimed. From the political head's standpoint it is sure-fire, for the people who make it and the people who will pass judgment upon it are the same.

Under these circumstances, the city planning department will have two main functions: (*a*) to advise the mayor on the technical aspects of the various alternatives put before him by private groups, and (*b*) to assemble data justifying and supporting the privately-made proposals that the mayor decides to "merchandise," and to prepare maps, charts, perspective drawings, and brochures with which to "sell" the plans to the public.

This division of labor is illustrated in the Fort Dearborn case. There the Mayor, not satisfied with various private proposals that had been made to him, instructed the head of the City Planning Department and his adviser on housing and planning matters, Downs, to prepare a comprehensive plan for the central area. The plan they prepared was essentially a listing of the probable outcomes of several site selection controversies then underway, and it showed remarkable agreement with the views of a committee of big businessmen who had made a plan for the central area on their own. Actually, political and other circumstances had so narrowed the site possibilities that there was little the Planning Department could do but record the results of the battles that had been waged and — a very important function — legitimate them by conferring upon them an aura of technical impartiality. ("The plan," the commissioner of city planning told the Mayor in his letter of transmittal, "represents the basic thinking of the technicians.")

There are often fundamental differences of opinion among those whose approval the political head wants. Chicago is too big a place, and the interests in it too diverse, for agreement to occur very often. When there is disagreement within the "good government" forces, the rational strategy for the political head usually is to do nothing. Watchful waiting will offend no one, and to be negative when one does not have to be is (as Mayor Daley recognized in the Fort Dearborn case) bad politics. The political head is therefore inclined to let a civic controversy develop in its own way without interference from him, in the expectation that "public opinion" (the opinion of "civic leaders" and the newspapers) will "crystallize." Controversies like those described in this book serve the function of forming and preparing opinion; they are the process by which an initial diversity of views and interests is reduced to the point where a political head feels that the "community" is "behind" the project.

The political head, therefore, neither fights for a program of his own making nor endeavors to find a "solution" to the conflicts that are brought before him. Instead, he waits for the community to agree upon a project. When agreement is reached, or when the process of controversy has gone as far as it can, he ratifies the agreement and carries it into effect.

In the Branch Hospital case, for example, President Ryan had no strong personal views for or against a South Side hospital. Had he tried, he might have found a course of action satisfactory to everyone (he might, for instance, have asked the General Assembly to offer capital grants to private hospitals willing to take county patients on a non-discriminatory basis). However, he made no effort to find a "solution" to the problem. Instead, he postponed matters as long as possible by assuring the Welfare Council that it would be heard in due course. When further postponement was impossible, he appointed a committee of "civic leaders" to bring in recommendations. In these ways he managed to avoid antagonizing either the radical or the conservative Negroes and to make it appear that he was honest, impartial, and tax-minded. To be sure, the question at issue remained unsettled and had to be fought over again two years later. Eventually, however, there might be agreement, and then Ryan would doubtless carry the agreement quickly into effect.

If this account of the structure of influence is correct, it should be possible to draw some inferences as to how the political head will respond to efforts to influence him.

It would be rational for the political head to pay a rather high "price" for newspaper support. If his only aim were to maintain himself in the machine wards of the inner city, he could afford to be indifferent to the newspapers. But he must lead his party to victory in the county and state, and to do this he must establish a good opinion both of himself and of it in the outlying wards and the suburbs. It is with the voters in these outlying areas that the newspapers can help him or hurt him. They can present him to their readers as the "boss" of a "machine" or as an honest and progressive administrator laboring mightily to make Chicago the greatest city in the world.

The behavior of the politicians seems to bear out this inference. The leaders of the heavily Democratic inner city wards — for example, Dawson, the Negro Congressman — are notoriously indifferent to criticism in the press. On the other hand, those politicians who have a county-wide constituency are very sensitive to it. In the public housing case, John J. Duffy as alderman paid no attention to the newspapers; when he decided to run for president of the Cook County Board, however, he became extremely amenable to pressure from the *Sun-Times*.[8] In the Branch Hospital case, Ryan compromised only when proponents of a South Side hospital threatened to start a newspaper campaign against the bond proposals. Mayor Daley and Governor Stratton both exerted themselves greatly in support of the Exhibition Hall, which was a *Tribune* "must."

It is to the advantage of the newspapers to harp on the faults of the boss and the "machine." The newspapers are all Republican, and of course it is "good politics" to make the Democrats look bad. Then, too, in enlarging upon the threat to civic virtue represented by the boss and his henchmen, they enlarge by implication — and sometimes expressly as well — upon the importance of their own role as guardians of that virtue. The embattled newspaper editor, fighting to save the people from crooks in office, is a popular culture hero whom the owners of newspapers, as well as the editors, would probably hate to see forgotten. Even if they were not attached, sentimentally and otherwise, to this image, they would not want their readers to forget that the mayor is the "boss" of a "machine," for their bargaining power with him rests largely upon his need for their assistance in eradicating the old image and creating a new one.

Whatever may be their reasons, the newspapers often attack the machine for doing what (as they well know) absolutely must be done in order to make a government so formally decentralized work at all. They want vast and controversial projects like the Exhibition Hall and the Fort Dearborn project pushed through at top speed, but at the same time they affect to believe that it is highly reprehensible for a party leader to impose discipline upon his followers in the General Assembly and the City Council. In general, they pretend that any departure from the formally prescribed procedures is an arrogant and probably corrupt usurpation of authority.[9]

The newspapers must be careful not to carry their attacks too far, however. It is one thing to pillory a ward boss and quite another to make an irreparable break with a political head who can give or withhold assistance in matters of great importance to the newspaper. Newspapers, no less than department stores and real estate operators, want favors from local government. Sometimes they want them for business reasons; sometimes for what they regard as public purposes. A political head who knows that he will not get a kind word from a newspaper under any circumstances is not likely to be very co-operative with it. If the newspaper wants a Fort Dearborn project or an Exhibition Hall, it must be moderate in its treatment of those in power in order not to deny them all incentive to co-operate. Violent as their Republicanism sometimes is in national matters, the Chicago papers get along well with the local Democratic political heads. The late Colonel Robert R. McCormick was on friendly personal terms with Mayor Kelly, and the *Tribune* today, although not failing in its duty to warn its readers of the evils of machine politics, sometimes praises Mayor Daley.

A Democratic political head can also be expected to pay a "price," although not a high one, for the support of the most prestigious "civic leaders." If it is known that prominent and respected men think highly of him and of his administration, something is gained toward overcoming the handicap of the machine's reputation and attracting the support that is needed in the outlying wards and the suburbs. What the most important of the "civic leaders" think influences what the civic associations do and thus what the newspapers report. Doubtless, too, the views of the more prestigious influence those of the less, and thus eventually help to shape middle-class opinion.

The number of "civic leaders" (unlike the number of newspapers) is large enough so that no one of them can ask a monopoly "price" for co-operation. Moreover, the "civic leader" (like the newspaper) wants something from the political head or expects to want something soon, and has, therefore, more incentive to get on good terms with the political head than the political head has to get on good terms with him. An overwhelming proportion of the "civic leaders" are Republican in national politics. Very few of them, however, are active in local Republican affairs, and still fewer are outspoken critics of the mayor. That Mayor Daley has conducted affairs well is not enough to explain this. There is always room for differences. Moreover, in other administrations, when there was much to criticize, the Republican "civic leaders" were not much more critical.

The influence structure that has been described is not stable. Although it has existed for many years without change, it is now moving rapidly toward a new and very different state.[10]

The principal dynamic factor is the tension between the demands for "good government" from the outlying areas and the maintenance requirements of the inner city machine. The outlying areas, as explained above, are constantly becoming more important to the success of the Democratic party in the metropolitan area. But all of the measures that will conciliate and attract the voters in these areas are in some way at the expense of the machine. In order to maintain itself in the outlying areas, the party must weaken the machine in its inner city heartland. Before long, it will have liquidated it altogether.

Even such a seemingly innocuous reform as the establishment of an information bureau in City Hall has weakened the machine. Helping a constituent find his way through the maze of local governmental organizations was one of the few favors the ward committeeman had left to give. When constituents found that they could get better service by calling the mayor's information bureau, another tie to the machine was cut. If a new tie took its place, it was to the mayor himself or to the City Hall bureaucracy.

The most serious blows to the machine have been the wide-scale extension of the merit system and the partial suppression of graft and corruption. There are still plenty of incentives for people at the top of the party hierarchy to give their time and effort: if the taste for "glory," "power," and being on the "inside" is not enough, there is still much "honest graft" to be had from the sale of legal service and insurance. At the lower levels of the hierarchy the case is very different. With few patronage jobs, and with those few much depreciated in value by the high level of general employment, there are not many incentives for ward and precinct workers. It is not surprising, then, that bribes and pay-offs tend to supplement the value of patronage. If putting an old uncle on the street-cleaning force is not a sufficient incentive to make the precinct worker work nowadays, then letting his brother, a policeman, take bribes from burglars may be necessary. This is an effect of inflation.

If it is to survive, the machine must tolerate a certain amount of corruption at least until such time as competent precinct captains can be induced to work from other motives than personal gain. At present, in the working-class districts at least, the other motives do not exist. Therefore the boss must — if he is to keep his organization from falling to pieces — "look the other way" to avoid seeing the inevitable corruption. If he saw it he would have to put a stop to it, and if he put a stop to it he would weaken both his personal political position and the whole structure of governmental power.

No matter whether he looks the other way or not, some corruption is inevitable in a city like Chicago. The inevitability of corruption — and therefore the inevitability of occasional exposures of corruption — is another element in the dynamics of the situation. An occasional scandal will keep the machine in ill-repute no matter what its achievements may be, and a large scandal occurring at a particularly inopportune time may possibly destroy it forever.[11]

The inner city machine, then, is being dismantled bit by bit in order to improve the position of the party in the outlying areas. Its liquidation will not result in a net loss in the Democratic vote in the county; on the contrary, it is being liquidated in the expectation of gaining votes or, at least, of cutting losses below what they would be if the reforms were not made. Democrats who run for county and for state office will be the special beneficiaries of its demise, for the inner wards will almost certainly continue to be heavily Democratic, and the party, by its reforms, will have gained much credit with the "independents" and the "good government" voters in the outlying areas.

The demise of the inner city machine, however, will nevertheless produce changes throughout the entire structure of influence — changes that are probably not anticipated by reformers and that in the long run may not be pleasing to them.

To the extent that the party is weakened, other means must be found for mitigating the effects of the extreme decentralization of formal authority that is so important a feature of government in the metropolitan area and the state. Chicago, like most large cities, has in recent years strengthened the formal powers of its chief executive (the mayor now prepares the budget and has control of purchases). But despite all of the reforms that have been made and all that are likely to be made, the formal decentralization is still so great that, unless it is somehow overcome by informal arrangements, the government cannot function effectively. When the mayor ceases to be a boss, he will not have power to run the city as it should be run, unless — a very unlikely possibility — fundamental changes are made in the constitution. In all probability, his loss of informal control will weaken the city government disastrously.

This weakening will both provoke civic controversies of the kind described here and prevent them from being settled. When every interest has a real chance of affecting an outcome by asserting itself vigorously, incitement to controversy is strong. When there is a very powerful political head, interests may make representations but they cannot bring *pressure* to bear (for the very powerful political head is impervious to pressure). Under the circumstances, the interests will accept, without challenge, decisions that they would contest bitterly if there were any chance of success. In the absence of a strong political head, the limitless opportunities for obstruction inherent in the system of decentralized formal authority will be used to the full. No decision will ever go unchallenged, and contests will often be fought to the draw because (as the Chicago Campus case suggests), with no strong political head to intervene, each side can check the others.

To the extent that the machine is weakened, the mayor will have to depend upon other means to get the heavy vote he needs from the inner city wards. There are two possibilities:

1. Voluntary associations — e.g., labor unions, organizations of businessmen, churches — may enter politics actively, using their resources to influence primary elections more or less as the machine does now. This, of course, would mean city administrations dominated by "labor" or "business," and probably sudden shifts back and forth between the two.

2. The mayor may make his appeal directly to the mass of voters. In this event — the more likely of the two — his power would depend ultimately upon his ability to manipulate a mass audience by television. If he appealed to the mass taste, perhaps by being "handsome," "folksy," or "colorful," he might have as much success with the voters as the machine ever had.[12] For such a candidate, one of the best formulas for success (but by no means the only one, of course) would be to appeal to ethnic pride and prejudice while at the same time distributing welfare services with a lavish hand.

Whether manipulating the inner city voter through television by appeals to ethnic pride is morally better than manipulating him through precinct captains with petty favors and phoney "friendship" may well be doubted. Certainly, there are dangers in "personality" politics, especially in a city highly charged with racial antagonisms. Relying as it has on its ability to buy the voter's support, the machine has never found it necessary to exploit these antagonisms. But a candidate who has no favors to give will have to deal with "issues," and one of these is likely to be race. The machine, moreover, must, like any organization, be preoccupied with its own maintenance and, therefore, with reconciling and harmonizing conflicting tendencies and with checking and subordinating extreme and erratic movements. The "personality" candidate will probably be a good deal freer to follow where the impulses of his mass audience lead.

Such a candidate will be constrained in one important way, however. He will require a very large campaign fund. (The boss pays for his campaign in part by promising his supporters an "in" at City Hall, but the "personality" must have cash for television time.) He will therefore be subject to the influence of large contributors. This may discourage him from some forms of demagoguery, but it will leave him little discretion in the matters that are of most interest to his backers. The boss has an extraordinary amount of discretion in important matters because his position depends upon doing petty favors for a large number of people. The "personality" candidates will have to do big favors for the big organizations — labor as well as business, perhaps — which alone can give the large sums required.

The difference between machine and "personality" politics is well illustrated by the Negro communities of Chicago and New York.[13] Negro political life in Chicago is dominated by an old-fashioned boss, Congressman William L. Dawson, who is not only extremely energetic in doing small favors for his constituents and in seeing to it that his precinct workers are "taken care of" but also quite indifferent to issues and principles, including those of special importance to the race. Dawson seldom speaks in Congress or from a platform, and when he does he never raises racial issues when he can avoid it. On some notable occasions, when others have raised racial issues, he has emphatically and publicly opposed the "race" position. In New York, an opposite style prevails. There, the leading Negro politician is Congressman Adam Clayton Powell, who has no organization to speak of (he is pastor of a large church) and who addresses the voters directly. Powell, unlike Dawson, is interested in nothing but race and never takes a position which is not an extreme "race" one. He is a vivid personality, an eloquent speaker, and an uncompromising rabble-rouser.

Chicago's influence structure has been formed to a large extent by the machine: the machine has been the dominant institution to which subsidiary ones have had to adjust. With its demise, the adaptations these subsidiary institutions have made will be obsolete, and new ones will have to be made.

This also can be illustrated by reference to Negro politics. The Dawson machine exists because the larger Democratic machine brought it into being and sustains it with patronage. (If Tammany

Hall were strong in New York, a Negro organization leader would probably soon displace Powell.) And because the Dawson machine exists, other institutions within the Negro community must take it into account and act accordingly. The NAACP, for example, is "practical" in its approach because Dawson arranged for the defeat of a president who was too "radical." The *Defender,* the Negro newspaper, is "reasonable" because Dawson helped its owner get credit. Conservatives like Robert E. Taylor[14] and Theophilus M. Mann (the Branch Hospital case) "represent" the Negro community in white-dominated organizations partly because they are acceptable to Dawson and his organization. Potential leaders know that anyone who wants recognition or who wants to achieve concrete gains must come to terms with the organization and must work through it. A Negro physician who is temperamentally a "race man" and an aggressive leader told an interviewer: "Now in Wisconsin, where I have a farm, I might very well be a Republican. You have to support the person who can get things done for you, and if the Republicans have the power then you have to be a Republican. But I can't see being anything but a Democrat in Chicago. I've never been anything but one here. . . ."

The influence of the machine on the Negro community is a special case of a more general phenomenon. The form and content of white politics, too, is affected by the presence of the machine. It is reasonable, then, to suppose that the demise of the machine and its eventual replacement by something else will produce a set of adjustments throughout the influence structure and that these will give rise to a different style of politics. If the new style were sure to be one in which every citizen's convictions on matters of principle were taken equally into account, no believer in democracy could doubt the desirability of the change. The alternative, however, is not that. Whether, in the long run, "personality" politics will be preferable to machine politics — whether the Powell style will be preferable to the Dawson style — is a question which each person may judge according to his own ideas of what is good and of what is probable. Where the electorate is largely middle-class, as it is in the outlying wards of the city and in the suburbs, it is reasonable to expect that voters will continue to be more discriminating in their choices and more exacting in their demands. In such places, the choice does not necessarily lie between "personality" and machine politics. In the slums of the inner city, however, the case is different; there it is likely to be many years before democracy, in something approaching the classical sense, can be made to work. Perhaps, in the final analysis, the Chicago machine should be judged by how well it facilitates the transition from itself to something better. By this standard, there is certainly much to be said against it. But here, too, the machine must be judged against real, not ideal, alternatives. If this is done, the case seems by no means clear.

9

The Process of Influence

Civic controversies in Chicago are not generated by the efforts of politicians to win votes, by differences of ideology or group interest, or by the behind-the-scenes efforts of a power elite. They arise, instead, out of the maintenance and enhancement needs of large formal organizations. The heads of an organization see some advantage to be gained by changing the situation. They propose changes. Other large organizations are threatened. They oppose, and a civic controversy takes place.

This is not the *only* way that a civic controversy arises in Chicago, but it is the simplest account of the cases reported here, and it fits them all fairly well. The county hospital proposed to expand at its present location; its expansion there was disadvantageous to a private hospital, which took the lead in opposition. A newspaper, in order to demonstrate its power, proposed building an exhibition hall; its proposal was opposed by the managers of an existing hall which would suffer from the competition. A state welfare agency proposed putting the city welfare department into the county welfare department, and the city department resisted. In other cases, a university, a forest preserve agency, a department store, and a metropolitan transit authority became key actors because their maintenance or enhancement was at stake.

This is not to say that the issues in these controversies had no reality or importance apart from organizational maintenance. In some instances they clearly did have other importance. In the Branch Hospital matter, for example, the question whether racial segregation by private hospitals should be tacitly encouraged was of lively interest to a large number of persons (as distinguished from organizations), and it would have had to be dealt with in one way or another sooner or later even if there had been no county hospital. The maintenance concerns of the opposing hospitals may be regarded as the instrumentality through which interests and concerns of larger public significance than mere organizational maintenance (even the maintenance of such important organizations as these) were raised and given concrete expression. In some other instances, however, there seems to have been little at stake except organizational maintenance or enhancement; it is plausible to suppose, for example, that if the *Tribune* had not needed to attract attention to itself by a conspicuous public service, the Exhibition Hall would never have been built.

The maintenance and enhancement needs of a large formal organization, moreover, can seldom be well served, and often cannot be served at all, by tactics which aim narrowly at the aggrandizement of the organization or which cynically disregard the interest of a larger public. Large formal organizations must offer their contributors (employees, members, customers, etc.) non-material incentives, like the opportunity to be of service to the community or to perform what Barnard has called "ideal benefactions."[1] Thus, paradoxically, the maintenance and enhancement needs of the organization can often only be served by showing that more than mere maintenance or enhancement is being aimed at. By taking a position which its contributors feel is in the public interest, the organization helps to earn their service and loyalty. If it takes a position contrary to what they feel is in the public interest, it must offer them some other inducements to make up for the deficiency. Frequently, no others will suffice.

Thus, because of tendencies inherent in organization, the maintenance and enhancement needs of a large formal organization are apt to be couched in terms of a conception of the public interest, or at least in terms of some goal or value having wider significance than mere organizational maintenance or enhancement.

Once raised, the issue acquires intrinsic importance by being a claim or assertion regarding the public interest. To say, for example, that the *Tribune* brought the Exhibition Hall controversy into being for reasons of organizational enhancement and that, otherwise, the matter would probably never have come up in a serious way does not explain the real significance of the controversy. It was only by performing a notable public service (or, at any rate, what a substantial part of the public would regard as one) that the newspaper could achieve its organizational ends. And once it advanced its conception of the public interest, the ensuing controversy concerned that conception and not the organizational exigencies which gave rise to it.

Civic controversies, then, are not "simply" the product of organizational needs. Some might arise in other ways: if the instrumentality of organizational maintenance did not bring them into existence, some other instrumentality probably would. But, however this may be, organizations generate issues, or give issues their specific character, precisely because the community believes the public interest is at stake or can be persuaded that it is at stake. It is for this reason that the matter becomes significant.

It will be noted that the organizations which play leading roles in these issues (they will be called here "affected organizations") are not civic associations like the League of Women Voters, the Urban League, or the Association of Commerce and Industry. Some are profit-making enterprises (e.g., the department store and the newspaper), some are public agencies which give free service (e.g., the welfare agencies and the forest preserve district), and some are public or semi-public agencies which sell services (e.g., the private hospital and the university). The one thing they have in common which differentiates them from the civic associations is that they are supported by people who are, in a broad sense, "customers," and not (as the civic associations are) by "members." This, perhaps, leads to a characteristic incentive system and, thus, to maintenance needs of a particular kind.[2] These are matters, however, about which the case studies have nothing to say.

The importance of organizations in precipitating civic issues implies the importance of the executives who run the organizations. In "business" organizations, even more than in "voluntary" ones, the chief executive has wide discretion. He decides — subject usually to the more or less *pro forma* approval of a board of directors — what is to be regarded as a threat to maintenance or as an opportunity for expansion, as well as how the threat or opportunity is to be met by the organization. He is employed to give his whole attention and energy to the management of the organization, he has a near monopoly of intimate knowledge about its situation as a whole, and he is the only one in a position to direct and co-ordinate its activity. Sometimes the executive is in the limelight; sometimes he merely decides whether or not the organization will precipitate the controversy, turning over the management of the issue to a subordinate when that decision has been made. (Thus, for example, the president of the University of Illinois left the conduct of the Branch Campus issue to a committee of the Board of Trustees, and the chairman of the Marshall Field department store assigned one of his vice-presidents to look after the Fort Dearborn Project). But whether he appears in the limelight or stands off-stage in the wings, he is always a principal actor.

In most of the cases described here the affected organizations are public ones, and their chief executives are career civil servants. Being a civil servant is no impediment to their acting politically, however. On the contrary, most of them are oriented not so much toward the impartial application of given rules (in the manner of Weber's ideal-type bureaucrat) as toward changing the distribution of power and, therefore, toward "fighting" (in the manner of Weber's ideal-type politician). Dr. Meyer,[3] Superintendent Sauers,[4] and Miss Wood,[5] for example, were extraordinarily alike in this regard. Each was quick to tell the politicians what they should and should not do. And each held — not very far out of sight — the possibility of giving trouble to any politician who acted contrary to his advice on a matter crucial to the organization.

Any one of the political heads — the president of the County Board, the mayor, or the governor — could, if he wished to exert himself, quickly impose his own settlement on any issue raised within his bailiwick. Ryan, for example, could decide the Branch Hospital dispute in any way he wanted. Daley could certainly have built the Fort Dearborn Project. The "Big Boys" of the City

Council (who were a collective political head during the transition from the Kelly to the Daley regime) could put public housing projects wherever they pleased. If the political heads agreed among themselves and tried hard, they could put almost anything through the legislature. The only issues which they could not decide to suit themselves were those upon which they disagreed and those which had to be passed upon by the courts or by the electorate. Issues in which none of the three intervened (e.g., the Chicago Campus and the Fort Dearborn Project) could not be settled at all, for although the contesting sides were strong enough to frustrate each other, none was strong enough to impose a settlement upon the others.[6]

One might expect that the chief executive of an affected organization would go directly to the appropriate political head to try to get what his organization wants. This, however, is not the way the process usually works. Instead, he employs intermediaries to present the organization's case to the political head and, simultaneously, to the newspapers, the civic associations, and the small but important body of citizens who pay attention to civic affairs. The intermediaries are prestigious persons — "civic leaders," they are called in the press — whose connections with the organization gives weight and legitimacy to its demands. Most large organizations maintain a formally co-opted body of such intermediaries; the Board of Trustees of the University of Illinois, the Board of Advisers of the Forest Preserve District, the Chicago Transit Authority board, and the Illinois Public Aid Commission are examples.

In the nature of the case, such formally co-opted "leaders" must occupy positions of at least nominal control over the organization. They take an interest in it and their prestige accrues to it because they are the heads of it. Whether their leadership is more than nominal depends somewhat upon the nature of the organization and upon the particular personalities involved. At one extreme, the "leaders" do no more than lend their names. The paid staff makes policy and, using the names of the co-opted "leaders" to get access, presents the organization's case to the newspapers, the civic associations, and political heads.[7] Although only the names of the "leaders" may be co-opted, this is sufficient to legitimate the organization and to give its executive the prestige he needs for access, on favorable terms, to those who must be influenced. But even when it is tacitly understood that the staff will run the organization, the co-opted "leaders" are likely to be a constraint upon it: their interests, opinions, and fixed ideas — ideas about the public interest as well as about the interest of the organization — set limits within which the executive must maneuver. In time, he may change these limits by "educating" his board or perhaps even by reconstituting it. In the short run, however, he is likely to be able to do little about it.

The co-opted "leaders" may serve very actively as intermediaries between the affected organization and its political environment, and they may also play leading parts in forming policy for the organization. In the Chicago Campus case, for example, Edward E. Brown, the chairman of the Advisory Board of the Forest Preserve District, and Wayne Johnston, chairman of the site selection committee of the University trustees, were not passive vehicles through which the executives — the superintendent of the Forest Preserve District and the president of the University — carried out their policies. Both of them made policy as well as legitimated it.

When special skills or access are required, intermediaries may be informally co-opted on an *ad hoc* basis. (Thus, the trustees of Michael Reese Hospital got Colonel Jacob Arvey, a super-salesman who was a leader in the Democratic machine, to plead their case with Ryan in the Branch Hospital dispute.) Knowing who can pull a particular string for the organization and being in a position to ask him to pull it are among the principal qualifications of the formally co-opted "leader"; a well-constituted board of trustees includes people with "contacts" in all quarters that may be needed.

Intermediaries are not always persons: they are sometimes civic associations, like the Civic Federation, the Metropolitan Housing and Planning Association, the NAACP, and the League of Women Voters. These pass resolutions, issue press releases, give testimony in legislative hearings, and make direct representations to politicians in support of or in opposition to proposals advanced by the affected organizations.

The relation between the affected organization and the civic association is often symbiotic. The civic association may serve as a "front" for the organization and as its ally. As a "front," it says things which the organization cannot well say for itself either because it would not be believed or because saying them would provoke a response from employees, competitors, customers, or others which the organization does not want. The organization's interest in the issue may be (or be thought) narrowly selfish, and its arguments, however well-founded, may be discounted on this account; the civic association, because it speaks for a broader interest, can appeal more plausibly to the public interest. (The trustees of Michael Reese Hospital felt that it was in the public interest, as well as in Michael Reese's interest, that the branch hospital be on the South Side. The advantage to Michael Reese of this was so great, however, that the trustees did not appear impartial. The Welfare Council, which *did* appear so, therefore made an effective "front".) As an ally, the civic association gives not only the advantage of another voice on the "right" side of the issue but, sometimes, also the assistance of its specially trained staff, the use of its mailing list, and even the loan of its own co-opted "leaders." In return, it gets from its association with the organization certain things that it values: these may include a cash contribution, the opportunity to recruit "leaders" and members from within the organization, and "good program material" which will maintain the interest of its members and give them a feeling of participation in important events and of accomplishment.[8]

In controversial matters, however, the civic association is likely to take no position at all, for fear of alienating some part of its support. In these circumstances the affected organization must create *ad hoc* bodies to serve its purposes. In the Fort Dearborn case, for example, none of the established civic associations took a stand for or against a dramatic redevelopment project that was proposed for the central city, and, accordingly, *ad hoc* bodies were brought into being to serve the purposes of both the proponents and the opponents.[9] Sometimes, too, an *ad hoc* association is created because it can devote its full time and resources to the particular matter at issue, something an established civic association ordinarily cannot do. Thus, in the Branch Hospital case, when it appeared necessary to carry on a prolonged publicity campaign, the proponents of the South Side hospital created a special committee for the purpose.

The political heads are slow to take up an issue presented to them by the "civic leaders." They know from experience that what one organization wants is almost certain to be opposed by others. Chicago is much too big a city, and the interests in it far too diverse ,to allow of quick and easy agreement on anything. By approaching an issue slowly, the political head gives opposing interests time to emerge, to formulate their positions, and to present their arguments. Before he commits himself he wants to see what the alignment on each side is likely to be and what is at stake politically. The longer the evil hour of decision can be postponed, the better he likes it; he has nothing to lose as long as the argument continues, and any settlement he imposes will make him enemies. What a public housing leader said of Mayor Kennelly — that his idea of a beautiful world was to sit around a table and have the opposing parties come to an agreement for which he would then take the credit without ever having opened his mouth[10] — can be said of the other politicians as well. Although he could settle the Branch Hospital dispute whenever he chose, Ryan moved very slowly; by doing so he was able to see (what the Welfare Council apparently missed) that there was opposition within the Negro community to a South Side hospital. In the Fort Dearborn case, Daley was equally cautious: year after year he resisted efforts to get him to commit himself, and the longer he waited the clearer it became that the business community was hopelessly divided. In the Transit Authority case, Governor Stratton made the mistake of deciding too soon and found it was necessary to renege on his promises.

The political head's reluctance to reach a decision is only in part a function of the situation in which he is placed. It is also a function of the conception he and his constituents share of the nature of the public interest and of the role of elected representatives. According to the Chicago view, a policy ought to be framed by the interests affected, not by the political head or his agents. In this view, the affected interests should work out for themselves the "best" solution of the matter (usually a compromise). The political head should see that all principally affected interests are represented, that residual interests (i.e., "the general public") are not entirely disregarded, and that no interest suffers unduly in the outcome. He is not expected to have decided views of his own (this might even be thought "undemocratic") or to "educate" others to accept a policy not to their liking. His role is supposed to be something like that of the chairman of a discussion group: to make sure that everyone is heard and to summarize the sense of the meeting at the end. In fact, of course, the political head may have very decided personal views. But if he has, he usually tries to hide them, especially if they are negative.[11]

In the Branch Hospital and Chicago Campus cases, for example, Ryan either had no position of his own or pretended not to have any, and he did not exert himself to find a compromise which everyone could accept. He looked for the course of action which would be least troublesome. In the Transit Authority case, the Mayor, the Governor and the President of the County Board acted as the agents of the affected interests in arranging the compromise; they did not try to impose a solution of their own upon these interests, and when the Governor found that the compromise was not popular with his suburban supporters, he immediately dropped it. In the Exhibition Hall and Fort Dearborn cases, Mayor Daley passed upon proposals that came from unofficial sources, and when he finally ordered a plan made, it was to a large extent a collection of decisions that private bodies had already made or were expected to make. Some opponents of the Exhibition Hall believed that the Mayor hoped they would bring sufficient pressure to bear upon him to cause him to block construction at 23rd Street. They seem to have misunderstood him, but it is nevertheless indicative of the prevailing view of things that they could suppose that a mayor with ample power to decide should secretly hope to be compelled to do what he thought he ought to do. In the public housing case, the "Big Boys" of the City Council had ample incentives to make a housing plan of their own; instead they accepted, rejected, and modified proposals made by the Authority.[12]

The political heads will ratify almost any proposal upon which the principally affected interests agree, and they will postpone as long as they can a decision upon any proposal about which they are not agreed. Knowing this, the interests try very hard to reach "out of court" settlements. Sometimes the political head tells them in so many words that unless they compose their differences and come to him with an agreed-up plan, he will not take action. The principal "civic leaders" are therefore constantly engaged in negotiations with each other, and skill in negotiation is an important base of influence among them.

"Out of court" settlements are not always possible, however, and the time eventually comes when the political head can avoid a decision no longer. When at last he imposes a settlement, it deals only with those aspects of the issue which cannot be put off; it does not go beyond the particular, concrete problem at hand in order to settle general principles or larger issues; and it is based, not on the merits of the issue, but on the principle that everyone should get something and no one should be hurt very much. The political head is satisfied to patch matters up for the time being. He makes no effort to arrange a general settlement of the fundamental issues, and so the basic conflict usually continues, renewing itself in a slightly different form after he has made his decision.

Ryan's handling of the Branch Hospital dispute illustrates the way this works. Ryan put the decision off as long as he could — a matter of many months — and then, instead of formulating a general policy or plan, he appointed a committee to work out a practical solution which he could ratify. In the end, he had to impose a settlement. It was a compromise. The County Hospital was assured that its bond proposals for repair of existing structures would be unopposed and that there would be no immediate development of a South Side branch. At the same time, Michael Reese and the Welfare Council were assured that the West Side branch would not be expanded and that money would be set aside for the eventual purchase of a South Side site. The compromise left the basic issue untouched, and in 1959 the same ground was fought over anew.

In offering an "out of court" settlement to the political head for his ratification or in presenting to him one side of an issue which is still disputed, it is usual to emphasize, so far as the facts of the case permit, the range and public importance of the interests that are allied. To be able to claim that these "represent a broad cross section of the community" is very advantageous, for in general the political head, in making a settlement, is expected to favor widely representative interests.

The "representativeness" of a position is judged in part by the number and character of the civic associations supporting it. The political head has some notion, although very likely not a well-founded or accurate one, of the number of members claimed by each organization, of the degree of their involvement in the particular issue, and of the association's ability to get attention in the press. No doubt he takes these factors into account. But there is another sense in which an association, or a coalition of them, is deemed "representative," and representativeness in this other sense is more important. Each association has created for itself a corporate personality and aura. It has made itself both the custodian and the symbol, as well as the spokesman, of certain values which are widely held in the community and in the name of which it feels especially entitled to speak. Thus, for example, the Welfare Council, in addition to representing as *agent* particular individuals and organizations which stand in a formally defined relation to it, represents as *symbol* the welfare-minded sectors of the community and indeed, in a certain sense, the whole community.

Achieving and maintaining the right symbolic significance is a matter of first importance to the association and one which requires a great deal of attention. The association's influence with the political heads and with prospective contributors, members, and supporters depends in part upon what it "represents" or symbolizes. Projecting the right image of itself is therefore essential to its maintenance as a going concern.

One way to project the right image is to have as officers and directors people who themselves, personally or through their organizational connections, "represent" some part of whatever it is that the association wants to symbolize. By the same token, it is necessary for the association to avoid connections which would introduce an element of inconsistency into its symbolism or make it less clear and intelligible. When the head of one of the civic associations was asked if there were any Negroes on his board, he replied:

> No. We haven't. There has been some discussion of that. And there has been some discussion of having some other groups that haven't been represented. We've stayed away also from ministers and priests. Of course, we did have a president of the Sunday Evening Club and Rabbi ———. We have a reason for that [i.e., not having Negroes or ministers and priests]. It is not because we are not anxious to have their support, but it is a matter of strategy. If there are too many people of that sort, people would say that we are a reform organization and we would lose effectiveness.[13]

The right choice of program material, and especially of issues on which to take a public stand, is another means by which the association projects the desired image of itself. A civic association, Ryan once observed to an interviewer, "has got to keep coming up with something." Unless its clientele feels that it is doing something, it will lose support. But the range of things that it may plausibly do at any given time is very limited. There are usually few, if any, concrete matters on which all elements within it are entirely agreed; taking a strong stand on anything will usually alienate some of its support. The conflicts among the interests it represents as agent are paralleled by others among the community values it represents as symbol: if it cannot have clergymen or Negroes on its board for fear of seeming too reform-minded it cannot, for the same reason, take part in controversies over racial justice or civil liberties.

Even when there are several suitable issues, an association can deal with only one or two at a time. There is a limit to the time of its staff and officers, and — what is usually more important — the press and the political heads will give it only so much of their attention. An association must, therefore, choose carefully how it will allocate its scarce resources: if it pushes this, it cannot push that. For example, a large mail order house, which generally played an active part in civic affairs and which wanted the University of Illinois campus located so as to improve its own decaying neighborhood, nevertheless failed to intervene in the site selection controversy. When asked why not, an executive explained that doing so would reduce the company's effectiveness in other matters:

It could [reduce the company's effectiveness]. Primarily in terms of the public officials. The general public doesn't have the details, but the public officials know what Sears is and is not doing. I might have a session with them on the University of Illinois one morning and that afternoon I might have one on housing. You can only carry so much water and get away with it. This in one of the great problems: knowing where to stop — what to take on and where to stop. You see things that need doing, and you get sucked in.

What has been said about civic associations applies as well to people who play civic roles as "individuals" rather than as spokesmen for associations. (In view of the continuity of their civic roles, these people are, perhaps, better regarded as "informal organizations" than as "individuals".) Like the associations, the "individuals" try more or less consciously to "stand for" or "represent" certain values or certain conceptions of the public interest. They also must continually "come up with something" if they are not to lose prominence, and they must invest their limited stocks of attention-getting devices economically.

The newspapers are in much the same position. They, too, represent certain elements of the community and certain conceptions of the public interest, and so they, too, must project the right images of themselves. Like the civic associations, they are required by the exigencies of organizational maintenance and enhancement constantly to put forward plans for civic betterment and to give the impression that they are accomplishing something. Whether this requirement arises from the professional pride of editors who have been brought up to believe that good journalism is crusading journalism or from reader interest, the fact is that the newspapers are also in search of what the civic associations call "good program material."

The political head's understanding of all this enters into his appraisal of the "representativeness" of the solicitations that are made upon him. He knows that those who come before him have carefully considered the effect upon their organizations (or upon their personal standing if they are "individuals") of taking this or that position. Their presence means that the position they endorse is popular with the membership, or at least that it is not so unpopular as to threaten the maintenance of the organization, and that the leaders think the matter important enough to justify an expenditure of their limited claim upon his attention. Accordingly, the political head, when he sees before him a particular configuration of support and opposition, finds it in clues by which to form an estimate of how the matter is viewed by the public at large. He feels that it is his duty to do what "a broad cross section of the community" wants, and these cues are one way he has of sensing what it is that the community wants.

The political heads employ "civic leaders" as intermediaries in much the same way that the affected organizations employ them. They find it useful to have prestigious laymen represent them with the civic associations, the press, and the public generally. When a controversial question arises, a political head may appoint a "civic leader," or a committee of them, to make a report or even to carry on negotiations for him with the affected parties. Ryan did this in the Branch Hospital case with the appointment of the Cunningham Committee. Daley did it in the Fort Dearborn case with the employment of Downs as a consultant.

Such appointments are usually for the ostensible purpose of giving the political head advice. In fact, however (as the example of Ryan and the Cunningham Committee suggests), the political head is likely to have his mind already made up or, at least, to make it up on grounds other than those supplied by the "civic leaders." He uses his intermediaries for other purposes than those that are publicly announced.

One of these may be to facilitate communication between him and some part of the public. The co-opted leader is someone who has a "following." He therefore becomes the communications link between it and the political head, explaining each to the other. This would be a function of importance in any political system in which unofficial persons play a large part in the making of public decisions. It is especially important in Chicago because differences of social class separate the political head from some sectors of his public and because his occupation — getting and keeping office — is little understood and much distrusted even by those few citizens who come into fairly frequent contact with politicians. There is a need, therefore, for persons who can "speak the language" of both the political head and of those parts of the public with which he must communicate (e.g., bankers, Negroes, social workers, physicians). To play the part of an interpreter effectively, a "civic leader" must have time and interest, a sense of political reality, and the trust and respect of the political head and of that sector of the public with which he is to deal. These qualifications are not easily met. Most business and professional people are oblivious of the local political scene or else contemptuous of it. Many feel uncomfortable in the presence of local politicians and convey the impression — perhaps rightly — of being snobs or stuffed-shirts. Consequently, the rare "civic leader" whose personality, interests, and symbolic attributes (name, dress, speech, church and other affiliations, and so on) enable him to bridge the gap between politicians and others or the gap between one part of the community and another (between Negroes and whites, medical men and patients, Catholics and Protestants) is very much in demand as an intermediary. Cunningham, Ryan's intermediary in the Branch Hospital case, may be taken as an example. A wealthy investment banker, a leading Republican, a prominent Presbyterian, and a Social Registerite, he had the attributes essential for dealing with the business and "old family" elites of Chicago. At the same time, his manner was so free and easy and he cultivated informality so assiduously ("Let's go to my office and get our feet up on the desk") that self-made men from the wrong side of the tracks could be entirely comfortable in his presence. Even his name was conveniently ambiguous: "Jim Cunningham" might be Irish-Catholic.

An even more important function of the co-opted "civic leader" is to legitimate the plans of the political head. In Chicago, politicians are regarded with distrust and career civil servants with mild contempt. If official acts are to have the confidence of the public, they must be approved by laymen whose competence and disinterestedness are considered to be beyond question. Those who have wealth and social position, who are highly successful in business or in a profession, and (what is not very different) who head civic associations are qualified to sanction the politician's acts. Committees of such people are therefore appointed by the political head to give his decisions their approval.

Thus, that Ryan, in the Branch Hospital case, followed, or appeared to follow, the advice of a committee of "civic leaders" — a committee which through no coincidence was predominantly Republican — gave the public assurance that all was well. Cunningham and other big businessmen had scrutinized the plans and endorsed them. That meant to the press and the public that the money was really needed and would be wisely spent.

The political head troubles himself to secure the seal of approval from "civic leaders" not because he could not otherwise get his measures accepted but because having them approved in this way disarms criticism. There was no doubt that the Democratic machine could get its bond proposals approved by the voters in the spring of 1957. Nevertheless, a few weeks before the election Mayor Daley appointed James C. Downs chairman of a committee of about eighty "civic leaders" whose task was to support the bond issue with the public. The "civic leaders," drawn from all neighborhoods, from both parties, and from a wide variety of occupations, were brought to City Hall, supplied with leaflets addressed by the heads of the departments that would administer the money to be voted, and urged by Downs and the Mayor to get the bond proposals endorsed by their civic associations. All this was done although there was no doubt that the Democratic organization could produce a safe margin at the polls. As one of the Mayor's assistants explained later:

The Democrats could have carried it anyway in a primary election. The Democrats can always carry a Chicago primary. But it would be inconceivable to put out a $113 million bond issue without a committee. We would naturally think in those terms.

Having a committee puts the power of "good" on our side and takes it out of politics. It is not a "political proposal" but a "good proposal." How could the press say that these proposals were for more patronage if the men who usually opposed patronage were for it and if the neighborhood committees were for it?

A third function of the co-opted "civic leader" is to draw upon himself pressure or criticism that would otherwise be directed against the political head. Edward Eagle Brown, the banker who headed the advisory committee of the Forest Preserve District, could well afford to ignore those who opposed the District in the Chicago Campus matter. Ryan could not. It was easy, therefore, for Ryan to take refuge behind Brown and the Advisory Committee and to claim that he could do nothing because he could not go against them. Having nothing to lose themselves, Brown and the Committee were glad to afford Ryan the protection he needed. Doing so not only relieved him of some political risks but actually enhanced his bargaining position, for if he could say that it was not within his power to make concessions — that the Advisory Committee had the power, not he — he could not be bargained with, and his position would have to be accepted.

Usually this function is performed by formally co-opted bodies like the Advisory Committee. But bodies which are *not* formally co-opted — civic associations, for example — sometimes deliberately shield a political head against demands that he will find hard to resist. Doing so serves their purpose as well as his. In describing the Civic Federation, a taxpayers' organization, one of its leaders told an interviewer: "Many people in the [local] governments will tell you that the Civic Federation is helpful. It helps them resist government expenditures. Often it is hard for them to say, 'no.' If they can pass the buck by saying that the Civic Federation is opposed, then they can say 'I can't go against the Civic Federation.' It is helpful to them."

The influence of the "civic leader," it has been suggested, depends mainly upon his ability to get the proposals of an affected organization accepted by one or more of the political heads. This, in turn, depends upon his ability to get other "civic leaders" to unite behind the proposals (for the political heads will try to avoid the issue if the community is divided) or upon his potential usefulness (as well as that of the proposals he advances) in conveying to the press and the public — in particular, to the public of the outlying wards and suburbs — an image of the political head that will help win him votes.

There is no telling who may be able to do these things in particular circumstances. In general, however, the requisite abilities are associated with three specialized roles. Every "civic leader" of importance functions now and then in one or more of them; a very few (no more than half a dozen, for, as will appear, the nature of the role itself limits the number who can occupy it at one time) are virtually full-time incumbents of one role or another.

1. *The adviser to the political head.* This is the "civic leader" who frequently serves as the political head's intermediary, who is called in often to advise him on particular problems, and who now and then conducts inquiries or makes plans for major undertakings on his behalf. The adviser must be someone who "speaks the language" of the politician and of the "civic leader," who is respected by the press and the public and trusted by the mayor (if he is too aggressively "on the make" in politics or business, he will not do), and who is able to devote a great deal of time to public affairs. Almost necessarily, he will be a leading executive of a big real estate, banking, architecture, engineering, or other firm which has much at stake in decisions made by the state and local governments.

The adviser is not a leading figure in any of the civic associations and is not closely identified with unpopular or controversial causes. He is near enough to being a member of the political head's administration to feel that he ought to do nothing that might compromise it. The influence that he *might* exercise in some matters is therefore very often rendered nugatory by his association with the political head.

The adviser must have a strong sense of political reality and must be ready to accept the compromises the political head thinks necessary. He is in no sense a politician, however, and his advice is never asked on purely political or party matters. For a Democratic political head, there is often an advantage in having advisers who are Republican in national affairs.

James C. Downs, chairman of the board of the Real Estate Research Corporation and Mayor Daley's planning consultant in the Fort Dearborn case, James A. Cunningham, the investment banker who assisted County Board President Ryan in the Branch Hospital case, and the late Ralph H. Burke, the engineer who figured in the Public Housing case, are examples par excellence of the adviser.[14]

2. *The negotiator.* This is the "civic leader" who characteristically finds the terms upon which other "civic leaders" will agree and who prepares "out of court" settlements for the political heads to ratify. He takes an idea which is generally accepted in principle, formulates it as a practical "project," gets the project accepted by all those interests håving a stake in it, and then "sells" it to the appropriate political heads. He is likely to be a big businessman — in fact, a chairman of the board (only presidents and chairmen can negotiate as equals with other presidents and chairmen, and presidents are often too busy for civic affairs) — and to be on first-name terms with all of the prominent men of the metropolitan area.

The negotiator avoids projects which are not "good for business" and, in this sense, good for the community. He also avoids those which are highly controversial or utopian. He wants to achieve concrete results. He is ready to make compromises where necessary, and therefore he is likely to be criticized by extreme partisans and by those who want to vindicate principles or to achieve victories of a symbolic sort.

The negotiator gets agreement by ingenuity in framing compromises and by skillful persuasion. He has no general stock of incentives from which he can draw to induce co-operation; at the most, he may "give and take" on the matter in hand. He relies mainly upon his ability to devise a plan which will serve all interests and upon diplomacy in presenting it in its most favorable light. He is likely to be one whose personality and experience incline him to try to bring people together in working relationships rather than to advance one interest at the expense of others by hard trading or by engendering conflict. One very successful negotiator told an interviewer:

I wouldn't say that the antagonistic method *never* accomplishes anything. It is just that I couldn't work that way. I'm psychologically unequipped for it. All the people that I've worked with are friends of mine. I made a comment like this to a *Tribune* editor. He said, 'That might be right for *you.*' He could use the meat-axe approach and also he could change his position. I have to maintain consistency.

Holman T. Pettibone, the first head of the Central Area Committee, is an excellent example of a negotiator.[15]

3. *The publicist of policy.* This is the "civic leader" who tries to create a public opinion favorable to certain undertakings. Whereas the adviser and the negotiators almost always work behind the scenes, the publicist is in the limelight, making speeches before civic associations, appearing on television, giving interviews to the press, and publishing endorsements and testimonials.

The publicist is likely to come from one of those occupations — real estate, advertising, public relations, entertainment, or law — in which smooth talking is at a premium. He is not likely to be the active head of a very large corporation. Generally speaking, the heads of big corporations do not seem to be particularly skillful in dealing with people in the mass. In any case, they are seldom willing to appear publicly in controversial matters.

The publicist is of great value to the political head when a "non-partisan" appeal must be made to the voters for approval of a bond proposal or a constitutional amendment.

James C. Downs is, and to a lesser extent the late Earl Kribben was, influential partly by virtue of being effective in this role.[16]

The influence of these roles, it should be noted, does not depend upon the incumbents' having "power" in the sense of great resources from which to apportion penalties and rewards. The publicist does not move the public by offering penalties and rewards. The negotiator does not secure agreement in this way either. The adviser, to the extent that his task is to get co-operation, also gets it by other means. It is true that one who functions well in any of these roles is valuable to the political head. It does not follow, however, that he can bargain to get a high "price" from the political head (i.e., that he can demand the privilege of influencing him); he is "paid" in other ways (e.g., in consultants fees or business advantage, in the satisfaction of doing a public service, and in the "glory" or "fun" of being on the "inside"). Therefore, even if he were inclined to bargain — and of course he may not be — he would have little bargaining power.

In the main, the influence of these "civic leaders" derives from the trust that others have in their judgment and in their disinterestedness. If they get their way, it is likely to be, as one of them put it, "by main force of being right" and not by promising rewards or threatening penalties. Moderate wealth, business position, and even social status are usually necessary conditions for the exercise of influence as a "civic leader." They are not, however, sufficient conditions. Along with them must go qualities that inspire confidence and respect.

It follows that the "civic leader" as such has very little discretion in the influence he exercises. He does not bend others to his will. If he influences them at all, he does so as the agent of an affected organization or of some group or entity, and it is their goals, not his personal preferences, that really count. He is constrained by those goals and by facts and logic. If he is to continue in his role and be influential, he must almost always subordinate his own values, tastes, whims, to these constraints. He can decide for himself whether to be active and whether to be enthusiastic. But that is about the extent of his discretion.

A common, indeed an almost invariable, feature of the process by which an issue is prepared for settlement is a ceremonial appeal to the authority of "objective facts" and "technical experts." Although the issue must, in the last analysis, always be settled on grounds that are political in the broad sense, and although the crucial judgments that are involved — judgments not only about values but about facts and probabilities as well — cannot possibly be made in a purely scientific or technical way, nevertheless the almost unvarying practice is to make it appear that the decision rests upon "objective" and even "factual" grounds. In the Branch Hospital case, the Welfare Council went through elaborate rituals of "research" to show that "from an objective standpoint" the hospital should be on the South Side. In the Chicago Campus case, those who favored and those who opposed the Miller Meadows site employed professional research organizations to prove "objectively" that they were right. In the Welfare Merger case, a firm of management consultants produced a "study" justifying the decisions a Republican senator had reached long before.

This extraordinary devotion to "facts" is often associated with an extraordinary determination to conceal what is really at issue and to direct the discussion along lines that are either irrelevant or less than fully relevant. The main question in the Branch Hospital case was what to do about the Negro. But all mention of the Negro was avoided in two days of testimony before the Cunningham Committee. ("There are," one of the witnesses told the Committee, "a lot of things underlying the surface in connection with this matter, which I hope do not come to the surface, the kind of things that should not be considered, and if they do come I sincerely trust that they will not be discussed.") In the Welfare Merger case, the elaborate factual material that was "picked out of the air" and presented to the legislative committee by the Illinois Public Aid Commission had nothing whatever to do with the reason for proposing the merger in the first place, namely, that the IPAC and the Chicago Commissioner of Welfare could not get along together. This, the cause of the controversy although not the only basis of it, was never alluded to in the testimony.

These strenuous efforts to bring forward "objective facts" and to conceal the underlying realities of the issue are certainly not made for the purpose of fooling the politicians. They are professionals at the game; they know what is at stake, and they are not likely to take facts and figures soo seriously. They are accustomed to using arguments that will seem relevant and convincing to an outsider and that will thus conceal what they — the insiders — know to be the considerations upon which the matter will really turn. The "impartial expert" and his "facts" are recognized by the politicians as forms of "cover"; it is only the amateur following the game in the newspaper who takes them at face value.[17]

The "civic leader," like the "impartial report" and the "expert," is sometimes himself a form of "cover." Whether he realizes it or not, he may be used to divert attention from real issues to spurious ones (or, perhaps more often, to such aspects of real issues as may be conveniently or usefully examined in public) and to provide, not arguments which will influence the decision, but arguments which will satisfy the public and give the politician concealment from which to make the decision on quite other grounds.

The importance of "cover" in these cases is to be explained, perhaps, by a peculiar feature of the American political style, namely, the belief that public business is everybody's business and that public decisions should be open and openly arrived at.

This principle is one that cannot possibly be lived up to in practice. There are many things that cannot be discussed truthfully, or even frankly, in public. Although he usually cannot admit doing so, the politician must look after his own interest and his party's interest. Even when he acts on purely public grounds, he cannot usually put the whole case before the public: there is not time, the public would not understand all the intricacies of it, some people would be unfairly injured by publicity, and conflict would be exacerbated. Even when the real motives of action *can* be explained, rationalizations may be more persuasive. In the Welfare Merger case, for example, it was more plausible to claim that savings would result from the merger than to maintain that Rose was an impossible man to work with. The latter argument would be easy to ridicule and would seem — without, of course, necessarily being — frivolous. "Cover," then, serves the function of giving the politician the privacy he requires in order to do his work. In a political system in which privacy is provided through formal devices, less attention would have to be paid to the various forms of "window-dressing."

1 0

The Mythology of Influence

MANY Chicagoans, including some who are generally well informed about civic affairs, believe that a little group of private persons whose names are in some cases unknown to the general public have ample power to decide any public matter whatsoever. These alleged "top leaders" are the multi-millionaires who control the largest businesses, own the newspapers, and dominate the boards of directors of the civic associations, universities, hospitals, and other public service bodies. They are said to be at the top of a hierarchy of influence the lines of which are so well drawn as virtually to constitute a formal organization. When they give the word, lesser figures below them in the hierarchy — including other business leaders as well as politicians, university heads, clergymen, and so on — are supposed to hasten to do their bidding. According to one businessman who knows his way around Chicago (he owns a firm that grosses more than $100 million a year), the city is run by only four men: "Do you know who really runs Chicago? Who has the real money and power? Four young men: Brooks McCormick of International Harvester; Hagenah of Wrigley's; Calvin Fentress, son-in-law of General Wood, you know; and Marshall Field, Jr. These four young men control the wealth of Chicago. Not many people know that."

The head of a Negro civic association set the number of "top leaders" a little higher. According to him, "There are a dozen men in this town who could go into City Hall and order an end to racial violence just like you or I could go into a grocery store and order a loaf of bread. All they'd have to do is say what they wanted and they'd get it."

Sometimes the "top leaders" are regarded as a conspiracy of the rich to frustrate the workings of democracy.[1] More often, it is assumed that they exercise their influence for the good of the community. The "top leader" — according to this view — is rich enough to put aside his private advantage in most matters (certainly in all small ones), and he is accustomed, by training and position, to take a statesmanlike view of public questions. He may be the representative of a family — the Fields, McCormicks, Ryersons, Swifts, or Armours, for example — that has devoted itself to public service for generations, or he may be the head of a large corporation — Inland Steel, Sears-Roebuck, Field's Department Store, the Chicago Title and Trust Company, for example — that has a long-standing tradition of "civic responsibility." In any case, he is trusted to have good intentions. The Negro leader quoted above was confident that if the facts about racial violence were brought to the attention of the right men, they would give the necessary orders. It was reasonable for him to take their goodwill for granted: most of his organization's support came as gifts from corporations owned or controlled by them.

In Chicago, big businessmen are criticized less for interfering in public affairs than for "failing to assume their civic responsibilities." They themselves seem to agree with this view; those of them who do not exercise influence in civic affairs are apt to reproach themselevs for failing in their duty. The general view seems to be that the "top leaders" ought to unite on some general plan for the development of the city and the metropolitan area.

Frequently, efforts are made in American cities to give official standing to the hierarchy of influence that is presumed to exist. The independent, unpaid planning commission, which is the organizational form into which the city-planning function has been cast in most cities, is, in intention (but not in practice), "top leadership" brought out from behind the scenes and made official. The assumption is that a plan can be carried into the effect if —

and only if — the principal private interests of the city agree upon it.[2]

It may be, as Norton E. Long has conjectured, that "top leadership" is talked about because people feel the need of a government that has power to solve community problems, to deal with community crises, and to make and carry out comprehensive plans. Where the politicians who hold the offices do not regard themselves as governors of the municipal territory but largely as mediators or players in a particular "game" (the great game of politics), the public finds reassurance in the notion that there exists a "they" who are really running things from behind the scenes.[3]

The notion that "top leaders" run the city is certainly not supported by the facts of the controversies described in this book. On the contrary, in these cases the richest men of Chicago are conspicuous by their absence. Lesser business figures appear, but they do not act concertedly: some of them are on every side of every issue. The most influential people are the managers of large organizations the maintenance of which is at stake, a few "civic leaders" whose judgment, negotiating skill, and disinterestedness are unusual and, above all, the chief elected officials. Businessmen exercise influence (to the extent that they exercise it at all) not so much because they are rich or in a position to make threats and promises as, in the words of one of them, "by main force of being right."

These findings do not, however, prove that there is no "they" behind the scenes. Possibly, they were not sufficiently interested in what was at stake in these cases to bestir themselves. Or, possibly they were well satisfied with what was done and saw no need to interfere. Or, again, they may, from considerations of policy, have restrained a desire to interfere (they may have thought interference "undemocratic" or "poor public relations"). Any of these theories, or all of them together, would explain the absence of "top leaders" from the scene and, incidentally, would leave open the possibility that in some future case — one in which their vital interests *are* at stake — they may issue the orders necessary to set in motion the lower echelons of the alleged influence hierarchy.

There is yet another possibility. It may be that the "top leaders" did not exercise their influence, or did not exercise it in earnest, for want of organization and that this want could easily have been supplied if they had cared to take the trouble. If, for example, the four young men who "have the real money and power" had got together for lunch one day and had talked things over, they might have set "policy" with regard to the Fort Dearborn Project, the Branch Hospital, the Exhibition Hall and, for good measure, racial violence. If they had done so, their decisions (according to the theory) would have been quickly communicated down the hierarchy of lesser business leaders, elected officials, managers, and civic association professionals. That they did not get together for lunch was — on this theory — only a matter of "accident" or "mere circumstance." (One of the young men may perhaps have been confined to his home with a painful case of gout, while another was busy skiing in Switzerland). On this theory, there was nothing to prevent the "top leaders" from running things except the difficulties that normally stand in the way of concerting the activities of four busy people. Their failure to exercise influence, then, is to be explained as "mere want of organization." This theory leaves open the possibility that the four young men may some day meet for lunch. If they do, presumably they will then run the city.

With such qualifications as these, the "top leadership" theory is widely held in Chicago. Probably no one with any knowledge of civic affairs supposes that the "top leaders" actually meet frequently to set policy and issue instructions to those beneath them in the hierarchy of influence. But there are many who think that the "top leaders" could do so if they wished and that, for the most part, it is "mere circumstance" that prevents them. The Negro leader quoted above and a white businessman were in fact, trying to arrange a meeting of "top leaders" at which the Negro would present the case for ending racial violence. The white businessman intended to invite some "top leaders" to his home and to introduce the Negro to them there. Lack of communication between the white leaders and the Negro, and among the white leaders themselves, was, the businessman and the Negro believed, the strategic factor in the situation.

These theories are all plausible. It is unquestionably true that

a very small number of men control the principal industries of
the metropolitan area and, if they wish, can have a great deal
to say about how civic associations and other private bodies are
run. No doubt, any four of at least forty men could, if they acted
together and if they exerted themselves fully, exercise a great, and
probably a decisive, influence in such matters as have been
described here. In the Branch Hospital dispute, for example,
Maremont and others raised several thousand dollars to fight
for a South Side site. They could have raised not thousands but
hundreds of thousands or even millions if they had wished. (To
have done so would have been out of proportion to any public
or private benefit, of course, but it would have been possible all
the same). If they had gone to such lengths, the outcome of the
controversy would probably have been different. It is not unlikely,
for example, that if the Urban League had been given a very
large contribution on condition that it support the South Side
branch, its directors would have decided that strengthening the
organization justified a sacrifice of ideological principles. Similarly,
if Ryan had been told that a very large addition to his campaign
fund was contingent upon his support of a South Side branch, he
might have been more sympathetic to it. Evidence that the biggest
businessmen of the metropolitan area were sufficiently aroused
to make such an offer would no doubt of itself have put the matter
in a different light in his eyes.

The political heads, even in the rather rare instances when they
have decided policy preferences of their own, believe that they ought
to be responsive to the wishes of the public and especially to the
wishes of that part of the public which has the most at stake in the
particular matter. As a rule, therefore, the "top leaders," if they
were united and ready to back to the limit a project which was
not obviously contrary to the interest of the community, would
find the political heads ready to co-operate. And even if the
political heads opposed, the "top leaders" might have their way,
although perhaps not in the very short run. For if the twenty or
thirty wealthiest men in Chicago acted as one and put all their
wealth into the fight, they could easily destroy or capture the
machine.

These remote and even fantastic possibilities are mentioned

only to show that the notion of an elite having the abililty to run the city (although not actually running it) is not inherently absurd. Indeed, if influence is defined as the *ability* to modify behavior in accordance with one's intention, there can be little doubt that there exist "top leaders" with aggregate influence sufficient to run the city.

What, then, accounts for their failure to do so? Are the factors that prevent the "top leaders" from exercising their full influence accidental features of the situation — are they "mere circumstance" — or are they an inevitable and necessary part of it?

Business leaders (including some who are at the top of the alleged hierarchy of influence) offer several explanations. Some say that big business is nowadays mainly run by managers rather than by owners. A generation or two ago, the principal enterprises in Chicago were run by owners who took a proprietary interest in the affairs of the community. Now the principal enterprises are run by salaried managers in behalf of stockholders many or most of whom live in other places and who, even if they lived in Chicago, would probably have no common interest in anything except dividends. The managers of today do not identify with the city as fully as did the proprietors of a generation ago: for some of them, Chicago is only an interval in a career that will take them ultimately to New York, Washington, or Los Angeles. Even if the managers did identify fully with the city, they could not exercise as much influence as did the old proprietors because they are subject to boards of directors. "There are not a dozen men in this town who could commit $25,000 without asking a board," Don Maxwell, the editor of the *Tribune,* told an interviewer. "Colonel McCormick could do it, but I can't. There are three of us [trustees of the newspaper] instead of one: that's the difference."

Because his life history and his position in the firm are different, the whole mentality of the manager is different from that of the proprietor, according to this theory. Not only does he lack the proprietor's strong sense of responsibility to the community, but he also lacks his taste for power and for asserting his individuality. He does not want to "run" the community any more than he wants to "run" the business; he is essentially a staff man and a member of a management "team."

This explanation of the absence of effective "top leadership" is weakened by two circumstances. One is that there are still a number of large proprietors on the scene. Henry Crown and Arnold Maremont, for example (not to mention the four young men who "have the wealth and power"), could commit millions of dollars without consulting a board of directors. The other is that many of the managers show both a very decided sense of civic responsibility and a marked taste for power, and are inhibited little, if at all, by their boards of directors. McBain, as head of Field's department store, could back the Fort Dearborn Project extensively without asking anyone's permission. Pettibone, as head of the Chicago Title and Trust Company, had the same freedom. So did the managers of the Inland Steel, Sears-Roebuck, and other large companies. That the *Tribune* was managed by three trustees rather than by a single proprietor did not prevent it from taking the lead in the promotion of the Exhibition Hall.

These objections are not conclusive, however. As James C. Downs has pointed out, most of those who are now managers formed their standards under the tutelage of the proprietors of the last generation. (The trustees of the *Tribune,* for example, got their notions of a newspaper's role from Colonel McCormick, the proprietor who was their boss for many years.) In a sense, then, the present managers are anachronisms: they are living by the standards of the past. As they pass from the scene — and in another decade most of them will have passed from it — their places will be taken by men who will have no firsthand acquaintance with the ways of the old proprietors and who will always have been staff assistants, never dominating personalities.

This process, some say, has already gone so far that the prevailing ethos today is that of the staff assistant, not that of the proprietor as remembered by the manager who worked with him. This new ethos, it is said, has spread to those who, like the four young men who have the "real money and power," are from a legal standpoint proprietors themselves. Having absorbed the prevailing mood and spirit of the times — a mood and spirit set

by the staff men whose style is in the ascendant — today's proprietors are utterly unlike those of a generation ago.

Whether from this cause or from some other, the significance
of the businessman's civic activity may have changed even when
its outward manifestations are the same as they were a generation
ago. If today's manager does the things that were done by the
proprietor of a generation ago, he may do them for different
reasons. What the proprietor did because he believed it good
for the community or for his business, the manager may do because it is good public relations. The proprietor was interested
in objective results and was indifferent to what people thought.
The manager, perhaps, is interested primarily in what people think
and only secondarily in objective results. This may explain why
Field's department store entered so readily into the Fort Dearborn
Project, an undertaking that was of dubious advantage to the
store or to the city. To be good public relations — to demonstrate
that the store took an enlightened interest in the welfare of the
community — it was not necessary that the Project be sound: it
was only necessary that it be plausible.[4]

The absence of effective "top leadership" is sometimes explained
by defects of character on the part of those who are in a position
to lead. Businessmen tell each other that it is only because they
are selfish ("lacking a sense of responsibility to the community")
or without vision that they do not make and carry out comprehensive plans for dealing with fundamental city problems. "The
general attitude is: 'Leave it to the other fellow; send him a check
and hope that it works out.' "

A businessman who thinks only of building his business and of
making money for his stockholders is unfashionably "narrow."[7]
One who sends a check and "leaves it to the other fellow" is not
much better. The man who is admired — the man of "broad"
outlook — gives a large part of his time and energy and much
of his stockholders' money to advance a variety of civic causes.
The trouble is (the business community thinks) that there are
not enough such statesmen at the top of the influence hierarchy.
Most big businessmen, while acknowledging that they "ought"
to "do more for the community," stop far short of doing what
would be necessary to make and carry out a general plan for

the development of the city. Accordingly, they are apologetic about not dealing with fundamentals like the race problem.

I see lip service given in a lot of businesses. But if they were thinking. . . . Hell man, the Commercial Club would form one of these secret fifteen committees: They used to have one on prostitution. They'd talk facts to each other and get at it. . . .

. . . [among businessmen] the most widely discussed topic is the current economic situation, and then politics, and then fishing, and hunting, and hobbies. So it [race relations] is pretty far down the list. By and large, I don't think that very many people bring it up.

Many people told me at the ———— Club, after the presentation, "This is the most important meeting the Club has ever had." I heard no adverse comment. And it was pretty risky to put this thing up in strong black and white terms. We recruited quite a few. . . .

If it is defects of character that prevent big businessmen from concerting their activity to make "policy" for the community, then, as the quotation above suggests, exhortation or "education" may some day improve the situation. This, at any rate, seems to be the assumption on which much of the rhetoric at business luncheons rests.

There are, however, at least three other important circumstances which would radically limit the ability of a business elite to make fundamental decisions. These circumstances would exist if all big businesses were run by proprietors rather than by managers and if all of the proprietors were men of the "broadest" (i.e., the most community-serving) outlook.

1. There exist fundamental conflicts of interest and opinion among the business leaders. Even if only the few men at the very top of the alleged hierarchy of influence are taken into account, these conflicts are such as to make concerted action among them impossible. In part, the conflicts arise on purely business grounds: e.g., what is good for the owners of the downtown hotels is not good for the owners of the amphitheatre, and what is good for the owners of real estate on the north side of the Chicago River is not good for the owners of real estate in the Loop. To suppose that these conflicts would be resolved if the "top leaders" met at lunch is naive. Business is a continuing process of bargaining in which every actor tries to get into the position that is best for him; mutual advantage is constantly being discovered and bargains

struck accordingly. There is no reason to believe, however, that bargains struck by "top leaders" around a luncheon table would represent any improvement in the situation from the standpoint of the community as a whole. There is, moreover, some presumption that where mutual advantage has not already been discovered, there is none to discover.

Where there is no mutual advantage, discussion can lead to nothing unless at least one party is willing to sacrifice his interest from a sense of "civic responsibility." Small sacrifices of business interests are made often, as this study shows, but it is not to be expected that a great or vital sacrifice will be made. Yet little of importance can be done in the city without great or vital sacrifices of some interests.

Even where business interests are not at stake — even in those matters where all actors are sincerely motivated by public-serving ends — there are conflicts that make concerted action impossible. People hold different conceptions of the public interest, and even those who hold the same conception may disagree entirely in their judgments about probabilities.

Race relations, for example, might possibly be improved without impairing the vital interests of any big business. But the differences of opinion among "top leaders" on that subject probably run at least as deep as do the conflicts of business interest. The Negro civic leader who was quoted above may recruit some "top leaders" to his cause. But other "top leaders" will meanwhile have been recruited by the white civic leader whose complaint about "lip service" has just been quoted. This man, an executive of a utility company, fears that Chicago will someday elect a Negro mayor. It will then, he says, be an intolerable place in which to live and do business.

2. Even if there were no such conflicts, the amount of communication that would be required to concert activity in making and carrying out a comprehensive plan would be so great that no time would be left for anything else. Even if there were, in fact, only four "top leaders" in Chicago, the communications problem would not be insignificant. (The problem would exist not only with respect to the four principals but also — and mainly — within the vast empire which each of the four controls.) But Chicago, being

a very large city, has a very large number of autonomous actors who would have to be taken into account; the number of these would certainly be not four but several hundred.

Even if there were a common purpose to which all would willingly subordinate themselves (which of course there is not), so many actors could co-ordinate their behavior only by exchanging a vast number of messages. The number of these would, of course, increase with the number of actors, with the complexity of the co-ordination required, and with the unwillingness of the actors to take direction from a common source.

The amount of communication that would be required to make and carry out a "policy" with regard to just one matter — race relations, for example — would probably overload the capacity of the influence hierarchy, even supposing its members were amenable to making "policy" on that subject. Anyone who has ever tried to get the key members of a large organization to enunciate a new policy and then to communicate that policy down the line to the "field" knows how many days of meetings with vice-presidents, branch managers, supervisors, salesmen, and foremen are necessary and how many conferences must be held to prepare the way for each meeting. If this is the case within a single organization where there is agreement on a common purpose as well as morale and discipline, how much greater is the task where communication must go on outside of a hierarchy and even outside of adherence to a common purpose!

3. Once conflict has been overcome and communication established, organization is necessary to concert activity: a group of "top leaders" who undertook to make and carry out a plan for Chicago would constitute an organization *ipso facto*. But organization, the evidence of this and other studies suggests, soon becomes an obstacle in the way of comprehensive action on fundamental matters. This is because the desire to maintain and enhance the organization tends to displace the ends for which it was formed: the organization becomes unwilling to act on these ends for fear that by acting it may weaken or destroy itself. Not only this, but preoccupation with the maintenance or enhancement of the organization, or with the kind of subject matter that is amenable to being "acted upon by an organization" rather than "thought

about by an individual," tends to turn attention from these ends altogether.

The civic associations that played a part in the cases presented here were generally ineffective because of their preoccupation with their own maintenance. They avoided controversy in order to maintain themselves. Almost without exception, they were split down the middle by the issues raised in these cases. To avoid being weakened (in the conventional formula, "loss of effectiveness"), they did not take positions in important matters. When the proponents or opponents of a position found organization necessary, they usually created *ad hoc* ones. If the *ad hoc* organizations survived to become permanent, they soon became as rigid as the others: they could not go beyond the fixed and narrow limits of the agreements under which they came into existence; sometimes they could not reach even to these limits.

The civic organizations, then, are not likely to deal with controversial problems except in the few uninteresting cases where virtually all members are on the same side. They are likely not only to avoid controversy but even to prevent its arising.

The civic associations, moreover, may get in the way of serious thought and discussion about fundamental problems. When the problem is clear-cut and its solution well understood, they may be an instrumentality for getting something done quickly. But with regard to the most important problems — race relations, for example — it is seldom at all clear what ought to be done. The first need is for persons of exceptional intelligence, information, and judgment to think out the problems together and to come to some general agreement about what ought to be done. Organizations get in the way of this. They feed on activity and publicity, whereas serious discussion must be carried on privately and without much regard to immediate and practical results. As one big businessman — himself the head of an important civic association — explained to an interviewer:

Businessmen are giving more support to the Urban League but they are not basically tackling the race relations issue.

There are no forums where you can discuss it and no vehicles. And you don't want to just stir up something irresponsibly and then not be able to follow through. When you study civic activity, where do you get the *reflective* aspect? People just want action. Most of them just grab an issue pronto and move on. I don't advocate the approach of Plato, but we do need men who can reflect. There is such a difference between seeing the need for a sewer or park and the delicate problems of human relations. This must be more deliberative. . . .

There is the problem of how to set up the civic mechanisms. Where could I sit down in a group and not stir up the newspapers? It must be done carefully to be productive. Where can I sit down with prominent Negro leaders and find out what they want and what the reasonable solutions could be? This [racial and religious problems] is getting into a different sphere of problems. Most people say, "Hip, hip for the merit system" or "let's have more parks." But these problems require more perception.

The staff people, who have the time and are paid to think, spend their time trying to raise money and to maintain the organizations. They just crystallize issues. Where can you get men of talent?

So much is done under the glare of publicity and so much of the publicity is inspired by the organizations themselves. They say, "In 1957 we did blah, blah, blah, blah. . . ." Suppose you said to some people "Let's take a weekend in some hotel and talk things over." What a lack of enthusiasm you'd get!

I know I once spoke to a prominent woman civic leader. I said, "Let's just sit around and chew it over." She was interested for a while and then she lost her interest. It doesn't have quite the dramatic qualities that are needed. They want *action, progress.* . . .

This is not just true of businessmen. It is true because of organizations. Their lifeblood is specific actions. Philosophy has become obsolete, except in the Great Books course. There you can have philosophy. Of course, make sure you don't localize it — don't let it spread over into real activities.

People want to know, "What did you do?" If civic organizations said, "We talked," people would just laugh.

As this suggests, the tendency of the business leader to express his interest in civic affairs by participating in civic organizations focuses attention on those matters which make "good program material" for the associations (that is, matters on which there is general agreement and some prospect of immediate "accomplishment") and tends to withdraw from consideration matters which are too controversial or too difficult to be treated in the few minutes that are left after the monthly luncheon. In lieu of the really significant problems (which often cannot be made into "good program material" *because* of their significance), the civic association atmosphere tends to produce spurious problems. The rhetoric of the "civic leader" is full of plausible-sounding but essentially empty generalities. Here, for example, is the reply of a prominent Chicago attorney to an interviewer's question, "What are the most important things to be done in Chicago?"

I think that in general planning and every phase of civic and community activity should be better integrated and far more broadly based. . . . Planning in the physical sense. The use of land that is embraced in the metropolitan area. That includes the rehabilitation of community areas, a reorientation of land use — all on a comprehensive basis. And it also includes the planning of a political structure that will be comprehensive and inclusive. The present political structure is a hodge-podge. Also in the area of . . . the structure and functions and scope — ah — of those elements of the community organization which are strictly political. There are a great many voluntary agencies that have enormous responsibilities, that operate extrapolitically. And there should be a similar co-ordination of their functions, again on a broad, comprehensive area, wide basis . . . on the metropolitan area basis.

To a considerable extent, "civic leadership" consists of such platitudinizing. (The attorney who made this statement may have been tired or bored during the interview; perhaps in another mood he would have done better. But "civic leadership" often comes from men who are tired or bored.) When, as sometimes happens, such talk results in concrete proposals for action, these usually have to do with problems that are, if not altogether spurious, at least of secondary importance and, in any case, politically hopeless.[6] Nevertheless, there is no denying that such activity serves a social function. In our society, everyone who has attained to a certain standing in the community is under some obligation to interfere in the conduct of public affairs in order to show that he is "civic-minded." Civic "activity" and civic "leadership" afford these people the opportunity to meet this obligation in ways that are, on the whole, innocuous.

The experience of Central Area Committee exemplifies rather well how the three factors to which attention has here been called limit the effectiveness of "top leadership" under even the most favorable of circumstances. The Committee, it will be recalled, consisted of the heads of all the principal businesses having a large stake in the central area of the city. It was formed as an *ad hoc* committee because the civic associations, notably the Association of Commerce and Industry, could not deal with central-area problems without risking internal divisions that might "endanger their effectiveness." The circumstances under which the Committee was created were remarkably auspicious. It had the advantage of limited objectives (to protect real estate values in the inner city) that were of business importance to all of its members. There was available to serve as its full-time chairman the retiring head of the Chicago Title and Trust Company, Holman D. Pettibone, who knew the downtown business community intimately and who possessed extraordinary skills as a negotiator. The city was governed by an all-powerful political machine under Mayor Daley, whose general outlook and political situation disposed him to favor the general objectives of the Committee.

One would think that if there ever was an occasion when the "top leadership" of a big city would make and carry out a comprehensive plan, this was it.

In fact, as the evidence of these cases shows, the Committee did not accomplish very much. It helped create an atmosphere in which the Mayor was encouraged to move a little faster than he might otherwise have moved. It enlarged somewhat the area of agreement among its members, or, at least, it helped find terms on which they would compromise; no doubt this removed some obstacles that might have slowed the Mayor, and no doubt it gave him incentive to press forward. The Committee did not, however, make a plan for the central area nor did it cause the Mayor to have one made. The big decisions with respect to such matters as the Fort Dearborn Project, the branch of the University of Illinois, and the Exhibition Hall turned mainly on considerations of parochial and sometimes private advantage and not at all on any grand strategic conception laid down by Pettibone or other "top leaders." If there existed any guiding conception at all, which is very doubtful, it was in the minds of the Mayor and of James C. Downs, a businessman (but not a "top" one) who functioned as an adviser to the Mayor and not as one of a clique of "civic leaders."[7]

Not only did the Committee fail to make a general plan for

development, but it failed also to take a decided stand on those particular matters — the CTA subsidy and the Fort Dearborn Project, for example — that were clearly of decisive importance to the future of the central city. As the case studies show, conflicts of interest and opinion cut across the business community in so many directions that effective action was out of the question. But even if the business leaders agreed, there were others (e.g., the Mayor and the General Services Administration in the Fort Dearborn case) who had contrary views and without whose cooperation no agreement could be carried into effect. Despite the energetic and talented efforts of Pettibone and others to bring all of the parties to these issues together, failures of communication were often decisive. (In the Fort Dearborn case, for example, the Mayor and the Sponsors seem never to have understood each other's basic positions.) And, as its pusillanimity in the CTA case showed, the Committee was prevented by considerations of organizational maintenance from doing some of the most important things that it was set up to do.

Although the businessmen, who have so much at stake in the metropolitan area, cannot themselves, because of the nature of their ends and the constraints upon their roles, make or carry out a plan for the area, they believe that local government can and should do so. One of the largest real estate men in Chicago told an interviewer:

I think that with the tremendous changes that have taken place in technology and living, it has become a matter of rebuilding cities. And I don't think most of them [the very wealthy] visualize this. And for some reason or another — and this is awfully hard to see — neither do the public servants. The things the city is doing, with the exception of the expressways and the garages . . . amount to very little. It is a piecemeal program. Certainly the public servants are providing no leadership. And the one place where there should be leadership is in the Plan Commission, and they've done damn near nothing. What planning there is, is by small groups here and there and it is *forced* on the city. For example, the Medical Center, Michael Reese, the University of Chicago area, and the housing authority programs. . . .

When the businessman tries to account for the failure of government to give the general direction he thinks is needed, he speaks of defects of organization — defects which in principle might easily be corrected and which are thus, in a sense, accidental or extraneous features of the situation — and of defects of character on the part of officials. These same factors are, of course, according to the mythology, all that stands in the way of informal government by a "power elite" of businessmen. But businessmen, even those of them who see clearly that business cannot formulate a plan for community development, often fail to see that government, for much the same reasons, cannot formulate one either. In the quotation above, the speaker complains of lack of leadership by public officials. When he was asked how he accounted for this lack, he said:

Well, I think many of the wrong people are appointed and many of the good ones get discouraged. Here is a case in point. It happened very recently. The Mayor said to Bach [the commissioner of planning], "Call a meeting and approve the 23rd Street site for the Convention Hall." So the Department of Planning calls a meeting and tries to put that over. If Bach had any guts, he wouldn' take that. He's too much of a Milquetoast guy.

The idea that there would be effective planning in Chicago if only the mayor had the "right attitude" or if only the planning commissioner had more "guts" is on a par with the idea that businessmen themselves could make and carry out a plan if only they had a stronger sense of civic responsibility. The fact is that some essential features of the political system, among them the structure of influence and certain deeply ingrained political habits and traditions, constrain all participants, the mayor no less than the planning commissioner, to act very much as they do. If the planning commissioner defied the mayor, he would at once be replaced by a commissioner who would not defy him. If the mayor had a planner's cast of mind (he would not have one, of course, for if he did he would never get to be boss in the first place), he would not be able to make the trades that keep him in office and give him power. To be sure, his power is great enough, thanks to the machine and to his ability to make the trades the planners deplore, so that he can exercise wide discretion in almost any matter. But being able to exercise discretion in almost any matter does not mean that he can exercise it in *all* matters. With respect to any one or two, or any few, moves, he is free. But if he wishes to stay in the game and to win, most of his moves, like most of the moves of the "civic leaders" and the businessmen in *their* games, must be determined by the exigencies of the game itself. Like them, he must act as the game requires or else get out of it.

PART III

I I

Concerting Action
by Influence

I_N earlier chapters, attention was centered upon the extreme formal decentralization of authority which is so striking a feature of the Chicago political system.¹ This formal decentralization, it was pointed out, must somehow be overcome by an informal centralization before anything can be done. The case studies may therefore be read as accounts of how informal centralization is achieved, or, more precisely, how it is attempted. The paradigm is as follows: the actions of many persons, each of whom has independent authority, must be concerted for a proposal to be adopted; the proponents of the proposal try to concert these actions by exercising influence — by persuading, deceiving, inveigling, rewarding, punishing, and otherwise inducing; meanwhile the opponents exercise influence either to prevent the actions from being concerted or to concert them in behalf of some alternative proposal which they prefer.

In this chapter, this simple conceptual scheme is elaborated into a formal model having application to all situations in which the activity of two or more actors, each of whom is free to give or withhold his activity, is to be concerted. Although intended primarily to describe politics in a metropolitan area, the model treats what Barnard and some others make the defining characteristic of all organization, namely, the conscious concerting of action to achieve a purpose.

307

It will be seen that the frame of reference, the principal concepts, and the basic assumptions and hypotheses about relations among concepts (approximately the first three-fourths of the chapter) are all based upon the empirical findings of the earlier chapters. These empirically-grounded assumptions and hypotheses are not "proved" by the data of these chapters (strictly speaking, they could only be disproved), but the data do not contradict them and they give some support to some of them. Some additional hypotheses (presented in the remaining fourth of this chapter) are derived by logical deduction from the empirically-grounded ones which constitute the basic framework of the model. If when tested — and some of them cannot be tested by any data in this volume — these derived hypotheses prove false, doubt will be cast upon the factual premises from which they were deduced. Thus the model is both a way of generating hypotheses (for some of the derived hypotheses could not possibly have been suggested by the data and others would probably have been overlooked if attention had not been turned in the right directions by the model) and of testing the basic assumptions and hypotheses upon which it is built. Some of these assumptions and hypotheses cannot be tested directly: disproving what is logically implied by them is the only way of disproving them; here the model is particularly useful.

To explain to the reader what support the findings of this volume give each of the premises of the model and how far each of the logically derived hypotheses accords with the evidence would involve much repetition and would get in the way of the explication of the model itself. It is left to the reader, therefore, to decide for himself how far the data of this and other studies fit the assumptions and hypotheses. References in this chapter to the case studies are intended only to illustrate the meaning of statements, not to supply evidence of the truth of them.

The frame of reference, then, is one in which a proposal is to be adopted or not adopted. In Chicago, proposals arise, proximately if not ultimately, from the maintenance and enhancement needs of large formal organizations. This fact, however, need not enter into the model: it is enough for present purposes that a proposal exists and that it is to be adopted or not adopted.

Performance of a specified set of actions by specified actors, or by a specified number of, or proportion of, the actors who constitute a specified group,[2] constitutes *adoption,* i.e., adoption is defined as the performance by these actors of these actions, which will be called *requisite* actions. (In the Branch Hospital dispute, for example, the casting of affirmative votes by a majority of the county board and by a majority of voters in a referendum were the requisite actions.) An actor who can perform a requisite action has *authority* over the action. He may perform it or not as he likes, or, in the language to be used here, he may *give* or *withhold* it from the system of activity being concerted toward adoption of the proposal.

An actor may, if he chooses, place himself under the control of another, either of one who has authority or of one who has not. One actor is under another's *control* when he gives or withholds action at the other's direction, i.e., becomes the other's agent. (The Democratic majority of the County Board gave and withheld its vote according to instructions from Ryan; it was therefore under his control.)

Control may be pyramided. That is, an actor who has authority may accept control by a second actor, who in turn accepts control by a third, who in turn accepts control by a fourth, and so on. (The Cook County Democrats in the legislature were controlled by Senator Lynch, who was himself controlled by Mayor Daley.) Such a situation is represented in Diagram 1.

Diagram 1

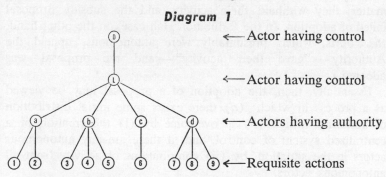

←— Actor having control

←— Actor having control

←— Actors having authority

←— Requisite actions

When, as in Diagram 1, all requisite actions are under the control of a single actor, control is *centralized.* Centralization decreases as the number of requisite actions under separate control increases. Thus if L were to lose control of a, there would be a decrease in centralization, and if D were to lose control of 8, there would be a further decrease.

In any situation there may be (but not always are) actors who cannot be controlled. These will be called *autonomous*. (A judge who bases his decisions solely upon the law is autonomous; so is a voter who votes on principle rather than in return for favors.) An autonomous actor may or may not take a position with respect to a proposal.[3]

There is no way of knowing in advance whether an autonomous actor will give or withhold his action.

Unless control over all controllable actors is centralized and unless all autonomous actors give the requisite actions under their control (either by affirmative action or by their failure to withhold them), a proposal cannot be adopted. Adoption (by definition) is constituted by the contribution of the entire set of requisite actions.

It follows that whether a system of activity can be concerted for the adoption of a proposal always remains uncertain until it has been discovered whether there are autonomous actors in the situation and, if there are, whether they will give their activity. (In the Chicago Transit Authority case it turned out, contrary to the general expectation, that the Governor's chief legislative leaders were — if their story be believed — autonomous in that matter; they withheld their activity, and the subsidy proposal failed of adoption. In the Exhibition Hall case, on the other hand, the courts, which presumably were autonomous, upheld the Authority — "gave their activity" — and the proposal was adopted.)

Essentially, then, the adoption of a proposal may be viewed as a process in which: (a) there exists some initial distribution of authority, which (b) is overcome by (i) the creation of a centralized system of control, and, if there are any autonomous actors in the situation, by (ii) contributions of activity from all antonomous actors.

If we think not of a single proposal but of a flow of them, we may describe two stages by which the system of control comes into being. In the first stage there occurs a partial centralization, which is stable from proposal to proposal, and in the second, centralization is completed (or not completed) by the laying down of *ad hoc* lines of control.

1. When two or more actors come under the control of another on a continuing basis, i.e., from proposal to proposal, a *structure* of control exists. (Thus, for example, the Mayor's control of the city council, the Governor's control of the legislature, and a newspaper's control of "civic leadership" constitute structures, since they exist with respect to all proposals in a series.)

Centralization of control therefore necessitates a linkage of structures where structures exist. In the situation presented in Diagram 2, some requisite actions are controlled on a continuing basis by A (the mayor), others by B (the governor), others by C (the president of the county board), and still others by D (a newspaper). Control is thus partially centralized in four structures, and a proposal may be adopted if the action of the four actors (A, B, C, and D) who control the structures can be concerted.

Diagram 2

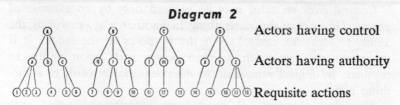

Actors having control

Actors having authority

Requisite actions

2. In the second stage of centralization, the remaining elements of decentralization must be overcome by the creation of *ad hoc* lines of control. In other words, structures must be linked by control relationships established to secure adoption of a particular proposal (when structures are linked on a continuing basis they constitute, by definition, a single larger structure); this in a given case may involve the laying down of many *ad hoc* lines of control or of few. If, for example, in the situation presented in Diagram 3 the newspaper (D) were to establish control with respect to a particular matter (an exhibition hall, let us say) over the three political heads (A, B, and C) and thus over the structures they control, control would thus have been centralized by the laying

Diagram 3

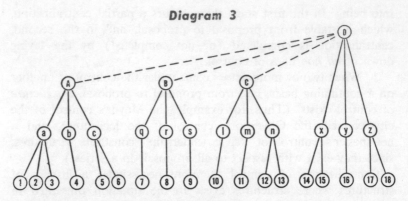

down of three *ad hoc* lines of control.

There must always be at least one *ad hoc* relationship in a centralized system of control. This is because sets of requisite actions, although they may be nearly the same from proposal to proposal, cannot be exactly the same. (If they were, one centralized structure of control would suffice for the adoption of all proposals, and the problem under discussion here would cease to exist.)

Control over an actor may be secured only by an exercise of power. Or, to say the same thing in another way, *power* is the ability to establish control.[4] For the purposes of the model, it is not useful to distinguish whether power rests upon ability to persuade by logical argument, to offer material reward, or something else.

No actor — except, of course, an autonomous one — ever gives a requisite action unless control over him has first been established by an exercise of power. That is to say, the actor must be persuaded, deceived, bribed, or otherwise induced to accept control, or else he will not give the requisite actions.

An actor has a limited stock of power which he gives up piecemeal, or "spends." His power is like capital: he can either "consume" it or "invest" it.[5] If he consumes it, it is "used up," and he does not have it any more. To say, then, that a certain actor could by exercising all of his power achieve a certain effect is seldom much to the point. For there are likely to be circumstances — especially the need to maintain a stock of power for use on future occasions — which prevent him from exercising all of it.

(In the Chicago Transit Authority case, for example, the Governor probably could have induced his legislative leaders to support the subsidy proposal by offering them large favors in return. But he had to think of the other things he could do with the same expenditure of his limited stock of influence — other items of his legislative program that he could get adopted, for example —, and he may have concluded that he could not afford to pass the subsidy proposal, even though it was within his ability to do so.)

Every actor seeks to maintain or increase his stock of power. That is, capital is always "invested," never "consumed." An actor exercises power only when he thinks doing so will improve his net power position (he may, of course, invest to minimize losses); when there are alternative investment possibilities, he always chooses the one he thinks will be most profitable.

To maintain control of a structure, repeated investments of power are required. (Daley, for example, could maintain control of the City Council only by continual outlays of patronage to ward committeemen.)[6] It is not useful to try to specify in the model how frequent these outlays must be; it is enough to say that the maintenance of a structure is a continuing cost to the actor who controls it.

In making his choice of investments, an actor takes into account the uncertainty of the return as well as its probable value. Uncertainty characterizes the situation in three ways particularly:

1. It is seldom clear who controls requisite actions. (In the Chicago Campus case, for example, it was not clear whether Ryan could dispose of Miller Meadows or whether he had given control of it to the Advisory Committee.) Power may be wasted by establishing control over actors who, it turns out, do not control requisite actions. Or an actor may fail to acquire control because he guesses incorrectly either that the other does not control certain requisite actions or that the actions are not worth the price asked for them. (The Chicago Housing Authority, for example, vastly underrated the value to it of control over the leading aldermen.)[7]

2. The terms upon which control may be acquired (assuming that it may be acquired at all) are established through a process of bargaining.[8] Therefore the terms cannot be known in advance.

The actor may waste power in futile efforts to acquire control, or he may spend more power than he would have to spend if he had perfect information. (There was no doubt that Mayor Daley was the key to the situation in the Fort Dearborn case, but how he could be influenced and whether he could be influenced were matters of great uncertainty.)

3. These and other uncertainties (e.g., how the actor will evaluate the investment opportunities open to him) make it difficult or impossible to predict whether or not an actor will exercise power in a given situation. (The Exhibition Hall controversy, for example, was sustained for a time by the proponents' hope that the Mayor would intervene to prevent building on the lakefront.)

The matter is further complicated because there are various *kinds* of power, and an actor who will respond to one kind may not respond to another. Even if an actor does respond to a certain kind of power, a larger (i.e., costlier to the powerholder) investment of it may be required to secure control over him. In other words, the kinds of power (and this is the defining characteristic of a kind) are very imperfectly substitutable one for another; the terms of substitutability, when substitutability exists, are unique to the transaction. This, of course, introduces additional uncertainty into the situation.

For present purposes, it is useful to distinguish four kinds of power. These belong to two (cross-cutting) categories, each of which is comprised of two classes:

CATEGORY I

Class A. Power which arises from the sacrifice of a proposal. A proposal is sacrificed when it is either killed or compromised. It is *killed* when its adoption is rendered impossible; it is *compromised* when an anomaly or inconsistency is introduced into it. Compromises may occur incrementally: the proposal has, so to speak, detachable features which can be given up one at a time to "buy" control. Power of this kind will be called *proposal-costly*. (In the Branch Hospital case, Ryan was able to get the proponents of the South Side branch to withdraw their opposition to the bond issue only by dropping plans for building on the West Side and by promising to build eventually on the South Side.

Thus this exercise of power depended upon a sacrifice of his initial proposal: it was the sacrifice which generated the only power which would work in the circumstances.)

Class B. Power which arises otherwise than from the sacrifice of proposals. This kind of power, which will be called *proposal-costless,* is a residual category.· It is not necessary to inquire where it comes from.

CATEGORY II

Class A. Power which makes its effect by offering gains or losses which the responding actor values for his own sake or for the sake of some small private circle belonging to him (e.g., family, friends). Power which operates in this way will be called *private-regarding.*

Class B. Power which makes its effect by offering gains or losses which the responding actor values for the sake of something (e.g., value, group, public) that transcends (although it may include) him and his small private circle. Power which operates in this way will be called *public-regarding.* (If Mayor Daley had had only public-regarding power, he could not have controlled the City Council. For the councilmen, in most instances, responded only to private-regarding power, e.g., jobs, favors, and recognition. Daley himself, on the other hand, responded to public-regarding as well as to private-regarding power: in the Fort Dearborn case, for example, considerations of the public interest had more weight with him than did private political advantage.)

In some situations a rule specifies that certain types of private-regarding power may not be exercised (offered or responded to). Violation of this rule is *corruption.* Whether in particular circumstances control can be secured corruptly is always problematic. The larger the bribe, however, the better the chance that it will succeed. Even where corruption is possible, the cost of it may be so high that the powerholder finds the investment unprofitable.

Although the several kinds of power cannot be used with perfect interchangeability, there may exist in the situation mechanisms by which one kind is linked to another. In Diagram 4, A (a civic association) has only public-regarding power and B (a mayor) will respond only to public-regarding power. But B's control of x, y, and z (councilmen) depends entirely upon private-regarding power: that is, x, y, and z will not respond to public-regarding power. Thus A is able to control x, y, and z because — and only because — B responds to one kind while exercising another. An actor (or a grouping of actors) who performs this function will be called a *connector*.

Diagram 4

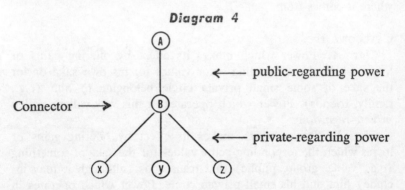

Any proposal is likely to be opposed. An opponent follows one or more of five strategies.[9]

1. He may attempt to prevent the centralization necessary for adoption of the proposal which he opposes. This he may do: (a) by discouraging a key actor from acquiring control over some requisite action (e.g., by raising the "price" of that action through competitive bidding or by offering the actor other and more profitable opportunities for the investment of his power) or (b) by himself acquiring control over a requisite action and then withholding the action. (In the Exhibition Hall case, the opponents hoped to control the newly elected State Treasurer and thus to withhold the requisite action — purchase of the Authority's bonds — over which he had authority. In the Branch Hospital case, opponents of the West Side branch threatened to withhold votes needed in a bond referendum.)

2. He may by an act of power establish *ad hoc* control over the centralized system. He may, in other words, secure control over that single actor who can give or withhold the entire set of requisite actions and may then use this control to kill the proposal. (This happens when someone persuades the governor to veto a bill.)

Diagram 5

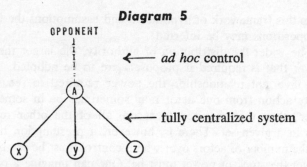

Such a situation is represented in Diagram 5.

3. He may exercise power so as to cause autonomous actors to take positions (as, for example, by appealing to a court for an injunction). Since there is always some chance that an autonomous actor who takes a position will withhold his action, it is to the opponent's interest both to discover which actors in a situation (if any) are autonomous and to cause them to take positions.

4. He may secure adoption of an alternative proposal which will vitiate the one he opposes. To do this he must of course establish control over the set of actions requisite to the alternative. (In the Branch Hospital case, for example, one set of actors tried to centralize control on behalf of a South Side site; another set tried to centralize control on behalf of a West Side one, and still a third set — the "race men" — tried to centralize control on behalf of having no county hospital at all.)

5. He may secure adoption of a proposal changing the set of actions requisite for adoption of the proposal he opposes. This is *constitutional revision*. Ordinarily an opponent finds it more difficult to revise a constitution than to kill a particular proposal: the set of requisite actions needed for revision is usually large and difficult to centralize. But if the opponent can change the set of actions requisite for adoption, he may make adoption more difficult, or perhaps altogether impossible, either by increasing the distribution of authority or by introducing autonomous actors. (If, for example, the opponents of the Exhibition Hall could have revised the constitution to require voter approval of such expenditures, they might have rendered adoption impossible.)

From this framework of hypotheses and assumptions the following propositions may be inferred:

1. The wider the distribution of authority, the larger the stock of power that is required if proposals are to be adopted. This is not an invariant relationship: the power required to secure one requisite action from one actor may sometimes be in some sense "greater" than that required to secure all of the other requisite actions in a given set. There is, however, a presumption that the larger the number of actors over whom control must be established, the larger the stock of power must be. One can imagine a political system in which there is seldom or never enough power to overcome the decentralization of authority. Similarly, one can imagine one in which authority is so highly centralized that little power need be exercised to secure adoptions. One would expect fewer proposals to be adopted in the first than in the second.

In Chicago, the previous chapters have shown, the distribution of authority is so wide that a large apparatus of informal power — notably the Democratic machine — is required to overcome it if anything is to be done. Mayor Daley, it was suggested, could cease being a boss if his authority were very greatly increased. On the other hand, if the machine were dismantled without there occurring any compensating centralization of authority, the city government would be paralyzed.[10]

2. As the number of autonomous actors in a situation increases, the probability of adoptions decreases. This is so because there is some probability that an autonomous actor will choose to withhold a requisite action.

3. As the number of autonomous actors increases, control tends to become less structured. Structures of control, i.e., relationships which are stable from proposal to proposal, are expensive to maintain. The value of a structure — and thus the amount that will be invested in it — tends to decline as the outcome of the process (viz., adoption or non-adoption) becomes less and less subject to control. If, for example, it is made easier to bring a proposal before the voters or the courts (assuming these to be autonomous), the value of a political head's control of the legislature (i.e., a structure) is thereby depreciated, and his incentive to maintain control is reduced.

4. In a situation where there are good investment opportunities (e.g., wide distribution of authority, few autonomous actors or none, relatively small structures of control, scarcity of capital, little uncertainty, and many proposals), there is a tendency toward capital accumulation and investment: large numbers of actors try to enter the game and by the investment of small amounts of power to acquire more. Throughout most of its history, the political system of Chicago (as contrasted with that of, say, London, where authority is highly centralized and most actors are autonomous) has favored political entrepreneurship. To be sure, Mayor Daley has in recent years created a monolithic structure of influence. But, as an earlier chapter explained, he encourages efforts to influence him because such efforts give him a sense of the intensity with which views are held and of the representativeness of the would-be influencers.[11] Thus, although he has a virtual monopoly of the final decisions, there remain strong incentives for others to get power and to bring it to bear upon him. As the case studies show, many people play hard at this game.

5. Conditions causing uncertainty (e.g., presence of autonomous actors, absence of structures, and specialization in kinds of power) tend to encourage investment by those who want to make quick gains ("speculators")[12] and to discourage investment by those who are content with relatively small and safe returns.

6. Circumstances which tend to increase the level of investment (particularly, perhaps, of speculative investment) tend also to increase the probability that any given proposal will be opposed. Opposing proposals in order to extort a payment from the proponents (e.g., perhaps a compromise on another, logically unrelated, proposal) may in some situations be a most profitable form of investment. If so, it will be one of the channels into which new investment is attracted. (In the Exhibition Hall case, Craven sued the Authority in order to improve his bargaining position with the State Department of Agriculture on another matter. Thus, presumably, the possibility of influencing the Department of Agriculture — i.e., an opportunity to make a good investment of power — had the effect of engendering opposition to the Exhibition Hall.)

7. An actor who controls a structure (i.e., whose control is maintained from proposal to proposal) can trade control over

requisite actions belonging to one set (i.e., having reference to one proposal) for control over requisite actions belonging to another set (i.e., having reference to a different proposal). Control of a structure also puts an actor in a position to "borrow": he can secure control of certain actions now by pledging to give control over other (perhaps unspecified) actions at a later time. Such trading and borrowing increase the amount of power available to the actor with respect to a particular proposal, or at a particular time, over what it would be if there were no trading or borrowing. This gives him an advantage over actors who, since they do not control structures, must operate on an *ad hoc* basis.

8. The more power an actor has, the less he will be affected by uncertainty in his efforts to secure control. For the small powerholder, there may be uncertainty *whether* he can obtain the control he wants. For the large one, the uncertainty is only as to the amount of the investment that will be required.

9. The more kinds of power an actor has, the greater the probability that he can secure control in a given case. An actor who has only one kind runs the risk, no matter how much of that one kind he has, that it will prove to be the "wrong" kind: i.e., that it will not work in particular cases.

10. The probability of adoptions (and the probability that there will not be much compromise) tends to increase as the correspondence improves between the kinds of power that powerholders have at their disposal and the kinds to which actors will respond. The probability is highest where the kinds are perfectly matched.

11. Where the distribution of power is highly specialized by kind (i.e., where the actors over whom control is sought respond differentially to many kinds of power) and where the kinds of power at the disposal of powerholders do not match this distribution well, connectors perform an indispensable function. In such situations, the more connectors (up to a point) the greater the probability that proposals will be adopted (and that they will be little compromised).

12. The "economies of scale" that arise from controlling a structure and from having a large and varied "inventory" of power give a cumulative advantage to certain actors and thus may lead

to structural centralization: i.e., oligarchy or dictatorship (oligopoly or monopoly). (Mayor Daley's power, for example, has "snowballed": having control of a few key wards, he got control of the party machinery in the county; having that, he elected himself mayor; being mayor he could give or withhold jobs, favors, and advantages of all kinds; his position thus became so pre-eminent that political possibilities — "investment opportunities" — are presented to him first as a matter of course.)

13. The structuring of control (i.e., creation of a stable partial centralization) may make possible adoption of proposals which could not be adopted if control were completely unstructured. A proposal which would not attract investments of power if it were necessary to construct an entirely *ad hoc* system of influence to secure its adoption may attract investment if it is possible to make use of a partial centralization which is already in existence and which will cost no more to maintain because of the added use. (Daley maintains complete control of the City Council; all but two of its members are Democrats and no Democrat has ever voted against a Daley proposal. The costs of maintaining this structure are fixed ones: to have an additional measure passed by the Council does not ordinarily cost the Mayor anything extra. If he did not maintain control on a continuing basis — if he had to establish it *de novo* for each proposal — the cost of passing an additional measure would seldom be negligible.)

14. In situations where there is a shortage of power in relation to profitable opportunities for its exercise (i.e., a shortage of investment capital), there will be a tendency to kill some proposals and to compromise others in order to increase the supply of power. It need not be assumed that powerholders will (assuming interchangeability) exhaust their stocks of proposal-costless power before using any of their proposal-costly power: whenever proposal-costless power is used up, the other — if there is any of it left — *must* be resorted to. It follows that an increase in the supply of power may — but need not necessarily — reduce the sacrifice of proposals. (The Mayor never sacrifices proposals to get them through the City Council: in the Council he has ample proposal-costless power resting upon patronage and favors. In his dealings with the Governor, on the other hand, he does not have, or cannot

use, patronage and favors. To get power to bargain with the Governor, he must therefore sacrifice proposals. If his stock of proposal-costless power were to increase — as it would, for example, if occasion arose for him to decide whether to slate a strong or a weak candidate against the Governor — it would then be possible for him to make fewer sacrifices in proposals. He might, however, choose to sacrifice them rather than to employ the other power at his disposal.)

15. When public-regarding power does not suffice to meet the needs of a system (either because there is not enough of it or because those over whom control is to be established will not respond to it), there will be a tendency to employ private-regarding power in its place. Where this is against the rule, corruption occurs (by definition). Other factors (especially the supply of and demand for public-regarding power) being held constant, corruption will tend to increase as the distribution of authority widens. (To get anything done in Chicago, numerous independent office-holders must be induced to act otherwise than as their official roles prescribe. In some cases reasonable argument based upon a conception of the public interest is a sufficient inducement. But the number who must be induced is usually large, and there are likely to be some who must be offered patronage, favors, and other bribes. Many kinds of bribes are generally considered legitimate [it is not dishonorable, for example, for a political head to endorse a legislator as the price of getting his vote][13] and most of them are technically legal. But legitimate bribes shade off by imperceptible degrees into illegitimate and illegal ones, and even though the illegality of a bribe is beyond question, it may as a practical matter be impossible to establish that it has been given. For example, a mayor may much against his inclination tacitly tolerate inefficiency and even graft by "looking the other way" because to do otherwise would destroy informal control essential to his main purposes. If he had more authority, or if the independent office-holders would respond to arguments about the public interest or to legitimate bribes, he would not find it necessary to tolerate graft.)

It will be seen that the model may be employed normatively.

Any political system incorporates or exemplifies values lying along continua having the following extreme positions:

1. All proposals should be adopted (radicalism).
2. No proposal should be adopted (conservatism).
3. No proposal should be compromised (planning).
4. The distribution of authority should be very wide (checks and balances).
5. All actors would be autonomous (democracy, classical conception).
6. Only public-regarding power should be employed.
7. There should be no corruption.

Obviously these requirements cannot all be met at once. Any political system must somehow compromise the competing values; even if overwhelming importance is attached to one value, the others cannot usually be entirely neglected: some weight must be accorded to all, even though this be at the expense of the most valued. Gains in terms of some values must be weighed against losses in terms of others. (Chicago might decrease corruption, but doing so would either require centralization of authority or — since the supply of power would be less — would make adoption of proposals harder and compromise of them more frequent.) It is very difficult to judge in even an approximate way how a change in respect to one value would affect the situation with respect to all of the others. And if these functions were known, it would be even more difficult to judge what should be the terms of the compromise.

I 2

Influence and the
Public Interest

Sometimes will say that a political system such as has
been described here can rarely produce outcomes that are in the
public interest. If actions profoundly affecting the city's development are based not on comprehensive planning but on compromises patched up among competing parochial interests, if
political heads are less concerned with the content of policy than
with maintaining a voting alliance between the machine-controlled
inner city and the suspicious suburbs and if the possessors of great
private fortunes and the heads of big corporations cannot, despite
all their talk of "civic responsibility," act concertedly for public
ends — if all this be the case, then Chicago's future welfare depends (some will say) not so much upon the processes of government as upon that special providence that is reserved for fools and
drunkards.

The great defect of the Chicago political system (those who
take this view will say) is that it does not provide sufficient central
direction. There are many special interests on the scene, each of
which looks after itself and cares only incidentally, if at all, for
the welfare of the community as a whole. Action in public matters
is largely a by-product of the struggles of these special interests
for their own advantage. What is needed (the critics will conclude)
is a central public authority which will survey the entire metropolitan scene, form a comprehensive, internally consistent conception

of what must be done for the good of the whole, and then carry that conception into effect without compromise. This is what the advocates of "planning" and "efficient metropolitan organization" have in mind.

It seems clear that there is a tension between the nature of the political system, on the one hand, and the requirements of planning — of comprehensiveness and consistency in policy — on the other. In part, this tension arises from the decentralization so characteristic of the Chicago political system; despite the trend of recent years toward formal centralization and despite the extensive informal arrangements for overcoming decentralization, no one is in a position to survey the city — much less the metropolitan area — as a whole and to formulate and carry out a comprehensive policy. (Mayor Daley, despite his great power as boss, can do little even in the city proper without at least tacit support from the governor.) In part, too, the tension arises from a general premise of our political culture: the belief that self-government consists, not in giving or withholding consent at infrequent intervals on matters of general principle, but rather in making influence felt in the day-to-day conduct of the public business. So long as particular interests can prevent the executive from carrying out his policy, or so long as they can place hazards and delays in the way of his carrying it out, they can demand concessions from him as the price of allowing him to act. It is the necessity of constantly making such concessions — of giving everyone something so as to generate enough support to allow of any action at all — that makes government policy so lacking in comprehensiveness and consistency.[1]

The tendency in the United States has long been towards strengthening the executive: in Chicago as elsewhere the formal centralization of executive power is much greater than it was a decade or two ago. It seems highly unlikely, however, that this strengthening will go far enough in the foreseeable future to change the essential character of the system. Chicagoans, like other Americans, want their city's policies to be comprehensive and consistent. But they also want to exercise influence in making and carrying out these policies; they want to be able to force the government to bargain with them when its policy threatens particular interests of theirs. It will be a long time, probably, before they will be willing to sacrifice as much of the second end as would be necessary to achieve the first. The tension between the nature of the system and the requirements of planning is, for all practical purposes, ineradicable.

This conclusion would be discouraging if it were perfectly clear that a comprehensive and consistent policy is necessarily better (i.e., more productive of "welfare" or "the public interest") than one which is not. We are apt to take for granted that this is the case. We are apt to suppose that a "correct" or "consistent" policy must be the product of a mind (or minds) which has addressed itself to a "problem", and, by a conscious search, "found" or "constructed" a "solution." Most of our study of political and administrative matters proceeds on the assumption that all of the elements of a problem must be brought together within the purview of some single mind (whether of a person or team) and that the task of organization is partly to assemble the elements of the problem. The more complicated the matter, the more obvious it seems that its solution must depend upon the effort of a mind which perceives a "problem" and deliberately seeks a "solution."

It will be convenient to make a fundamental distinction between "central decision" and "social choice." Both are processes by which selections are made among the action possibilities open to some group or public. A *central decision* is in some sense purposeful or deliberate: it is made by someone (leader, chairman, mayor, planning commission, council, committee of the whole, etc.) who, in making the selection, is trying (although perhaps ineffectually) to realize some intention for the group. From the standpoint of this decision-maker, the selection of an action, or course of action, for the group represents a "solution" to a "problem." A *social choice*, on the other hand, is the accidental by-product of the actions of two or more actors — "interested parties," they will be called — who have no common intention and who make their selections competitively or without regard to each other. In a social-choice process, each actor seeks to attain his own ends; the aggregate of all actions — the situation produced by all actions together — constitutes an outcome for the group, but it is an outcome which no one has planned as a "solution" to a "problem." It is a "resultant" rather than a "solution."

It may seem to common sense that because it is the product of intention, indeed of conscious and deliberate problem-solving, a central decision is much more likely to "work" than is a social choice. The social choice is, after all, an "accident": it was not designed to serve the needs or wishes of the group, whereas the central decision *was* so designed.

And yet, despite the presumptions of common sense, it may be that under certain circumstances the competition of forces which do not aim at a common interest produces outcomes which are more "workable," "satisfactory," or "efficient" than any that could be contrived by a central decision-maker consciously searching for solutions in the common interest. Charles E. Lindblom has observed that while it is customary to think of the analysis of a policy problem as going on in the mind of one man or of a small group of men, it can also be seen as a social process. "Fragmentation" of analysis (i.e., analysis that goes on among many individuals or groups, each of whom approaches the problem from his distinctive and limited point of view) may be an aid to the correct weighting of values in a choice.

Just how does the weighting take place in fragmentation? Not, I have suggested, in any one analyst's mind, nor in the minds of members of a research team, nor in the mind of any policy-maker or policy-making group. The weighting does not take place until actual policy decisions are made. At that time, the conflicting views of individuals and groups, each of whom have been concerned with a limited set of values, are brought to bear upon policy formulation. Policies are set as a resultant of such conflict, not because some one policy-making individual or group achieves an integration but because the pulling and hauling of various views accomplishes finally some kind of decision, probably different from what any one advocate of the final solution intended and probably different from what any one advocate could comfortably defend by reference to his own limited values. The weighing or aggregation is a political process, not an intellectual process.[2]

The evidence of the cases presented here makes it plausible to search for some such underlying logic not obvious to common sense. For if the outcomes alone of these cases are considered — that is, if the outcomes are considered apart from the seemingly "irrational" way in which they were reached — one might conclude that the political system is remarkably effective. It is impossible, of course, to come to any conclusion on this without making a large number of highly subjective judgments — not only judgments about values, but about facts and probabilities as well. Admitting this, the writer conjectures that most reasonable people who put themselves in the role of "statesman" and consider carefully all of the relevant circumstances will conclude that the outcomes are by no means indefensible. For himself, the writer can say that they are essentially what he would have favored had he been making "decisions." In every case, it seems to him "wrong" reasons (i.e., reasons which were irrelevant, illogical, or improper as a basis of a "decision" in the public interest) were controlling, but in every case these "wrong" reasons led to outcomes that were essentially "right" or "sound."

Others may not agree. But it is only necessary to establish that "obviously wrong" reasons led to outcomes that are "not obviously wrong" in order to raise the question: are such outcomes "lucky accidents" or is there some principle at work — an "invisible hand" — that leads a choice process to a result better than anyone intends?

The case for central decision rests upon the assumption that it is possible for a competent and disinterested decision-maker to find in any situation a value premise that uniquely determines the content of the public interest. If there existed several incompatible but equally desirable courses of action, a decision-maker would obviously have to employ some "arbitrary" procedure — e.g., flipping a coin, consulting his own or someone else's personal tastes, or assessing the relative influence of the interests having a stake in the matter — in order to arrive at the decision. But the assumption of administration-minded or planning-minded persons is that this embarrassing situation seldom arises. A competent and well-intentioned decision-maker, so they suppose, can usually find in the situation some premise that clearly ought to rule. The problem of good government, therefore, is to put into office men who will look for the proper premise and use it when they find it (i.e., who seek the public interest rather than private or party advantage) and who have the technical competence necessary to apply the premise correctly in the particular circumstances.

This assumption is wrong. No matter how competent and well-intentioned, a decision-maker can never make an important decision on grounds that are not in some degree arbitrary or non-logical. He must select from among incompatible alternatives each of which is preferable in terms of a different but defensible view of the public interest. If there is a single "ultimate" value premise to which all of the lesser ones are instrumental, if its meaning is unambiguous in the concrete circumstances, and if he can know for sure which lesser premise is most instrumental to the attainment of the ultimate one, he can, indeed, make his decision in an entirely technical and non-arbitrary way.[3] But these conditions can seldom be met, and when they can be, the matter is not "important" and usually does not require "decision." Matters come before high officials for decision precisely when it is not clear which value premises ought to be invoked, what the premises imply concretely, or what is most instrumental to their achievement. If such questions do not arise, the matter does not present itself as a "problem" at all.

In the Branch Hospital case, for example, there were at least three defensible value premises, each of which implied an altogether different decision: (*a*) "relieve overcrowding expeditiously" implied expanding on the West Side where a site was available; (*b*) "improve service" implied building on the South Side in proximity to the service area; and (*c*) "eliminate racial discrimination" implied not building at all in order to put pressure on the private hospitals. There was no higher premise to which each of these stood in an instrumental relationship and by which they could be judged. (There were slogans, of course, like "the greatest good of the greatest number," but these meant nothing concretely.) Clearly, then, the decision could not be made on technical or non-arbitrary grounds.[4]

In such cases, where the decision-maker must select among alternatives without having any "higher" value premise by which to judge their relative importance, he must, wittingly or unwittingly, employ a criterion which has nothing to recommend it except use and wont or professional acceptance (e.g., "this is the way it is done in standard professional practice") or which expresses only his own (or someone else's) tastes or advantage, or else he must enact in imagination a choice process, imputing preference scales to the interested parties and striking, on their behalf, that compromise which he thinks "fair," productive of the most satisfaction, or the best reflection of the distribution of influence.

Thus, for example, a city-planning technician faced with the competing value premises of the Branch Hospital dispute and seeing no "higher" premise by which to decide the claims of the "lesser" ones, would, following the usual professional practice, gather a great deal of factual information on the distribution of potential hospital users, travel time, the optimal size of hospitals, etc., and then in all likelihood "find in the data" some reason — e.g., economy of travel time — for putting the hospital on the South Side. The chances are that the planner would not be as sensitive to the value, "relieve overcrowding expeditiously," as to the professionally sanctioned one, "minimize cross traffic." And it is very likely that the value, "eliminate racial discrimination," would not occur to him at all or that, if it did, it would not seem to him to be an appropriate ultimate criterion. If it were expressly called to his attention, he might even say that it is a "political" factor which should not be allowed to influence the decision.[5]

There is likely to be a systematic bias in a technician's choice of value premises. He will, it seems plausible to suppose, minimize the importance of those elements of the situation that are controversial, intangible, or problematic. He will favor those value premises upon the importance of which there is general agreement (e.g., travel time), and he will ignore or underrate those that are controversial or not conventionally defined (e.g., eliminating racial discrimination); he will favor those that can be measured, especially those that can be measured in money terms (e.g., the cost of transportation), and he will ignore or underrate those that are intangible and perhaps indefinable as well (e.g., the mood of a neighborhood); he will favor those that are associated with reliable predictions about the factual situation (e.g., the premise of accessibility is associated with relatively reliable predictions about population movements and consumer behavior), and he will ignore or underrate those that are associated with subjective judgments of probability (e.g., that it will be harder to get political approval for a South Side site).

In a social choice process, by contrast, there is a single ultimate criterion: the distribution of influence. The importance accorded to each alternative in a choice process depends, then, upon the relative amount of influence exercised on its behalf.

This may appear to be a highly inappropriate criterion in most situations. There are, however, a number of things that can be said in its favor:

1. The distribution of influence may be viewed as the outcome (as of a given moment) of a continuing "game" which has been going on under rules that a majority of the players have been free to change at any time. That the rules are as they are implies that they seem fair, over the long run, to most of the players. Accordingly, the outcome at any particular time is also fair, even though some players are losing. A player exerts himself to win only because winners receive rewards that are not given to losers. If, therefore, the winners have no more weight in a choice than do the losers — i.e., if the criterion does not reflect the distribution of influence — they will have that much less incentive to enter the game and to fight hard to win it. If the game is, on the whole, good for the society, it is foolish to reduce the incentive to play it. In other words, a society that wants people to exert themselves to get influence must not limit, unnecessarily, opportunities to exercise it once it has been obtained.

2. A criterion which reflects the distribution of influence also reflects, although roughly, the intensity with which the competing values are held.[6] This is so because the choice process takes into account "real" influence, i.e., not the ability of each participant to modify the behavior of others, but the ability *which each sees fit to expend, out of his limited stock, for the sake of the particular value in question.* In the Fort Dearborn case, for example, the opponents had less influence than the Sponsors in the sense that if all had exerted themselves to the utmost, the Sponsors would

have had their way. But the opponents were more intensely moved. Accordingly, they exercised a larger part of their influence potential than did the Sponsors. To the extent that the process was one of bargaining, it registered a compound of influence and intensity of interest. If it is considered appropriate to maximize "total satisfaction" of those whose views are taken into account, then it is essential to have some indication of how intensely each value is held. The choice mechanism forces each bargainer to give up something (the amount of influence he "spends"); this something can therefore be taken as a measure of the value to him of what he seeks. (If the influence distribution is "incorrect," the measure will of course be, to that extent, "wrong." But, as was maintained in the paragraph above, there is some reason to assume that the distribution is "correct.")

3. The character of the influence exercised may afford additional grounds for considering the distribution of influence to be an appropriate criterion. In one situation or set of situations, influence may consist of "forcing others to do one's will even when that will is anti-social." In another it may consist of "persuading others on reasonable grounds to accept a view of the common interest." There are circumstances in which one can exercise influence only by being (or seeming to be) intelligently concerned with the common good ("by main force of being right"). So far as this is the case in a given society or situation, the criterion of influence has further justification.[7]

The appropriateness of the criterion of influence is, however, only one aspect of the larger question, namely, the appropriateness of the social-choice process as a whole. It would be a point in favor of the choice process and a point against the decision process if it could be shown that while neither is clearly undesirable as a procedure for selecting an ultimate criterion, the former is more likely to bring all relevant considerations to the fore and to give them the attention they deserve.

There is indeed much reason to think that this is the case. A decision-maker, even one of long experience and great capacity, is not likely, when an issue first arises, to be fully aware of all of the interests that are at stake in it or of the importance that is attached to each interest by those who hold it. He gets this information (except with regard to the most obvious matters) only as the interested parties themselves bring it to his attention. The effort an interested party makes to put its case before the decision-maker will be in proportion to *the advantage to be gained from a favorable outcome multiplied by the probability of influencing the decision*. Thus, no matter how high the stakes, an interested party will invest no effort at all in putting its case before a decision-maker who cannot be influenced. On the other hand, if there is a virtual certainty that the decision can be influenced, an interested party will have incentive to expend, in the effort to influence the decision, almost all of what may be gained from a favorable decision.

If the decision-maker is surely going to make the decision on purely public grounds, the possibilities of influencing him are relatively small. The interested party may present the facts of its case in the best possible light. It may argue that the public interest is to be understood in this way rather than that. But it cannot go much further than this. It cannot do more than try to persuade. In some cases the probability of success by persuasion may be sufficient to induce it to put forth a considerable effort. In others, however, its effort will be perfunctory because it knows that the decision-maker will pay little attention. In still others, it will make no effort at all because it knows that the decision-maker is not open to persuasion.

If, on the other hand, the official[s] is open to influence by other means than persuasion, the probability of influencing the outcome may be vastly increased. If, indeed, it is possible, by a large enough expenditure of influence, virtually to compel him to select the favored alternative, then the incentive to make the effort is limited only by the advantage to be had from its success. In these circumstances, the affected interests will almost literally bring their cases "forcibly to the attention of" the official.

In a system of government in which the possibility of influencing outcomes is great, a vast amount of effort is spent by very able people in the attempt to do so. This expenditure of effort has some socially valuable results. It leads to the production of more information about the various alternatives and to a clarification

of the values that are involved. Not only are the officials compelled to take into account more than they otherwise would, but
the interests themselves are brought to examine their own and
each other's positions with great care. Of course, in an instance
where there exists some obviously appropriate and concretely
meaningful value criterion upon which it is apparent, once the
information is all at hand, that the official's decision ought to turn,
the ability of an interested party to force the official to decide
by some other criterion introduces error into the selection process.
The argument here, however, is that such criteria almost never
exist in matters of importance, and that when they do not exist,
it is socially desirable that interested parties have incentive to
vigorously assert value principles which will compete with those
necessarily arbitrary ones (e.g., professional use and wont) which
officials, wittingly or unwittingly, must fall back upon.

In a political system in which there exists no possibility whatever of influencing an outcome by an exercise of power (as distinguished from persuasion), it is unlikely that an interested party
whose value position is not widely accepted as a plausible ultimate basis of decision will exert itself to put that position forward.
Berry and Calloway, for example, would probably not have appeared upon the scene in the Branch Hospital dispute if the
Chicago political system had been such as to make clear that the
decision would be entirely in the hands of planners or technically-
minded people; but had they not exerted themselves, it is likely
that the "race" position would have been entirely overlooked or
given little weight. (The Welfare Council's planners, it will be
remembered, virtually ignored it.) A "decision" reached without
the racial aspects of the matter having been taken fully into
account would have been deficient, although it might well have
seemed (the deficiency not being called to anyone's attention)
more "rational" than the social choice that was actually made.

In summary, then, it has been maintained: (1) that when, as is
the case in important matters, there exists no concretely unambiguous criterion which clearly ought to rule, the distribution of "real" influence, as revealed in competitive exercises of
influence, may be the appropriate criterion; and (2) that a selection process (or political system) which allows of the exercise

of power other than that of persuasion by affected interests produces a wider canvas of policy alternatives and a more thorough scrutiny of each alternative than does a process which allows the affected interests only the opportunity to persuade. A corollary of these propositions is that the "rationality" of the process in which only persuasion is possible (i.e., the decision process) is often a simplification secured by overlooking or radically undervaluing some alternatives.

The social-choice process, however, suffers from at least two inherent limitations of great importance:

1. It takes into account only such ends as actors of influence see fit to assert, and it weights these ends according to the amount of influence behind them and without regard to their intrinsic value. In many circumstances, the distribution of influence may be an entirely inappropriate criterion. There may be ends which are not asserted in the choice process at all or which are asserted only weakly (e.g., ends which pertain to the community "as a whole") but which nevertheless ought to determine the outcome, ought to enter into it along with the ends which are asserted by influentials, or ought to serve as criteria by which the appropriateness and relative value of these and other ends are established.[9]

2. There may exist an outcome which represents the "greatest total benefit" of the parties to the choice process but which is not likely to be found if each party seeks only his own advantage. There may, for example, be two ways in which A can attain his end equally well and between which he is indifferent. One of these ways may be advantageous to B and the other disadvantageous to him. A may not perceive the opportunity to increase total satisfaction by acting so as to benefit B; even if he does perceive it, he may have no incentive to act upon it.

It is a disadvantage of the choice process that no one has either an incentive to devise "greatest total benefit" solutions or the information about the preferences scales of the various interested parties that would be needed in order to do so.

In the Branch Hospital dispute, an arrangement whereby the county paid its clients' hospital bills in full, gave them freedom of choice in hospitals, and offered subsidies for expansion of those private hospitals which agreed not to discriminate might have represented a "greatest total benefit" solution. (It would presumably have suited both the left and the right wings of the Negro community, and the white hospitals as well.) But this solution was not likely to be devised by any of the parties to the struggle; each was too much committed to the solution implied by its own ends to look for one which would serve the ends of all.

The distribution of influence may be such as to paralyze action altogether. (In only two of the six cases described in the book — the Exhibition Hall and the Welfare Merger — was a course of action carried out as planned by its proponents; in the other cases, the outcomes were essentially the checking of action.) This tendency to paralyze action is sometimes regarded as a defect of the choice process. In certain circumstances it may be, of course. But from a general standpoint, there is no presumption that "inaction" represents a less desirable outcome than "action."

Certainly, a social-choice process is not always to be preferred to a central-decision process. Which is more appropriate will depend upon the circumstances of the case, especially the following: (a) the complexity of the policy problem to be solved, including especially the number of elements that must somehow be taken into account or weighted (and thus the amount of conflict in the situation) and the time and other resources that can be employed in looking for a solution; the more complicated the problem, the stronger the case for the choice mechanism; (b) the visibility of the factual and value elements that should be taken into account; where there is reason to believe that all relevant values (and their intensities) are not known, the play of influence should be allowed in order to assist their being made known; (c) the presence or absence of an appropriate "ultimate" criterion which is sufficiently definite in meaning to afford a basis for selection among the competing values that are instrumental to it; where such a criterion exists, a decision process is indicated, and the play of influence on the decision-maker is clearly undesirable; and (d) the appropriateness of one or another procedural criterion (e.g., that the settlement should reflect the distribution of influence, that it should accord with professional use and wont, that it should be "fair"); if the distribution of in-

fluence, or the bases upon which influence rests, are clearly undesirable, and if a decision-maker can be expected to employ procedural criteria which are *not* clearly undesirable, there is, of
course, a presumption in favor of the decision process.

The discussion so far will have suggested the possibility of a
selection process which combines features of both central decision
and social choice and which therefore has some advantages (or,
it could also be, disadvantages) of both. In a *mixed decision-choice*
process, there are two or more interested parties each of whom
seeks its own advantage without regard to any common intention. But there is also on the scene a central decision-maker who
intervenes in the selection process to perform one or more of the
following functions:

1. The central decision-maker may regulate the selection
process so that "public values" are achieved or, negatively, not
disregarded. He may, in the first place, decide whether the matter
is one in which only the self-regarding ends of the interested
parties should be taken into account (i.e., whether they are the
only relevant value stuff) or whether there are corporate ends or
"public values" that ought to be taken into account instead of, or
along with, the self-regarding ends of the interested parties. He
decides, in other words, whether selections ought to be made by
social choice, central decision, or a mixed process. If he decides
either that only "public values" or only "self-regarding ends" are
relevant, the process then ceases to be "mixed": it becomes either
central decision or social choice. But he may decide that what is
appropriate is an aggregation of both public values *and* self-
regarding ends — an aggregation in which certain public values
and certain self-regarding ends are given greater or lesser weight.
(He may, for example, decide that the matter is one in which a
"qualified individualist" conception of the public interest is appropriate, and, accordingly, he may disregard "tastes" of "private-
spirited" persons while giving great weight to the "settled convictions" of "public-spirited" persons.[10] Thus, the selection may
be made through a social-choice process, but through a social-
choice process *which operates within a limiting framework laid
down by central direction.* The outcome of such a process is there-

fore both a "resultant" (from the standpoint of the interested parties) and a "solution" (from the standpoint of the central decision-maker, who decided which interested parties should be allowed to enter the process, how their ends should be weighted, and what importance should be accorded to "public values").

2. The central decision-maker may co-ordinate the activities of the interested parties in order to help them find positions optimal in terms of their (self-regarding) ends — i.e., positions such that no possible reallocation would make anyone better off without making others worse off. The central decision-maker keeps track of external economies and diseconomies, which are not visible to the interested parties, and he watches for "saddle-points." He may, for example, guide the interested parties to a greater total "welfare" merely by supplying information (e.g., he may know that A is indifferent as between states x and y, whereas B much prefers state y; by pointing out that someone will gain and no one will lose by choosing state y, he increases welfare), or he may be the agent through which interpersonal comparisons of welfare are made or other agreed-upon rules are applied (e.g., if state x would mean great gains to A and small losses to B, he may intervene to impose the loss on B.)

3. The central decision-maker merely records the relative influence exercised by the competing interested parties. In this case, he is merely an environment which facilitates the working out of a social-choice process. The interested parties make their influence known by putting pressure upon him; his action is entirely in response to these pressures (he is a weathervane, responding equally to all the breezes that blow), and it constitutes the resultant of the selection process.

In the first two of these three roles — but not in the third — the central decision-maker may eliminate inconsistencies and anomalies from the outcome. Therefore, in these two types of mixed process the outcomes are both resultants (they are this insofar as they are the unintended product of competition among interested parties) and at the same time solutions (they are this insofar as they are the product of an intention — that of the central decision-maker).

It will be seen that the Chicago political system is of the type that has been called "mixed decision-choice." It has, therefore, in principle, and to a large extent in practice, the advantages of both polar types — social choice and central decision. In the writer's view, in its general features it is a reasonably close approximation of the logical model that is preferable.

One great advantage of social choice is that it involves a thorough canvas of all the elements — both the factual and the value elements — in a selection situation. The better their opportunities to influence an outcome, the more carefully will interested parties examine a situation for its effect on them, and the more vigorously will they assert their interests when they have identified them. In Chicago the opportunities to exercise influence are great enough to call into play the best abilities of many extremely able people. Nothing of importance is done in Chicago without its first being discovered what interests will be affected and how they will be affected and without the losses that will accrue to some being weighed carefully against the gains that will accrue to others. It is easy for Americans to take this kind of thing for granted, but there are cities — London, for example — where great decisions are made with little understanding of the consequences for those interests which are not plainly visible to the decision-makers.

Another great advantage of social choice is that, where there exists no concretely meaningful criterion of the public interest and where, accordingly (whether they realize it or not), central decision-makers must employ some standard (e.g. professional use and wont) that is essentially arbitrary, the competition of interested parties supplies a criterion — the distribution of "real" influence — which may be both generally acceptable and, since it puts a premium upon effort to acquire influence, serviceable to the society. In the cases reported here, there were not, in the writer's opinion, criteria from which central decision-makers could have obtained clear directions with regard to the main questions. (There was not, for example, any way by which a central decision-maker could have known whether "racial justice" or some other general end ought to be made decisive in the Branch Hospital dispute.) There being no "public values" which obviously ought to be decisive, the distribution of real influence was, it seems to the writer, as defensible a basis for decisions as any other. This judgment is strengthened by the character of the influence that is exercised in Chicago. For the most part, as previous chapters have shown, the interested parties in Chicago find it hard to take positions which cannot be defended in terms of some conception of the public interest.[11]

The advantages of central decision are that the central decision-maker can assert the supremacy of "public values" and can find the outcome that is "best for all." On the Chicago scene there is, to be sure, no one central-decision-maker who can do this in all of the most important matters. The mayor and the governor, whose tacit collaboration is essential in anything of importance, are required by the logic of their positions to disagree. Antagonism between mayor and governor, Democrat and Republican, Cook County and downstate, is the very basis of the political system. (Even in the rare intervals when the governor is a Democrat, the antagonism is not removed, for even then the Senate is dominated by downstate and is almost sure to be Republican.) There is, nevertheless, an important element of central decision in the Chicago system. The governor, the mayor, and the president of the County Board are all in positions to assert the supremacy of "public values" and, in general, to regulate the workings of the social-choice process. Although their practice is to let the social-choice process work itself out with as little interference from them as possible, each of them has in some matters the power to impose a settlement when he thinks doing so is necessary. Sometimes, as in the Fort Dearborn Project case, a political head's intervention is a conspicuous feature of the situation. At other times, a political head merely registers the influence exerted by the competing interests. (In the Branch Hospital dispute, this seemed for a long while to be Ryan's main function; in the end, however, he intervened to patch up a last-minute compromise without which all parties would have been worse off. Some observers were left with the suspicion that the clash of interests in that affair was not as important as it seemed — that it was, in fact, nothing but a public show staged by Ryan to justify a decision he had reached long before on the basis of his view of "public values.")

That the mixed-decision-choice process, as it works in Chicago, takes more time to produce an outcome than, presumably, a central decision process would take and that the outcome, when reached, is likely to be a stalemate cannot, of course, be held against it.Time spent discovering and evaluating the probable consequences of a proposal is not necessarily wasted; and if in the end nothing is done, or not much is done, that may be because it is in the public interest to do little or nothing.

Notes

CHAPTER 1

INTRODUCTION

1. It should be noted that two important classes of phenomena often included in definitions of influence are here excluded: (1) the production of *unintended* effects, and (2) the production of effects upon things as distinguished from actors. There may be some objection to including "thinking" and "feeling" in the definition. But mental activity, of course, is very relevant. "We certainly act," Professor Knight has written, "largely if not predominantly and more or less intelligently and successfully, with a view to changing the 'mental content,' the attitudes and feelings of other human beings, rather than in order to produce some desired physical end. The universe of meaning, which is the universe of most purposive human life, is the universe of intercommunication. This is the main form of power, the 'world' in which power is chiefly exercised (or voluntarily not exercised) and with which a 'social analysis' of power must be primarily concerned." Frank H. Knight, "Bertrand Russell on Power," *Ethics*, XLIX (April, 1939), 257.

2. See Chester I. Barnard, *The Functions of the Executive* (Cambridge, Mass.: Harvard University Press, 1938).

3. A step in this direction was taken by Peter H. Rossi in "A Theory of Community Structures," a paper delivered at the 1959 meeting of the American Sociological Society.

4. See two long case studies: Martin Meyerson and E. C. Banfield, *Politics, Planning and the Public Interest*, (Glencoe, Ill.: The Free Press, 1955), and Peter H. Rossi and Robert A. Dentler, *Rebuilding a City* (Glencoe, Ill.: The Free Press, 1960).

5. James Q. Wilson's *Negro Politics: The Search for Leadership* (Glencoe, Ill.: The Free Press, 1960), deals largely with Chicago. Peter B. Clark is completing a study of "The Big Businessman as a Civic Leader," which is also based largely upon observations made in Chicago.

6. When a person rather than a role is meant, his name will be used or his title capitalized (e.g., Mayor Daley or the Mayor). When the role is meant, the title will not be capitalized (e.g., the mayor).

CHAPTER 8

THE STRUCTURE OF INFLUENCE

1. For an account of the Chicago machine (although in the transitional period just before the rise of Mayor Daley), see Martin Meyerson

343

and E. C. Banfield, *Politics, Planning, and the Public Interest* (Glencoe, Ill.: The Free Press, 1955), especially Chapter 3.

2. In this and the following chapters, the term "political head" will be used to refer to one who is both the chief executive of an administration and the "boss" of a party machine; the three political heads on the Chicago scene are the governor, the mayor, and the president of the Cook County Board.

3. See the Chicago Home Rule Commission, *Modernizing a City Government* (Chicago: University of Chicago Press, 1954).

4. Having formal authority to discharge an employee, although it may sometimes be a necessary condition for controlling him, may not be a sufficient one: there may be many reasons why the political head cannot "afford" to discharge him. But if he has authority, he can discharge him *if he is willing to pay the price,* whereas if he lacks authority he may not be able to get rid of him in any way at all. Usually, therefore, having authority gives the political head some measure of control that he would not otherwise have, for the employee knows that there is a point beyond which he cannot go without convincing the political head that it would pay (in the sense of minimizing his losses) to get rid of him.

It may be useful to employ the concepts "costless formal authority," the exercise of which is not attended with any disadvantages or "costs" at all, and "net formal authority," which in the circumstances the possessor can "afford" to exercise, notwithstanding certain attendant costs. The statements in the text may then be made more precise: if the political head had costless or net formal authority commensurate with the requirements of his tasks,

he would not have to engage in trading. To this it may be added that if surrounding ("cost") conditions are held constant, an increase in formal authority produces an increase in net formal authority.

5. The Leader of the London County Council, although he dominates the LCC very much as the Mayor dominates the Chicago City Council (the Leader consults a policy committee, but its members are selected by him), does not have to bear the onus of being a "boss." His position, much more than that of the Mayor of Chicago, is extra-legal; he is not elected at large, and nothing in law gives him the right to call the tune. But while his influence is extra-legal, it is not informal. There are explicit understandings which give him a right to issue orders; consequently, he need not "buy" control in the Chicago manner.

Nevertheless, a Democrat in the Chicago City Council is a paragon of independence compared to his opposite number in the LCC. As the chief whip of the LCC recently explained to a visitor:

"It rarely happens that a member votes against his party. If it did happen, we would probably say, 'We are prepared to overlook it this time, but not again.' If it happened a second time, we would not admit that person to party meetings and he would be reported to the London Labour Party. In effect, it would bar him from standing again.

"We do have what we call the 'conscience rule.' If there is something that a member can't vote for because of religious or conscientious scruples—for example, selling liquor in public parks, or Sunday games in parks—he will be allowed to absent himself from the vote. The Party is always very generous about that."

6. This argument is developed and

applied to other metropolitan areas in E. C. Banfield, "The Politics of Metropolitan Area Organization," *Midwest Journal of Political Science,* I, No. 1 (May, 1957), 77-91.

7. According to Robert Moses, "Smith and LaGuardia had quite a lot in common. First and foremost, they shared the same fierce determination to demonstrate to skeptics and bigots that boys from the sidewalks of lower Manhattan could run great governments honestly, intelligently, progressively and, to an astonishing degree, without degrading politics, and thus wring reluctant admiration from the sticks, the crossroads, the Southern Tier and Park Avenue. One had the curious sense in observing Governor Smith that he was living up to a model or an example he had established for himself and that the executive was something apart from and superior to the man. It was the same with LaGuardia." (*New York Times Magazine,* September 8, 1957).

8. Meyerson and Banfield, *op. cit.,* pp. 196-99.

9. Here, for example, is a *Chicago Tribune* editorial (April 13, 1955) which ridicules the City Council without acknowledging that in a body of fifty formally independent representatives shortcuts may be indispensable:

"Ald. Keane (31st) arrived 11 minutes late for a meeting Tuesday morning of the council committee on traffic and public safety, of which he is chairman. The committee had a sizeable agenda, 286 items in all to consider.

"Ald. Keane took up the first item. For the record, he dictated to the committee secretary that Ald. A moved and Ald. B seconded its approval, and then, without calling for a vote, he declared the motion passed. Neither mover nor seconder had opened his mouth. He followed

the same procedure on six more proposals, again with a word from the aldermen whose names appeared in the record. Then he put 107 items into one bundle for passage, and 172 more into another for rejection, again without a voice other than his own having been heard.

"Having disposed of this mountain of details in exactly 10 minutes, Ald. Keane walked out. The aldermen he had quoted so freely without either their concurrence or their protest, sat around looking stupid.

"Most likely they are."

10. The argument that follows develops some points made in Meyerson and Banfield, *op. cit.,* Chapter 11.

11. In 1959 and 1960, scandals in the traffic court, the assessor's office, and the police department put the Chicago machine in a very bad light. Mayor Daley was not personally involved; there was no question regarding his integrity. Nevertheless, the scandals prohibited him from running for governor at that time (he might not have run anyway, of course). If he had been up for re-election just then against a strong candidate, he might possibly have been beaten.

12. New York's Mayor LaGuardia is a good example of a mayor who appealed directly to the mass. As Robert Moses has written (*op. cit.*):

"It must be admitted that in exploiting racial and religious prejudices LaGuardia could run circles around the bosses he despised and derided. When it came to raking ashes of Old World hates, warming ancient grudges, waving the bloody shirt, tuning the ear of ancestral voices, he could easily out-demagogue demagogues. . . . He knew that the aim of the rabble-rousers is simply to shoo into office for entirely extraneous, illogical and even silly reasons the municipal officials who clean city streets, teach in schools, protect, house, and keep healthy, strong and happy the millions of people crowded together there."

CHAPTER 9

THE PROCESS OF INFLUENCE

1. See his discussion of the importance of non-material inducements in Chester I. Barnard, *The Functions of the Executive* (Cambridge, Mass.: Harvard University Press, 1938), especially Chapters 7 and 11.

2. Organizations which distribute services (whether for pay or not) to a large number of "customers" are much more numerous than civic associations, and this fact in itself may be sufficient to account for their prominence in these cases. It seems likely, however, that there is a fundamental difference in the maintenance strategy of what may be called "customer-oriented" and "member-oriented" organizations. The latter rely largely, if not exclusively, on what Chester I. Barnard, in *The Functions of the Executive*, has called non-material incentives, e.g., "associational attractiveness" and "the sense of enlarged participation." Because of this, perhaps, they are more adaptable and less powerful than the "customer-oriented" organizations. Moreover, "member-oriented" organizations are especially subject to immobilization by disagreement within the membership. This aspect of the matter is discussed later in the text.

3. See above, pp. 25-27.

4. See above, pp. 172-75.

5. Meyerson and Banfield, *op. cit.*, p. 148.

6. See above, p. 158 and 189.

7. The professional head of a voluntary association said of his

13. See the much more elaborate discussion of these matters in James Q. Wilson, *Negro Politics: The Search for Leadership.*

14. Meyerson and Banfield, *op. cit.*

board: "They chair meetings . . . head up committees. They have very little contact with politicians or with the press. We use them internally rather than with the outside. I line up the politicians. Our board doesn't try to cover the waterfront [concern itself with a wide range of issues] and there is little policy. I've had to struggle often to get them to take a position. They say to me, 'You work it out.' I prepared some legislation which was controversial, but the Board didn't even question it. Which was fine with me. Mr. A. opposed it, but he wasn't there that day. I got to the position of taking things to them and asking for their O.K. Very rarely did they take the initiative."

8. Meyerson and Banfield, *op. cit.*, pp. 144-45, 180.

9. See above, pp. 141-42.

10. Meyerson and Banfield, *op. cit.*, p. 81. In a profile of Mayor Daley, Keith Wheeler wrote that the Mayor laughed and giggled when it was suggested to him that he had never, in his whole life, committed himself to anything whatever until he absolutely had to. "That's a pretty good way to be, don't you think?" Wheeler quoted Daley as saying. "Pretty good way to run any business." ("Last Big Boss on U. S. Scene," *Life*, February 8, 1960, p. 140).

11. See above, p. 136.

12. Meyerson and Banfield, *op. cit.*, p. 255.

13. See also above, p. 19, and

Meyerson and Banfield, *op. cit.*, pp. 138-47.

14. Meyerson and Banfield, *op. cit.*, pp. 204-14.

15. See above, pp. 145-46; also Chapter 5.

16. Downs' chairmanship of the committee to win voter approval of the bond issue was mentioned earlier in this chapter. For Kribben, see above, p. 137.

17. In a valuable work on the Illinois legislature, Steiner and Gove tell of a witness who made an extremely persuasive argument before a legislative committee and then remarked privately to a legislator that he had no illusion that his argument would change votes. The legislator agreed, but he said, ". . . do

not undersell the significance of the presentation. Our arrangements [for votes] were concluded before the hearing ever started, but it was absolutely essential that members who had agreed to vote against the bill be furnished with a 'cover' — with an impressive witness whose competence was unquestioned so that they could offer an explanation of their votes. The professor furnished that 'cover.' The more consistently a legislator can furnish a good 'cover' to support his position, the easier it is for him to enter into logrolling arrangements." (Gilbert Y. Steiner and Samuel K. Gove, *Legislative Politics in Illinois* [Urbana: University of Illinois Press, 1960], p. 77.)

CHAPTER 10

T H E   M Y T H O L O G Y   O F   I N F L U E N C E

1. See Meyerson and Banfield, *op. cit.*, especially the footnote, p. 115.

2. In practice, "top leaders" have played little part in plan commissions, and the commissions have rarely been of consequence. For an account of them see Robert A. Walker, *The Planning Function in Urban Government* (Chicago: University of Chicago Press, 1950), especially Chapter 5.

3. Norton E. Long, "The Local Community as an Ecology of Games," *American Journal of Sociology*, LXIV, No. 3 (November, 1958), p. 255.

4. According to Peter B. Clark, it is the vice-presidents in charge of public relations who are mainly responsible for the corporations' growing interest in racial problems. Supporting race reform would seem to be as little likely to increase profits as supporting urban renewal; pre-

sumably, race is another field in which the corporation can demonstrate that it is "enlightened" and "responsible."

5. When he read a first draft of "The Fort Dearborn Project" and thought he found in it the implication that the Sponsors were trying to make money, Hughston McBain, chairman of Field's, protested in a letter to the writers that this imputation was "sophomoric," He was right, of course.

6. The attorney whose platitudes are quoted was one of an earnest group that persuaded Governor Stratton and Mayor Daley to have the 1957 legislature create a metropolitan planning commission. The late Earl Kribben was appointed chairman of the commission, and it employed a professional staff to gather facts and to lay the groundwork for a plan. Whether Stratton and Daley, or any governor and

mayor, would ever pay any heed to its recommendations (and whether it would be a good thing if they did!), the reader of this book may well doubt. Setting up machinery for the making of plans and, in general, the reorganization of metropolitan government to make it more "logical," are almost everywhere popular civic activities. Their popularity is often to be understood not so much by the objective needs of the community as by their suitability as "program material" for the "civic leaders." For a case in point, see Ralph Conant, "The Politics of Metropolitan Reorganization in a Michigan City," unpublished Ph.D. dissertation, University of Chicago, 1959.

7. See especially the concluding section of Chapter 5.

CHAPTER 11

CONCERTING ACTION BY INFLUENCE

1. Especially Chapter 8, pp. 235-41.

2. The specified group might be "registered voters" and the specified proportion "a majority." If there are 100 voters, any 51 who vote in favor contribute all of the requisite actions. If more than 51 vote in favor, it is impossible to say which favorable voters contributed the requisite actions. The actions of voters other than the 51, whether these actions are in favor or opposed, are not requisite and so do not enter into the situation at all.

3. There is a special class of autonomous actor (empirically, the courts) whose activity is counted as given unless it is withheld by affirmative action. (A court's contribution of activity is not withheld if the proposal does not come before it; it is withheld only if, when the proposal comes before it, the court decides negatively.)

4. The following glossary may be helpful: (a) *Authority* is the right to give or withhold action requisite to adoption of a proposal; only an actor who can perform such actions (who is "authorized") has authority. (b) *Control* is the ability to cause another to give or withhold action; one who is controlled acts as the agent of the one who controls. (c) *Power* is the ability to establish control over another. (d) *Influence* is a generic term including authority, control, and power.

5. See Chapter 8, especially p. 242.

6. If Daley does not mean to use this control eventually to acquire more control, this is not an "investment." The assumption here is that he *does* mean to use it so.

7. Meyerson and Banfield, *op. cit.*, p. 260.

8. See the discussion of the logic of bargaining by T. C. Schelling, in *The Strategy of Conflict* (Cambridge, Mass.: Harvard University Press, 1960).

9. See Chapter 8, especially pp. 238-40.

10. See Chapter 8, especially pp. 258-59.

11. See Chapter 9, pp. 275-76.

12. See, for example, the important part played in the public housing site controversy by George Stech, the truckdriver who wanted to get into politics (Meyerson and Banfield, *op. cit.*, especially pp. 109-11).

13. Cf. Lincoln Steffens, *Autobiography* (New York: Harcourt, Brace & Co., 1931), p. 577.

CHAPTER 12

INFLUENCE AND THE PUBLIC INTEREST

1. This does not imply that consistency is possible only in a system in which no one except the executive has power (i.e., dictatorship). In principle, and in some countries execution of policy once one has been chosen. The only necessity, from the standpoint of those who want comprehensiveness and consistency in policy, is that the executive be powerful enough not to need to bargain.

2. Charles E. Lindblom, "The Handling of Policy Norms in Analysis," in Moses Abramowitz, et al., *Allocation of Economic Resources* (Stanford, Calif.: Stanford University Press, 1959), p. 174. See also Lindblom's article, "Policy Analysis," *American Economic Review*, XLVIII (June, 1958), and his RAND research memorandum, "Bargaining: The Hidden Hand in Government," RM-1434-RC, February 22, 1955.

3. See the discussion of these matters in Simon, Smithburg, and Thompson, *Public Administration* (New York: Alfred A. Knopf, Inc., 1950), p. 434.

4. This argument does not depend upon the assumption that values are subjective and relative. The believer in natural law will have a hard time finding by logical means the concrete implications of the law for many cases. Can it be assumed that all prudent believers in natural law would come to the same decision in the Branch Hospital dispute?

5. It may be felt that this is un-in practice, there may be a lively play of influence in the choice among alternatives each of which is comprehensive and consistent, and *no* play of influence in the fair to the "intelligent" planner. But the point is that a clear-cut ultimate criterion is rarely given in the situation and that, therefore, the decision must usually rest upon value premises selected in an arbitrary if not in a political way. This is as true for "intelligent" planners as for others.

6. See above, p. 275.

7. See above, pp. 264-65.

8. It is necessary now to refer to an "official" rather than a "decision-maker" because, to the extent that the outcome is the resultant of a bargaining process rather than a course of action logically implied by a given set of ends, the process is one of "choice."

9. Cf. the discussion of conceptions of the public interest in Meyerson and Banfield, *op. cit.*, pp. 322-29. The social-choice process implies what is there termed a "quasi-Utilitarian" conception, the utility of the individual being weighted according to his influence. "Unitary" or "qualified individualist" conceptions require a mechanism embodying other criteria than the distribution of influence.

10. See Meyerson and Banfield, *op. cit.*, pp. 325-26.

11. See Chapter 9, especially pp. 264-65.

Index